Elusive
Alliance

Elusive Alliance

Treatment Engagement Strategies With High-Risk Adolescents

Edited by
David Castro-Blanco
and Marc S. Karver

American Psychological Association • Washington, DC

Published by
American Psychological Association
750 First Street, NE
Washington, DC 20002
www.apa.org

To order
APA Order Department
P.O. Box 92984
Washington, DC 20090-2984
Tel: (800) 374-2721; Direct: (202) 336-5510
Fax: (202) 336-5502; TDD/TTY: (202) 336-6123
Online: www.apa.org/books/
E-mail: order@apa.org

In the U.K., Europe, Africa, and the Middle East, copies may be ordered from
American Psychological Association
3 Henrietta Street
Covent Garden, London
WC2E 8LU England

Typeset in Goudy by Circle Graphics, Inc., Columbia, MD

Printer: United Book Press, Baltimore, MD
Cover Designer: Mercury Publishing Services, Rockville, MD

The opinions and statements published are the responsibility of the authors, and such opinions and statements do not necessarily represent the policies of the American Psychological Association.

Library of Congress Cataloging-in-Publication Data

Elusive alliance : treatment engagement strategies with high-risk adolescents / edited by David Castro-Blanco and Marc S. Karver. — 1st ed.
     p. cm.
 Includes bibliographical references and index.
 ISBN-13: 978-1-4338-0811-1
 ISBN-10: 1-4338-0811-0
 ISBN-13: 978-1-4338-0812-8 (e-book)
 ISBN-10: 1-4338-0812-9 (e-book)
 1. Problem youth—Mental health—United States. 2. Problem youth—Mental health services—United States. 3. Adolescent psychotherapy—United States. I. Castro-Blanco, David. II. Karver, Marc S.

 RJ501.A2E48 2010
 616.89'140835—dc22
                                        2009048096

British Library Cataloguing-in-Publication Data

A CIP record is available from the British Library.

Printed in the United States of America
First Edition

CONTENTS

v

CONTRIBUTORS

Sasha Collins Blackwell, MA, MPhil, The Graduate Center of the City University of New York, New York, NY

Julie Boergers, PhD, Department of Psychiatry and Human Behavior, Alpert Medical School, Brown University, Providence, RI

Nicole E. Caporino, MA, Department of Psychology, University of South Florida, Tampa, FL

Annalise Caron, PhD, American Institute for Cognitive Therapy, New York, NY

Louis G. Castonguay, PhD, Department of Psychology, Pennsylvania State University, University Park, PA

David Castro-Blanco, PhD, ABPP, Adler School of Professional Psychology, Chicago, IL

Joseph Chiechi, PhD, Connecticut Valley Hospital, Whiting Forensic Division, Middle Town, CT

Brian C. Chu, PhD, Graduate School of Applied and Professional Psychology, Rutgers University, Piscataway, NJ

Michael J. Constantino, PhD, Department of Psychology/Clinical Division, University of Massachusetts at Amherst, Amherst, MA

Torrey A. Creed, PhD, Children's Hospital of Philadelphia, Center for Family Intervention Science, Philadelphia, PA

Joan DeGeorge, MS, Department of Psychology, University of Massachusetts at Amherst, Amherst, MA

Deidre Donaldson, PhD, May Institute, Randolph, MA

Richard Gallagher, PhD, Parenting Institute, New York University Child Study Center, New York, NY

Marc S. Karver, PhD, Department of Psychology, University of South Florida, Tampa, FL

Philip C. Kendall, PhD, ABPP, Department of Psychology, Temple University, Philadelphia, PA

Steven Kurtz, PhD, ABPP, New York University Child Study Center, New York, NY

Alec L. Miller, PsyD, Montefiore Medical Center, Bronx, NY

Julie S. Nathan, PhD, New York, NY

Karen Kovacs North, PhD, Annenberg School for Communication, University of Southern California, Los Angeles, CA

Joanna Robin, PhD, Department of Psychiatry, Columbia University Medical Center, New York, NY

Stephen R. Shirk, PhD, Department of Psychology, University of Denver, Denver, CO

Anthony Spirito, PhD, ABPP, Department of Psychiatry and Human Behavior, Alpert Medical School, Brown University, Providence, RI

Cynthia Suveg, PhD, Psychology Department, University of Georgia, Athens, GA

Elizabeth E. Wagner, PhD, White Plains, NY

Sanno E. Zack, PhD, Department of Psychiatry/Behavioral Medicine, Stanford University Medical Center, Stanford, CA

PREFACE

Many adolescents are vulnerable to mental health problems peculiar to this age group. Scores of these adolescents are additionally plagued with risk factors that increase their susceptibility to mental illness—and the same risk factors typically prevent these adolescents from receiving the treatment they need. These are *high-risk* adolescents because they need mental health treatment services but do not have access to these services or drop out of treatment prematurely. Treatment engagement with this high-risk population is an important but elusive topic, daunting clinicians and researchers alike. The knowledge base of methods and techniques for just engaging adolescent clients in therapy—let alone treating them—remains stultified, resulting in the failure of effectiveness studies to replicate findings of carefully controlled trials, in high dropout rates in clinical practice, in treatment manuals that state nothing more than "form a therapeutic alliance" (but provide no instructions on how to do so), and in the woefully inadequate attention devoted to the subject in the training of mental health professionals. Currently, there is an extensive effort to manualize treatments for adolescents with common psychopathologies (e.g., anxiety disorders, depression, externalizing or disruptive behavioral disorders), and such therapeutic approaches may very well be the "best" treatments for this age group; yet even the best psychotherapeutic treatments in the world will not matter if no one is there to receive them. In the tentative and contingent world of the therapist and the high-risk adolescent client, practically everything revolves around engagement.

Over the past 2 decades, there has been a gradual increase in research looking at therapeutic relationship variables that predict treatment dropout and treatment outcome with adolescent clients. Reviews of the evidence are consistently finding that common factors such as the therapeutic alliance and treatment involvement appear to serve an important role in successful treatment outcomes for adolescents. The important role of the therapeutic alliance in adult psychotherapy has been known for quite awhile longer. The more recent interest in the alliance with adolescents appears to be driven by myriad forces: Prominent researchers have started to attend to how to engage adolescents in treatment. Frustrated clinicians have sought guidance on how to use evidence-based practices in a way that may be more likely to appeal to a culturally diverse and younger clientele but without sacrificing treatment effectiveness. Parents of adolescents have become increasingly concerned about their children staying in treatment and participating in treatment. Policymakers have become concerned about the low use of mental health services by adolescents, as well as the long-term costs associated with leaving these conditions untreated, and they have called on mental health professionals and researchers to address the problem of service and relational barriers in the treatment of this young clientele.

The purpose of this book is to examine the conceptual, theoretical, and empirical bases of these myriad forces by way of presenting some of the promising work that has been accomplished over the past 2 decades on engaging high-risk adolescents in psychotherapy. By getting a picture of the current state of the field while also getting an in-depth analysis of a few specific programs of research supported by evidence examining adolescent engagement, researchers and clinicians alike, we believe, will be able to establish a more robust and firmer knowledge base that should advance future treatment process research and thus further our knowledge of how to engage the challenging and underserved population of high-risk adolescents.

This effort actually began in 1996 at the annual convention of the American Psychological Association. One of the editors of this volume, David Castro-Blanco, presented an early version of his efforts to expand on a negotiation-based model of treatment engagement for high-risk adolescents. While at the conference, he met Karen Kovacs North, who suggested putting together a symposium in which several of those working toward enhancing engagement with high-risk adolescents could report their combined progress. At the time, North was finishing an executive fellowship at the White House Office of Science and Technology Policy, following an American Psychological Association–American Association for the Advancement of Science congressional fellowship in which she advised Representative Edward Markey on social science and social policy issues. During her White House fellowship, North consulted on a variety of behavioral science and mental health issues, including the initial policy deliberations on the surgeon general's major report on mental health published a few years later. North not only encouraged Castro-Blanco to convene the symposium but also began working with him on arranging the symposium's substantive agenda: North's training as a clinical psychologist and her experience in policy formulation and implementation gave her an invaluable insider's perspective on the nature of the problems associated with mental illness in youth, the need for evidence-based approaches in helping these young people and their families, and the ongoing dilemma of how to maximize the delivery of mental health services to this disordered population while bolstering treatment effectiveness.

Following the symposium, which was presented at the annual conference of the American Psychological Association in 2000, Castro-Blanco and many of this book's contributors agreed that researchers, clinicians, and policymakers could benefit tremendously from a book outlining the conceptual, theoretical, and empirically based efforts on engaging adolescent clients in treatment. Subsequently, Castro-Blanco chaired a symposium at the annual conference of the Association for Behavioral and Cognitive Therapies in 2004 on the therapeutic alliance; Marc Karver, this book's coeditor, was one of the presenters at this symposium. After a number of conversations, Castro-Blanco invited Karver to assist in the completion of this book.

The contributors to this volume are all clinical researchers specializing in treatment engagement, and their work spans a breadth of clinical problems. The editors sought their contributions because of their cutting-edge nature and the importance of demonstrating evidence-based approaches to treatment engagement with adolescents presenting with a variety of internalizing and externalizing problems and who are at the highest risk of not being engaged in treatment.

Beyond the practical appeal to researchers and clinicians, this book should also be of interest to scholars and practitioners concerned with adolescents and mental health treatment. In addition, policymakers at all levels who are involved in shaping mental health service delivery are likely to find this volume a highly informative and useful compendium of information and inspiration for making treatment for adolescents more accessible and more cost effective. We have also geared this book toward policymakers who control research funding for mental health, as too often research agendas focus on specific treatments for specific disorders rather than on the common factors that permeate both adolescent (and adult) disorders and the therapeutic approaches that result in positive outcomes in the treatment of such disorders.

The latter priority, we believe, bolsters the kind of research that ensures that our most effective treatments can actually reach more of our nation's high-risk adolescents.

In putting together this volume, we would like to acknowledge the contributions of several individuals who served very important roles in helping to form the work presented here.

David Castro-Blanco thanks Mary Jane Rotheram-Borus, Ray DiGiuseppe, and John Piacentini, whose mentorship put him on the road to recognizing the importance of treatment engagement with vulnerable teens. Joseph Chiechi's doctoral and postdoctoral research experience as a member of Castro-Blanco's Anxiety, Mood, and Psychopathology Lab helped focus attention on engaging young people with extensive histories of trauma; his insights into developmental theory have helped provide a richer context for treatment engagement research, and we have benefited from his work in the concluding chapter of this volume. Susan Reynolds, acquisitions editor for American Psychological Association Books, first recognized the potential for this work as a book topic, and her enthusiasm and patience helped guide its early development. Peter Pavilionis, the development editor for the book, offered both practical guidance and sincere enthusiasm for the project, and his feedback was both substantial and helpful. Marc Karver thanks his early mentors Leonard Bickman and Stephen Shirk, who encouraged him to look inside the "black box" of treatment to examine what therapists are really doing when they are delivering mental health services.

Of course, this book would not have been possible without the generosity of our contributors. Their shared enthusiasm for the topic, and their willingness to share their insights, allowed us to present a volume with remarkable breadth and currency.

We also thank our colleagues, past and current graduate students, postdoctoral fellows, and research assistants for their support and assistance. We thank in particular the National Institute of Mental Health and the Substance Abuse and Mental Health Services Administration, which have funded some of our work and some of the work of our contributors. We also extend a special thanks to our families, without whose support this book would never have come to fruition. Finally, we extend our gratitude to the adolescents and families whose efforts have helped pave the way for this work. This book is dedicated to them.

Elusive Alliance

INTRODUCTION: THE PROBLEM OF ENGAGING HIGH-RISK ADOLESCENTS IN TREATMENT

DAVID CASTRO-BLANCO, KAREN KOVACS NORTH,
AND MARC S. KARVER

The therapeutic relationship has been considered a vital element of successful therapy since the time of Freud's early theories about psychotherapy (e.g., Freud, 1912/1958). Since then, numerous psychotherapeutic paradigms have arisen, each emphasizing different models of change to be accomplished using a variety of different techniques. However, across these different treatment approaches, the therapeutic alliance (also known as the *working alliance*) has consistently been acknowledged as important to treatment delivery (e.g., Bordin, 1979; Greenson, 1971; Horvath & Symonds, 1991; Pinsof & Catherall, 1986; Rogers, 1951; Sweet, 1984). In the adult mental health treatment literature, the therapeutic alliance has been viewed as important because it might influence treatment outcomes in a couple of different ways: either as a necessary and direct relational change mechanism or as a facilitative mechanism that activates other treatment processes or techniques that lead to positive outcomes (Horvath, 2006).

Most discussion and research on the therapeutic alliance has focused almost exclusively on therapy for adults. In fact, when Division 29 (Psychotherapy) of the American Psychological Association formed the Task Force on Empirically Supported Therapy Relationships to determine which relationship variables are evidence based, it completely omitted any mention of treatment processes in the child or adolescent treatment literature (Norcross, 2002). Attention to the alliance with adolescents has really blossomed only in the past decade. For example, Shirk and Karver (2003) were able to find only 11 adolescent treatment studies that examined the linkage between a therapeutic relationship variable and outcome.

This book examines one of the most vexing issues among therapists today: How to get high-risk disordered adolescents engaged in psychotherapy; these adolescents are high risk because they need mental health treatment services but face many more formidable barriers to treatment or drop out of treatment prematurely. What is at work that limits the willingness of adolescents and their families to commit to, and follow through on, the need for active psychological intervention for problems? The risk or danger for these youths is that regardless of the psychological problems or of their varying severity, clinicians may not recognize the tenuous connection of these youths to treatment. We use the therapeutic alliance in the analytical framework for this volume in an effort to reveal some significant clues as to why it is so difficult for therapists to form a therapeutic relationship with this younger, troubled segment of the clinical population. More important, we explore what other common factors therapists could isolate that may predict positive outcomes for getting high-risk disordered adolescents engaged in therapy (even beyond the required number of sessions mandated by third parties such as courts and schools).

Much of the professional literature on psychotherapy research has suggested that the therapeutic alliance is a common factor and one of the best predictors of outcome across different forms of efficacious therapies among psychologically minded adult clients. With children and adolescents, however, the alliance is an elusive predictor of therapeutic outcome. In this volume, we endeavor not to reiterate why formal therapeutic alliances with troubled adolescents are so difficult to isolate but also to isolate those fundamental components of the therapeutic alliance that seem to offer the most promise for therapeutic engagement with members of this young, disordered clientele.

Two fundamental problems arise in such a task. The first is how to overcome treatment barriers and get high-risk adolescents into therapy. The second is how to get these high-risk adolescents involved in therapy once they make it into the therapy room.

A BURGEONING UNDERSERVED CLIENTELE

In a recent study, Roberts, Roberts, and Chan (2009), replicating earlier epidemiological studies, found that adolescent psychopathology is still a major problem, with close to 20% of sampled adolescents being found to have a psychiatric disorder in the past year. The ramifications of that figure bode ill for future additions to the U.S. labor force, the financial strain on insurance, corporate productivity, and social capital in general.

Culture Matters

Even more concerning, though, the figure does not reveal how many adolescents in the United States are at risk of mental illness. Kessler et al. (2007) found that an additional one third of individuals will face factors that will put them at lifetime risk of developing a mental health disorder. The surgeon general's major report on mental health acknowledges that

> there are children who are at greatest risk by virtue of a broad array of factors. These include physical problems, intellectual disabilities (retardation), low birth weight, family history of mental and addictive disorders, multigenerational poverty, and caregiver separation or abuse and neglect. (U.S. Department of Health and Human Services, U.S. Public Health Service [DHHS/USPHS], 1999, p. 193)

What is troubling about this tremendous number of potential adolescent clients is that a high percentage of them do not see even a single day of mental health services. Recent research has confirmed earlier studies, finding that only 25% to 35% of youths who meet diagnostic criteria for a disorder or for being at high risk (e.g., engaging in behaviors that have severely negative functional outcomes such as self-harm behavior, substance use, dangerousness to others, being suspended or expelled from school, getting in trouble with the police) have ever received any mental health services (Nemeroff et al., 2008). Unfortunately, this problem is even worse for adolescents in at-risk groups who exist in social and personal environments plagued with a host of pernicious risk factors—domestic and neighborhood violence, poverty, and substance abuse are among the most conspicuous and prevalent examples. This is the segment of the population most susceptible to mental health problems by dint of their environmental risk factors and their concomitant lack of personal assets, such as self-esteem and resilience. Such a lack of assets is reflected in their immediate social environment, but the impact of such deficits is magnified among children and adolescents in such environments who are still in a fragile developmental period in their lives.

The epidemiological links among environmental risk factors, ethnocultural groups, and the prevalence of mental health problems were made explicit in a supplement to the surgeon general's report on mental health:

> Ethnic and racial minorities in the United States face a social and economic environment of inequality that includes greater exposure to racism, discrimination, violence, and poverty. Living in poverty has the

most measurable effect on the rates of mental illness. People in the lowest strata of income, education, and occupation (known as socioeconomic status [SES]) are about two to three times more likely than those in the highest strata to have a mental disorder. (DHHS/USPHS, 2001, p. 10)

Barriers to Treatment

Culture matters not only in the epidemiology of mental health problems but also in the public health approaches aimed at effective service delivery of mental health care to populations that need it the most. Here, the surgeon general's approach relies on a two-pronged strategy: Locate preventive interventions in the community through consumer and family movements, and reduce barriers to treatment. Yet, with at-risk populations, the barriers to treatment are more numerous and formidable. According to the supplement to the surgeon general's 1999 mental health report,

> A constellation of barriers deters minorities from reaching treatment. Many of these barriers operate for all Americans: cost, fragmentation of services, lack of availability of services, and societal stigma toward mental illness. But additional barriers deter racial and ethnic minorities: mistrust and fear of treatment, racism and discrimination, and differences in language and communication. The ability for consumers and providers to communicate with one another is essential for all aspects of healthcare, yet it carries special significance in the area of mental health. (DHHS/USPHS, 2001, p. 2; citations and footnotes omitted)

As if this were not enough, interventions and referrals for racial and ethnic minorities living at the lower socioeconomic rungs with fragmented social support networks typically come during periods of crisis for these troubled adolescents; in other words, some violence typically precedes the involvement of the mental health care community, and referrals are usually done through the courts, schools, or the parents or guardians of the troubled adolescent, yet such interventions typically happen when the adolescent is not ready to be referred.

With these additional treatment barriers, it is perhaps not surprising that fewer than 20% of minority youths in need have been found to access mental health services (Malti & Noam, 2008). Spurred by these findings, Kazdin and Wassell (2000) investigated barriers impeding the referral and effective treatment of young people for mental health concerns. Among the barriers they mentioned most frequently are costs in terms of both money and time required for a commitment to treatment. Money and time are especially challenging barriers to low-income inner-city families (e.g., Bledsoe, 2008).

In addition, fears of being judged negatively or pejoratively by health care providers also figured prominently in family members' decisions about whether to follow through on a referral for psychiatric treatment. Although Kazdin and Wassell's (2000) findings pertain primarily to children referred for outpatient treatment, there is considerable reason to believe they are relevant to any discussion of adolescent engagement and entry into psychotherapy. More specific to adolescents, Meredith et al. (2009) found that one of the most prominent barriers to seeking treatment for adolescents was perceived stigma. The fear of being shamed or ostracized in the community for having a mental illness and for using treatment services can have a chilling effect on adolescent–family help seeking. Perceived need and the belief that treatment will actually work—and that the adolescent–family will be treated with respect and understanding—must be high enough to overcome the fear of stigma and other service barriers.

Although the reform of organization and financing policies may well help in addressing these service-related barriers that block access to preventive and effective mental health care, it is likely that widespread public health psychoeducational interventions that emphasize consumer empowerment and consumer and public knowledge will be needed to surmount barriers such as stigma, lack of perceived need, and lack of belief in the efficacy of mental health care (see DHHS/USPHS, 1999, p. 14ff.).

Relational Barriers

Effective mental health care for high-risk populations possesses its own special barriers to treatment, particularly relational barriers between the high-risk adolescent and the therapist. Thus, the second fundamental problem with engaging high-risk adolescents in therapy is how to get these adolescents to stay in therapy and be involved in therapy once they make it into the therapy room. It is important to keep in mind that an adolescent's physically being in a therapy office does not necessarily mean that the therapy is being presented in an accessible manner to that adolescent. In fact, across several studies, premature dropout rates of 40% to 75% have been reported; the rate for ethnic minority substance-abusing clients is more than 50% (Armbruster & Fallon, 1994; Austin & Wagner, 2006; DiGiuseppe, Linscott, & Jilton, 1996; Kazdin, 2000).

These alarming rates of attrition and treatment dropout do not appear to be limited to externalizing problems. For example, Spirito, Brown, Overholser, and Fritz (1989) reported that in a sample of consecutive adolescent visitors to a hospital emergency room following a suicide attempt, nearly 85% received fewer than three follow-up sessions in the year following the attempt. To be sure, across various symptomatology groups in the high-risk adolescent category, a common relational barrier emerges that likely drives problems with treatment dropout and participation: Adolescent clients often have a developmental mismatch with adult clinicians.

In one of the most cited articles describing the developmental period of adolescence, Spear (2000) suggested that over this period of ongoing and uncertain change and developmental transition between childhood and adulthood (approximately between the ages of 12 and 18), the adolescent experiences numerous physical, emotional, cognitive, and sociobehavioral changes. These changes lead adolescents to seek independence and social interaction but also to experiment with different identities and attitudes, take risks, and seek novelty. These changes are part of what makes adolescents such notoriously high-risk and difficult clients. They are at the age where they are trying to achieve autonomy and an independent identity—usually painfully and typically with some degree of conflict or persistent relational tension with authority figures. Unfortunately, high-risk distressed adolescents—referred for therapy not by their choice—often initially view the therapist as one more authority figure attempting to restrict their strivings for autonomy, get them to conform, and "tell them who to be." One can imagine trying to conduct therapy with James Dean while he is fighting to establish his own identity, facing what he sees as the choice of ostracism at the cost of his independence or loss of personal integrity as the consequence of conformity. It can be quite a challenge for a therapist to engage and validate an adolescent—and also validate the parent or parents—regarding less typical and problematic behavior that is beyond normative adolescence.

Effective treatment is predicated on effective engagement. The best treatment techniques will not work in an empty office or with a client who is present but not participating. This is particularly true of adolescents, whose experience (or lack thereof) with psychotherapy may well affect not only current psychological problems but also responses to problems in the future.

Treatment Effectiveness Dilemma

Since 1995, there has been a push in both the adult and the youth treatment literatures for prescriptions for better mental health care to be based on efficacious therapeutic interventions that work best for specific mental health problems (Chambless, 1996; Lonigan, Elbert, & Johnson, 1998). Yet the dilemma presented by this approach is that little is known about how these empirically supported treatments work with certain types of complex cases that have by and large been excluded from clinical trials—cases involving severe self-harm behavior and a host of typical environmental risk factors contributing to multiple stressors, including limited education and low income (Ruscio & Holohan, 2006).

The crucial issue of efficacious versus effective treatment was fore-shadowed years earlier by the surgeon general's 1999 mental health report and its 2001 supplement: More effective treatment of a burgeoning at-risk clinical population requires if not a proactive and salutary blending of values along preventive lines, then at least a special regard on the part of the clinical–therapeutic community for the values and concerns of the patient as a member of the community the clinician is treating. Quality mental health care for all Americans was both an assumption and a goal in the surgeon general's 1999 mental health report and its 2001 supplement. "Quality care," according to the supplement,

> conforms to professional guidelines that carry the highest standards of scientific rigor. To improve the quality of care for minorities, this Supplement encourages providers to deliver effective treatments based on evidence-based professional guidelines. . . . To be most effective, treatments always need to be individualized in the clinical setting according to each patient's age, gender, race, ethnicity, and culture. . . . At the same time, research is needed on several fronts, such as how to adapt evidence-based treatments to maximize their appeal and effectiveness for racial and ethnic minorities. While "ethnic-specific" and "culturally competent" service models take into account the cultures of racial and ethnic groups, including their languages, histories, traditions, beliefs, and values, these approaches to service delivery have thus far been promoted on the basis of humanistic values rather than rigorous empirical evidence. (DHHS/USPHS, 2001, p. 20)

Herein lies the dilemma: how to tailor the treatment of a mental health disorder to a specific clientele when the efficacy of the treatment across all those who suffer—regardless of race, ethnicity, age, gender, or case complexity—has not been proved through randomized controlled trials. Indeed, the juxtaposition of empirically supported treatments (which focus on specific disorders and seek to discover what works under specific circumstances) and evidence-based practices (which focus on the patient and ask what will achieve the best outcome, including randomized controlled trials) is the ideal clinical approach. However, the clinician–therapist does not work in an ideal professional world, especially when that workaday world is fraught with precious little accumulated scientific and clinical research data, as well as the urgency of dire—sometimes tragic—presenting symptoms of a severe mental disorder.

This is especially true in the case of therapists who specialize in high-risk adolescents because the therapist is dealing with, in most cases, highly resistant clients; getting them to attend a few initial sessions for just diagnostic purposes can seem like a clinical breakthrough. To be sure, information that could aid the engagement of these clients in psychotherapy is often a higher priority than information on what treatment worked best in a carefully controlled clinical trial. In fact, Bickman et al. (2000) found that clinicians who worked with youths considered information on the therapeutic alliance to be among the most critical components of the delivery of mental health treatment.

Recent health care reform, such as the Paul Wellstone and Pete Domenici Mental Health Parity and Addiction Equity Act of 2008, has emphasized a push for increased deliverability and accessibility of mental health care. However, the increased demand for services faces a new barrier: a lack of trained mental health professionals to work with a burgeoning clinical population that often includes some of the hardest-to-engage, high-risk adolescents. The need for new clinicians combined with the current emphasis on the use of more effective therapeutic interventions based on evidence-based practices will very likely mean that mental health services are delivered by a growing pool of inexperienced therapists who may rely on therapeutic manuals to assist them in delivering a course of treatment in fewer sessions (to accommodate a bigger caseload). Yet, although therapeutic manuals outline the broad contours, the fundamentals, and even the specific techniques of a particular therapy, they do not address how to get an adolescent client to engage in the specific activities of the treatment beyond the instruction to "form an alliance with the client" (Friedberg & Gorman, 2007).

With high-risk adolescent clients, however, existing therapeutic manuals are of little use if the therapist's efforts must focus on first getting the young client to attend sessions beyond a third-party sanction and then working with the client in agreeing on the goals and tasks of the therapy itself. If therapeutic effectiveness relies on the adolescent's engagement in specific treatment techniques for a client's specific disorder, perhaps a different type of manual may also be needed, such as one that details engagement strategies for disordered high-risk adolescents—or even for disordered adolescents in general. On that score, Addis and Cardemil (2006) addressed the manualization advantage per the therapeutic alliance:

> The value of manuals lies in their ability to specify and operationalize the assumedly critical ingredients of a therapeutic approach, be they "technical" or otherwise. We do agree . . . the therapy alliance is an important ingredient in treatment outcome and may be particularly critical in the treatment of certain disorders (e.g., depression). Thus, we would be interested in seeing a treatment manual for depression that focused on the therapy alliance; it would likely include a set of prescribed behaviors that therapists would use to enhance the therapist-client relationship and a set of proscribed behaviors that therapists should avoid to develop a strong therapy alliance. (p. 149)

To be sure, both psychotherapy and client engagement in the therapy rely a great deal on the personal qualities of the therapist: empathy, confidence, trust, speech, and body language. All serve to communicate and reaffirm to the client in various ways both the caring and collaborative relationship and the requisite behavioral changes the client must undertake to get toward wellness. So far, manuals have not provided guidelines on how therapists should relate to their clients—and they have not guided therapists on how to form a solid, engaging bond with adolescent clients (and their family members). So at least with an adolescent clientele, therapists are often left to their own professional and personal devices to make the young client want to keep returning to the therapist to continue with the treatment plan. The result is that some therapists do not know how to engage adolescent clients, whereas in other instances the therapist unwittingly sacrifices therapeutic content and effectiveness for likability. As DiGiuseppe et al. (1996) pointed out, however, adolescent clients perceive a therapist's focus on likability as fake and manipulative and prefer therapists who relate to them in a more collaborative, contractual manner, explaining and negotiating the goals of treatment.

Such is the dilemma with evidence-based practice, which relies on the "manualization" of proven engagement strategies. Yet, such manualization is viewed by some as inappropriate simply because they consider the delicate balance between therapeutic content and the interpersonal relational style of the therapist more of a creative endeavor than a matter of technical specifications as prescribed by a manual. The American Psychological Association's (2005) *Report of the 2005 Presidential Task Force on Evidence-Based Practice* reaffirmed the problem with rigid adherence to manuals and pointed out the importance of the therapist's personal attributes in terms of the therapeutic alliance's relational bond:

> Research suggests that sensitivity and flexibility in administering therapeutic interventions produces better outcomes than rigid application of manuals or principles. . . . Reviews of research on biases and heuristics in clinical judgment suggest procedures that clinicians might employ to minimize those biases. . . . Because of the importance of therapeutic alliance to outcome, . . . an understanding of the personal attributes and interventions of therapists that strengthen the alliance is essential for maximizing the quality of patient care. (p. 14; citations omitted)

SIGNIFICANCE OF ALLIANCE FORMATION WITH HIGH-RISK ADOLESCENTS

Numerous definitions and models of the therapeutic alliance have been proposed (for a comprehensive review, see Elvins & Green, 2008) since Bordin's (1979) model of the therapeutic alliance in adult treatment, which involves three fundamental components: goals, tasks, and the relational bond between therapist and client. In studies of the treatment of adolescent clients, Bordin's proposed alliance factor structure has not been supported (e.g., DiGiuseppe et al., 1996). Thus, there has been a call for models and measures that are not "downloads" from adult treatment theory and measures.

Karver, Handelsman, Fields, and Bickman (2005) proposed a definition–model of the therapeutic alliance in youth therapy that includes aspects of the Bordin (1979) model but also expands on the model on the basis of research on adolescent treatment. In their definition, the therapeutic relationship consists of three components: an emotional–affective connection (e.g., bond, trust, attachment, feeling accepted and understood), a cognitive connection (e.g., agreement on goals and tasks, hopefulness, believing in the therapist's credibility), and a behavioral connection (e.g., collaboration on tasks, openness in talking with the therapist, and other forms of client participation). The cognitive and behavioral components are negotiated, the result of the dyadic exchange between client and therapist on what the client wants from the therapy and what the therapist can assign to the client by way of a convincing and persuasive treatment rationale, specific change mechanisms, rehearsals, and reframings that the client undertakes during the course of the specific therapy.

The affective component—the relational bond between the client and the therapist—is likely a necessary but not sufficient condition for the formation of a healthy therapeutic alliance with an adolescent client. A strong bond with the therapist makes the adolescent initially want to come back to see the therapist again; the therapist is perhaps likable, a good listener, trustworthy, and so forth. Without this initial bond, treatment dropout is imminent. The therapist must get the adolescent client—self-referred or not—interested enough in the therapeutic endeavor to work with the therapist on a goals-and-tasks treatment agenda. And the therapist cannot assume the existence of the bond because research has shown that therapist–adolescent client agreement on measures of the bond is quite low.

The relational bond relies on the use of the personal qualities of the therapist, especially in the first therapeutic encounters, where listening skills, empathy, validations, trust, patience, confidence, support, and a host of other variables can instill in the adolescent client the fundamental belief that the therapist is indeed an advocate for him or her. Yet this is not enough: Adolescent clients will not participate in therapy just because they like the therapist. Building the cognitive connection becomes critical after the initial sessions because adolescents have many things they want to do with their time, and the therapist has a small window of time to "sell" the therapy to the client; otherwise, the client will not return (even to a likable, caring therapist).

In addressing service and relational barriers within the current zeitgeist of evidence-based approaches, the question is raised as to what is adequate evidence for methods of engaging adolescents in treatment. At this time, there are no set criteria that can answer this question. Some have proposed that correlational data are adequate evidence for process constructs. For example, the therapeutic alliance has been found to be one of the most robust predictors of both proximal (e.g., poor attendance, premature termination) and distal treatment outcomes for adult clients across disorders and types of therapies (Martin, Garske, & Davis, 2000). The alliance has even been found to predict outcome when controlling for prior therapeutic change (Castonguay, Constantino, & Holtforth, 2006).

Even in the more extensive adult treatment process literature, these issues have yet to be resolved. There have been minimal attempts in the adult literature to use experimental methods to manipulate the alliance to provide evidence for engagement methods (e.g., Acosta, Yamamoto, Evans, & Skilbeck, 1983; Constantino & Smith-Hansen, 2008; Safran, Muran, Samstag, & Winston, 2005) because critics point out that it is very difficult, if not impossible, to randomly assign therapist interpersonal approaches such as the use of empathy. Thus, most of what is considered the highest level of adult treatment process research has relied on quasi-experimental designs (e.g., Crits-Christoph et al., 2006). Nonetheless, this is far beyond the adolescent treatment process literature. With disordered adolescents, there is minimal evidence that the alliance is related to outcome or that there are replicable common-factors engagement strategies that consistently result in a positive therapeutic alliance. This, of course, raises another, more profound point.

One of the goals of valid psychological research is that findings be replicable. Can treatment-process research result in replicable findings that can guide clinician ability to form a therapeutic alliance with an adolescent? For those who see the delivery of therapy as more of an art, there is a high degree of skepticism. However, trying to discover and document the observable, objective elements of this art of engagement may be extremely important relative to the training of mental health professionals. However, it is not clear what engagement techniques should be related to. If the principal research concern here centers on engaging troubled youth in the therapeutic enterprise—discovering how to get them interested in working with a therapist on the goals and tasks of their therapy—then what exactly do we measure? What construct do we label as positive change, if not a therapeutic outcome (symptom change, functional improvement) but a pretherapeutic construct (motivation, resistance), an engagement variable (session attendance, treatment dropout, the therapeutic alliance, treatment involvement, verbal participation, completion of homework), and so forth? Moreover, if we can isolate an effect of relational variables on engagement constructs, the direction of that effect remains unclear, especially if the empirical basis of those engagement variables remains mired in confusion. In fact, as mentioned earlier, it is not even clear whether there is any consensus on what is meant by the *therapeutic alliance*.

Even though Bordin (1979) proposed three dimensions, most of the literature addresses only the relational aspect.

When we approach the alliance as a dyadic construct and a change mechanism in its own right, however, we encounter an array of more robust—and more useful—variables with which to assess the alliance's effectiveness per disordered adolescents. More important, though, such an approach encourages researchers and clinicians to ask the right kinds of questions about how to engage these troubled adolescents in a course of psychotherapeutic treatment. In short, what does the cumulative knowledge base tell us about best practices therapists have used to engage disordered adolescents—that is, what works in getting this young high-risk cohort to return (somewhat voluntarily) to the therapist's office?

When we consider the panoply of risk factors that high-risk adolescents have been exposed to, we are tempted to conclude that the clinical option is perhaps overstepping its bounds, offering psychotherapy for what amount to social problems. Social problems require good public policy and public health solutions to ameliorate (or at least mitigate) the environmental risk factors that promote psychopathologies and injurious and self-defeating behaviors. Yet, if we retain the mindset of containing or compartmentalizing mental health care in favor of social policy palliatives, we run the risk of contextualizing what really amount to pervasive and pernicious mental health issues—anxiety disorders, self-destructive behavior, substance abuse, and hyperaggression among the most prevalent. Moreover, good public policy looks perforce at the cost–benefit dimension of the problem: What kinds of service provisions and interventions are pervasive enough and effective enough to ensure that the particular adolescent disorder is thoroughly treated so that it does not recur—with perhaps more dire consequences—later in life?

AN OVERVIEW OF THIS WORK

In this volume, our approach addresses a public health perspective to the extent that we are talking about attenuation of barriers to reduce risk of not receiving services. This leads to a focus on service and relational barriers. In fact, our perspective on the problem of treatment engagement among high-risk adolescents, we believe, admits a crucial interface between the clinical and public health–public policy perspectives in that a better understanding of how to attenuate (and possibly eliminate) relational barriers in engaging and treating high-risk adolescents obviously leads to better therapeutic outcomes and more cost-effective mental health service delivery. Let's face it, youths who want to (or find it easier to) return to treatment sessions are better candidates for positive therapeutic outcomes. Funding for research on how to make the crucial initial sessions (or even pretreatment sessions) between a therapist and a high-risk adolescent client the anchor for a positive alliance—and thus an assured, successful course of treatment—is money well spent. However, as researchers–clinicians who specialize in the treatment of this troubled clientele, we approach the vexing problem of therapeutic engagement of high-risk adolescents primarily within a clinical framework, presenting some promising findings of empirically supported engagement strategies that have been used within the broad spectrum of types of disorders prevalent among these high-risk adolescents. In addition, this book also serves to demonstrate the type of research needed to make engagement processes with adolescents evidence based.

If the therapeutic alliance serves as a bellwether of the common factors that figure prominently across different forms of therapy for psychologically minded adult clients, perhaps an examination of other common factors across different disorders that are prevalent among high-risk adolescents can provide us with some important clues about what can make an engagement strategy more effective. As the surgeon general's mental health report supplement concluded,

> Cultural and social factors contribute to the causation of mental illness, yet that contribution varies by disorder. Mental illness is considered the product of a complex interaction among biological, psychological, social, and cultural factors. The role of any of these major factors can be stronger or weaker, depending on the specific disorder. (DHHS/USPHS, 2001, p. 1)

In the same manner, engagement strategies that work with adolescent clients may also vary depending on cultural and social factors and the specific disorder being addressed. The alliance with high-risk adolescents may be elusive, but it is not beyond the grasp of good empirical and clinical research designs.

Like Bordin's (1979) conceptualization of the therapeutic alliance, the work in this volume is designed to transcend rigid theoretical boundaries. Although many of the engagement strategies reported here proceed from a cognitive–behavioral base, the thread linking the chapters of this book is their reliance on empirical evidence. However, we set no precondition on what would be considered acceptable evidence, given the relative newness of the adolescent engagement literature. Instead, contributors were selected to write chapters relative to their clinical practices and programs of research with some of the adolescent populations that are considered high risk—that is, populations that are notoriously known to have poor treatment utilization (many not even making it to a single day of treatment services) and to be prone to treatment dropout. It is our sincere hope that therapists of all theoretical stripes will find these efforts helpful and worthwhile in their work with high-risk adolescents.

The reader will note that many of the chapters cover engagement strategies with subgroups of adolescents who are often considered among the hardest to treat (those with obsessive–compulsive disorder, self-harm behavior, oppositional and delinquent behavior). This book is designed to highlight approaches that have been attempted with these extremely challenging populations, what we have learned so far about engaging adolescents with these approaches, and what more we still need to learn. In addition, we have presented approaches that vary along the spectrum of evidence-based approaches, from untested approaches based on prior research and clinical experience to approaches that have been tested in at least one randomized controlled trial. The more developed and tested approaches serve as good examples of programmatic treatment engagement research for others interested in doing this type of research. These chapters will be useful in guiding future researchers on how to methodically investigate engagement in their own treatment populations of interest. The less developed approaches point out areas that are ripe for future investigation.

The initial chapters of this book provide an overview of the broad conceptual–theoretical issues in adolescent treatment process research and summarize what is known and what still needs to be learned. First, the therapeutic alliance construct is introduced, and information is presented on client characteristics and therapist actions that have been found to relate to the therapeutic alliance. Second, theoretical and measurement issues provide a broad foundation relative to what is known about the therapeutic alliance in adolescents and set the stage for what additional research is needed. Third, the critical constructs of engagement and involvement are introduced and explored with consideration of the importance of developmental issues in the treatment of adolescents.

The chapters that follow provide details from leading experts with specific programs of research on engaging adolescents in more narrowly defined areas of psychopathology. For these chapters, contributors provide an overview of the clinical problem that they are addressing, prior research and evidence on engagement of adolescents with the clinical problem (that of others in the field and their own), and descriptions of engagement strategies that are specific to adolescents with that clinical problem. The chapters provide useful and detailed information, sample engagement dialogue as it relates to disorder-specific treatment techniques, and guidance on implementing engagement approaches, skills, or tasks that are likely to be helpful in engaging high-risk adolescent clients.

Much of this detail on engagement does not appear in disorder-specific treatment manuals and has not been featured in journals about therapeutic alliance research. These chapters provide readers the opportunity to find out more about what the alliance really is and to find out what is really meant when they read "Form an alliance with your client." We intend for the strategies described in the book to pertain across adolescent disorders, at-risk adolescents, and adolescents with high-risk behaviors who are all at high risk of not receiving needed treatment services. We organized this book with chapters covering various disorders and high-risk groups, serving as examples that we hope can apply more broadly. In short, the intention of this book is to make alliance formation with high-risk adolescents just a little less elusive.

REFERENCES

Acosta, F. X., Yamamoto, J., Evans, L., & Skilbeck, W. (1983). Preparing low-income Hispanic, Black, and White patients for psychotherapy: Evaluation of a new orientation program. *Journal of Clinical Psychology, 39,* 872–877. doi:10.1002/1097-4679(198311) 39:6{872::AID-JCLP2270390610}3.0.CO;2-X.

Addis, M. E., & Cardemil, E. V. (2006). Does manualization improve therapy outcomes? In J. C. Norcross, L. E. Beutler, & R. F. Levant (Eds.), *Evidence-based practices in mental health: Debate and dialogue on the fundamental questions* (pp. 131–160). Washington, DC: American Psychological Association. doi:10.1037/11265-003

American Psychological Association. (2005). *Report of the 2005 Presidential Task Force on Evidence-Based Practice.* Washington, DC: Author.

Armbruster, P., & Fallon, T. (1994). Clinical, sociodemographic, and systems risk factors for attrition in a children's mental health clinic. *American Journal of Orthopsychiatry, 64,* 577–585. doi:10.1037/h0079571

Austin, A., & Wagner, E. (2006). Correlates of treatment retention among multi-ethnic youth with substance use problems: Initial examination of ethnic group differences. *Journal of Child & Adolescent Substance Abuse, 15,* 105–128. doi:10.1300/J029v15n03_07

Bickman, L., Rosof-Williams, J., Salzer, M. S., Summerfelt, W. T., Noser, K., Wilson, S. J., & Karver, M. S. (2000). What information do clinicians value for monitoring adolescent client progress and outcomes? *Professional Psychology: Research and Practice, 31,* 70–74. doi:10.1037/0735-7028.31.1.70.

Bledsoe, S. E. (2008). Barriers and promoters of mental health services utilization in a Latino context: A literature review and recommendations from an ecosystems perspective. *Journal of Human Behavior in the Social Environment, 18,* 151–183. doi:10.1080/10911350802285870

Bordin, E. (1979). The generalizability of the psychoanalytic concept of the working alliance. *Psychotherapy: Theory, Research, & Practice, 16,* 252–260. doi:10.1037/h0085885.

Castonguay, L., Constantino, M., & Holtforth, M. (2006). The working alliance: Where are we and where should we go? *Psychotherapy: Theory, Research, Practice, Training, 43,* 271–279. doi:10.1037/0033-3204.43.3.271

Chambless, D. (1996). In defense of dissemination of empirically supported psychological interventions. *Clinical Psychology: Science and Practice, 3,* 230–235.

Constantino, M., & Smith-Hansen, L. (2008). Patient interpersonal factors and the therapeutic alliance in two treatments for bulimia nervosa. *Psychotherapy Research, 18,* 683–698. doi:10.1080/10503300802183702.

Crits-Christoph, P., Connolly Gibbons, M. B., Crits-Christoph, K., Narducci, J., Schamberger, M., & Gallop, R. (2006). Can therapists be trained to improve their alliances? A pilot study of alliance-fostering therapy. *Psychotherapy Research, 16,* 268–281. doi:10.1080/ 10503300500268557

DiGiuseppe, R. F., Linscott, J., & Jilton, R. (1996). Developing the therapeutic alliance in child-adolescent psychotherapy. *Applied & Preventive Psychology, 5*, 85–100. doi:10.1016/S0962-1849(96)80002-3

Elvins, R., & Green, J. (2008). The conceptualization and measurement of therapeutic alliance: An empirical review. *Clinical Psychology Review, 28*, 1167–1187. doi:10.1016/j.cpr.2008.04.002

Freud, S. (1958). The dynamics of transference. In J. Strachey (Ed. & Trans.), *The standard edition of the complete psychological works of Sigmund Freud* (Vol. 12, pp. 97–108). London, England: Hogarth Press. (Original work published 1912)

Friedberg, R., & Gorman, A. (2007). Integrating psychotherapeutic processes with cognitive behavioral procedures. *Journal of Contemporary Psychotherapy, 37*, 185–193. doi:10.1007/s10879-007-9053-1

Greenson, R. R. (1971). The "real" relationship between the patient and the psychoanalyst. In M. Kanzer (Ed.), *The unconscious today: Essays in honor of Max Schur* (pp. 213–232). New York, NY: International Universities Press.

Horvath, A. (2006). The alliance in context: Accomplishments, challenges, and future directions. *Psychotherapy: Theory, Research, Practice, Training, 43*, 258–263. doi:10.1037/0033-3204.43.3.258

Horvath, A., & Symonds, B. (1991). Relation between working alliance and outcome in psychotherapy: A meta-analysis. *Journal of Counseling Psychology, 38*, 139–149. doi:10.1037/0022-0167.38.2.139

Karver, M. S., Handelsman, J., Fields, S., & Bickman, L. (2005). A theoretical model of common process factors in youth and family therapy. *Mental Health Services Research, 7*, 35–51. doi:10.1007/s11020-005-1964-4

Kazdin, A. E. (2000). *Psychotherapy for children and adolescents: Directions for research and practice*. New York, NY: Guilford Press.

Kazdin, A. E., & Wassell, G. (2000). Predictors of barriers to treatment and therapeutic change in outpatient therapy for antisocial children and their families. *Mental Health Services Research, 2*, 27–40. doi:10.1023/A:1010191807861

Kessler, R. C., Amminger, G., Aguilar-Gaxiola, S., Alonso, J., Lee, S., & Üstün, T. (2007). Age of onset of mental disorders: A review of recent literature. *Current Opinion in Psychiatry, 20*, 359–364. doi:10.1097/YCO.0b013e32816ebc8c

Lonigan, C. J., Elbert, J., & Johnson, S. (1998). Empirically supported psychosocial interventions for children: An overview. *Journal of Clinical Child Psychology, 27*, 138–145. doi:10.1207/s15374424jccp2702_1

Malti, T., & Noam, G. G. (2008). Where youth development meets mental health and education: The RALLY approach. *New Directions for Youth Development, 120*, 13–29.

Martin, D. J., Garske, J., & Davis, M. (2000). Relation of the therapeutic alliance with outcome and other variables: A meta-analytic review. *Journal of Consulting and Clinical Psychology, 68*, 438–450. doi:10.1037/0022-006X.68.3.438

Meredith, L. S., Stein, B. D., Paddock, S. M., Jaycox, L. H., Quinn, V. P., Chandra, A., & Burnam, A. (2009). Perceived barriers to treatment for adolescent depression. *Medical Care, 47*, 677–685. doi:10.1097/MLR.0b013e318190d46b

Nemeroff, R., Levitt, J., Faul, L., Wonpat-Borja, A., Bufferd, S., Setterberg, S., & Jensen, P. S. (2008). Establishing ongoing, early identification programs for mental health problems in our schools: A feasibility study. *Journal of the American Academy of Child & Adolescent Psychiatry, 47*, 328–338. doi:10.1097/chi.0b013e318160c5b1.

Norcross, J. C. (2002). Empirically supported therapy relationships. In J. C. Norcross (Ed.), *Psychotherapy relationships that work: Therapist contributions and responsiveness to patients* (pp. 3–16). New York, NY: Oxford University Press.

Paul Wellstone and Pete Domenici Mental Health Parity and Addiction Equity Act of 2008, Pub. L. 110–343, 122 Stat. 3881.

Pinsof, W., & Catherall, D. (1986). The integrative psychotherapy alliance: Family, couple, and individual therapy scales. *Journal of Marital and Family Therapy, 12*, 137–151. doi:10.1111/j.1752-0606.1986.tb01631.x

Roberts, R. E., Roberts, C., & Chan, W. (2009). One-year incidence of psychiatric disorders and associated risk factors among adolescents in the community. *Journal of Child Psychology and Psychiatry and Allied Disciplines, 50*, 405–415. doi:10.1111/j.1469-7610.2008.01969.x

Rogers, C. R. (1951). Where are we going in clinical psychology? *Journal of Consulting Psychology, 15*, 171–177. doi:10.1037/h0059653

Ruscio, A., & Holohan, D. (2006). Applying empirically supported treatments to complex cases: Ethical, empirical, and practical considerations. *Clinical Psychology: Science and Practice, 13*, 146–162. doi:10.1111/j.1468-2850.2006.00017.x

Safran, J., Muran, J., Samstag, L., & Winston, A. (2005). Evaluating alliance-focused intervention for potential treatment failures: A feasibility study and descriptive analysis. *Psychotherapy: Theory, Research, Practice, Training, 42*, 512–531. doi:10.1037/0033-3204.42.4.512

Shirk, S. R., & Karver, M. S. (2003). Prediction of treatment outcome from relationship variables in child and adolescent therapy: A meta-analytic review. *Journal of Consulting and Clinical Psychology, 71*, 452–464. doi:10.1037/0022-006X.71.3.452.

Spear, L. P. (2000). Neurobehavioral changes in adolescence. *Current Directions in Psychological Science, 9*, 111–114. doi:10.1111/1467-8721.00072

Spirito, A., Brown, L., Overholser, J., & Fritz, G. (1989). Attempted suicide in adolescence: A review of the literature. *Clinical Psychology Review, 9*, 335–363. doi:10.1016/0272-7358(89)90061-5

Sweet, A. (1984). The therapeutic relationship in behavior therapy. *Clinical Psychology Review, 4*, 253–272. doi:10.1016/0272-7358(84)90003-5

U.S. Department of Health and Human Services, U.S. Public Health Service. (1999). *Mental health: A report of the Surgeon General.* Washington, DC: Author.

U.S. Department of Health and Human Services, U.S. Public Health Service. (2001). *Mental health: Culture, race, and ethnicity, a supplement to Mental health: A report of the Surgeon General.* Washington, DC: Author.

1

ENGAGEMENT IN PSYCHOTHERAPY: FACTORS CONTRIBUTING TO THE FACILITATION, DEMISE, AND RESTORATION OF THE THERAPEUTIC ALLIANCE

MICHAEL J. CONSTANTINO, LOUIS G. CASTONGUAY, SANNO E. ZACK, AND JOAN DeGEORGE

Psychotherapy process researchers investigate variables in the therapeutic interaction that may facilitate or interfere with client improvement (Castonguay, Norberg, Schut, & Constantino, in press). Although psychotherapy process research has historically been initiated with adult populations (for a comprehensive review, see Orlinsky, Rønnestad, & Willutzki, 2004), it has recently extended into the realm of adolescence (for a review, see Karver, Handelsman, Fields, & Bickman, 2005). Drawing on both the ample adult and the smaller adolescent process research literatures, the major thrust of this chapter is to present some clinically informative empirical evidence regarding the measurement and impact of client engagement in psychotherapy, as well as factors that promote or interfere with such engagement.

PSYCHOTHERAPY ENGAGEMENT AND THE WORKING ALLIANCE

Of the many process variables that have been investigated to date, the client's engagement in psychotherapy might safely be considered the most robust change mechanism. In their seminal review of the psychotherapy process and outcome literature, Orlinsky, Grawe, and Parks (1994) affirmed that the "quality of the patient's participation in therapy stands out as the most important determinant of outcome" (p. 361). For instance, several studies (e.g., Gomes-Schwartz, 1978; Hartley & Strupp, 1983; Moras & Strupp, 1982) conducted within the landmark Vanderbilt research program (Strupp, 1993) consistently showed that patient involvement was the best predictor of client improvement, even after therapist conditions such as warmth and friendliness were removed from the analyses. More recent studies (e.g., Castonguay, Constantino, Przeworksi, Newman, & Borkovec, 2008; Stiles, Agnew-Davies, Hardy, Barkham, & Shapiro, 1998) have continued to support this notion that the client's engagement in, or receptivity or openness to, the psychotherapy process is a key determinant of successful treatment outcome. Willingness to participate and participation in treatment have also been identified as key factors predicting positive treatment outcomes in youth populations (Karver, Handelsman, Fields, & Bickman, 2006).

One construct that reflects a large facet of the client's (and therapist's) engagement in psychotherapy is the therapeutic alliance—also widely referred to as the *working alliance*. By far the most frequently studied aspect of the psychotherapeutic process, the working alliance has been pantheoretically defined as the perpetual negotiation of therapeutic goals and tasks between the client and therapist as a function of client and therapist characteristics, including their bond with each other (Bordin, 1979). Paralleling Bordin's (1979) influential conceptualization, Orlinsky et al. (1994) referred to the alliance as consisting of two dimensions: (a) the quality of the client–therapist teamwork (i.e., the "task–instrumental side") and (b) the quality of the personal rapport (i.e., the "social–emotional side").

Although there is not perfect correspondence among theorists and researchers regarding the exact elements that make up the working alliance or exactly how the alliance yields its therapeutic influence (see Constantino, Castonguay, & Schut, 2002), it is generally agreed that the alliance plays some role in the curative process as a pantheoretical principle of change (e.g., see Castonguay & Beutler, 2006; Castonguay, Constantino, & Holtforth, 2006; Hill & Knox, 2009; Horvath & Bedi, 2002; Norcross, 2002; Orlinsky & Howard, 1987). The clinical importance of the working alliance is also empirically supported in child and adolescent treatments (e.g., Shirk & Russell, 1996) as well as reflected in the self-reports of clinicians working with child and adolescent clients and of youth clients themselves. For example, Kazdin, Siegel, and Bass (1990) found that more than 90% of youth clinicians cited the relationship as extremely or very related to change, whereas Garcia and Weisz (2002) found that youth clients expressed failures of the relationship as being the most frequent reason for treatment discontinuation.

In the following pages, we summarize some of the most pertinent research findings related to the working alliance and briefly describe some of the clinically relevant implications of these findings. Specifically, we (a) present some basic clinical implications to be derived from the reliable and valid measurement of the working alliance; (b) highlight certain client characteristics that contribute to difficulties in establishing or maintaining a quality alliance; (c) underscore ways in which therapists can facilitate, interfere with, and restore the working alliance; and (d) highlight several general considerations of the current state of the alliance literature. We discuss findings from adolescent research as well as considerations from the more abundant adult research that may extend to the psychotherapeutic process as it relates to working with adolescent clients. Again, process research with adolescents has been relatively scarce compared with efforts aimed at explicating the role of the alliance in the treatment of adults (Kazdin, Bass, Ayers & Rodgers, 1990; Morris & Nicholson, 1993). However, despite the lack of a rich empirical base, the importance of a quality therapeutic relationship has certainly not gone unrecognized in the child and adolescent literature. In fact, paralleling the adult realm, child and adolescent theorists have for some time championed the importance of developing an effective, collaborative relationship with younger clients, including characteristics such as warmth, empathy, trust, acceptance, and respect (Freedheim & Russ, 1983; Levinson, 1973; Oetzel & Scherer, 2003; Shirk & Russell, 1996).

MEASURING THE ALLIANCE

Several instruments developed for use with adults have demonstrated the reliability and validity of the general working alliance construct (see Elvins & Green, 2008; Horvath & Bedi, 2002; Horvath & Greenberg, 1994). The most frequently used are the California Psychotherapy Alliance Scales (Gaston & Marmar, 1994; Marmar, Weiss, & Gaston, 1989), the Penn Helping Alliance Scales (Alexander & Luborsky, 1986; Luborsky, 1976; Luborsky, Crits-Christoph, Alexander, Margolis, & Cohen, 1983), the Therapeutic Alliance Rating Scale (Marziali, 1984), the Vanderbilt Therapeutic Alliance Scale (Hartly & Strupp, 1983; O'Malley, Suh, & Strupp, 1983), and the Working Alliance Inventory (WAI; Horvath & Greenberg, 1986, 1989; Kokotovic & Tracey, 1990). More recently, the Combined Alliance Short Form (Hatcher, 1999; Hatcher & Barends, 1996) has been factor analytically derived from items from several of the widely used alliance measures. Typically, these measures have respective client, therapist, and observer versions that have been used to provide a global assessment of the alliance over various amounts of time (e.g., entire sessions, segments of a session).

Alliance measurement in adolescent populations has largely been built on adaptations of the adult measures (Elvins & Green, 2008). Adaptations have ranged from changes in vocabulary and reading level (e.g., Adolescent WAI; DiGiuseppe, Linscott, & Jilton, 1996; Fitzpatrick & Irannejad, 2008; Florsheim, Shotorbani, Guest-Warnick, Barratt, & Hwang, 2000) to less frequent incorporation of developmental theory (e.g., Adolescent Therapeutic Alliance Scale [Faw, Hogue, Johnson, Diamond, & Liddle, 2005], Family Engagement Questionnaire [Kroll & Green, 1997]). Unlike adult alliance measures, however, adolescent-specific measures have to date lacked the volume of psychometric research establishing consistent reliability and validity. Moreover, meta-analysis of child and adolescent alliance and broader relationship measures has found the modal frequency of use to be one (Karver et al., 2006). Thus, the development and assessment of process measures and tools for assessing the therapeutic alliance with adolescents lags significantly behind that for adults. However, the trajectory shows a steep increase in focus over the past decade, with increases in both theoretical and empirical considerations of the alliance (Elvins & Green, 2008; Hawley & Garland, 2008; Zack, Castonguay, & Boswell, 2007). Initial validation studies have suggested that adolescent measures capture the global construct of alliance defined through adult research; however, the differentiation of task and bond has been less rigorously established (DiGiuseppe et al., 1996; Faw et al., 2005).

Other measurement systems aimed at a more fine-grained, moment-to-moment assessment of the interpersonal process have also been applied to the study of the working alliance with adults. For example, Benjamin's (1974) structural analysis of social behavior (SASB) has proven to be a valuable system for uncovering complex, reciprocal, and frequently subtle processes of affiliation (e.g., love, hostility) and interdependence (e.g., control, submission) during psychotherapy sessions (see Benjamin, 1996; Constantino, 2000; Henry & Strupp, 1994). Although the SASB has been used with adolescents to study family dynamics and dating relationships (Humphrey, 1989; Ybrandt, 2008), we could locate no published studies using the SASB to examine the adolescent alliance construct. Thus, examination of interpersonal processes at this fine-grained level reflects an important future direction for adolescent alliance research.

Although based on slightly different definitions of the alliance, the adult-derived measures appear to converge in their ability to tap (in reliable and valid manners) the two overarching facets of the alliance that we identified earlier: the client–therapist bond and their collaborative engagement in the therapy endeavor (Hatcher & Barends, 1996; Hatcher, Barends, Hanssell, & Gutfreund, 1995; Horvath & Bedi, 2002). Taken as a whole, the many studies conducted with these instruments have shown that alliance quality is predictive of client improvement across a variety of treatment approaches (e.g., psychodynamic, cognitive–behavioral), treatment lengths (e.g., short term, long term), client problems (e.g., depression, substance abuse), and areas of functioning (e.g., symptoms, self-concept; see Castonguay et al., 2006; Horvath & Bedi, 2002; Martin, Garske, & Davis, 2000) and that this association has been shown to be more than an artifact of client improvement before alliance measurement (e.g., Barber, Connolly, Crits-Christoph, Gladis, & Siqueland, 2000; Castonguay et al., 2008; Klein et al., 2004). Additionally, for adolescent clients, measuring caregiver alliance is often important because adolescents rarely refer themselves for treatment. Rather, treatment and goals for therapy are often first initiated by someone other than the adolescent client, such as a teacher or parent. Recent studies have examined the contributions of both adolescent and caregiver perspectives (e.g., Hawley & Garland, 2008; Hawley & Weisz, 2005).

As a whole, research with both adults and adolescents has demonstrated that alliance ratings from different perspectives typically have only low to moderate associations (e.g., Bachelor, 1991; Hawley & Garland, 2008; Hawley & Weisz, 2005; Hersoug, Hoglend, Monsen, & Havik, 2001; Hersoug, Monsen, Havik, & Hoglend, 2002; Tichenor & Hill, 1989) and that the predictive validity of the alliance is strongest when assessed by the client early in treatment (e.g., Hawley & Garland, 2008; Horvath & Bedi, 2002; Tichenor & Hill, 1989). For adolescents, however, initial evidence has suggested that caregiver-rated alliance may uniquely predict persistence and attendance in treatment as well as engagement in family therapy (Hawley & Weisz, 2005).

Although an in-depth discussion of each of the various adolescent- and adult-specific alliance measures and their points of convergence and divergence is beyond the scope of this chapter, the fact that all of the well-researched measures have provided sound psychometric support for the alliance concept has important clinical implications. The first (and perhaps most obvious) of these implications is that irrespective of whom they are working with, what they are working on, and how they are working toward it, clinicians need to make a systematic effort to establish and maintain a strong working alliance with their clients. This, of course, is likely easier said than done because research has suggested that clients and therapists might not always be aware of the interpersonal rifts that are occurring between them (e.g., Henry, Strupp, Butler, Schacht, & Binder, 1993). Rifts in the alliance may also be masked by incongruous overt disclosures of clients and therapists (e.g., Safran, Crocker, McMain, & Murray, 1990; Safran & Muran, 1996; Safran, Muran, & Samstag, 1994), making it difficult to address relationship problems adequately, even when participants are aware of them. Moreover, as Henry, Schacht, and Strupp (1986, 1990) have demonstrated, complex communications (i.e., communications that simultaneously convey different and usually contradictory information) can often occur within a dyadic exchange. Thus, even though a therapist may be convinced that the content of his or her message conveys empathy to the client, the process by which this message is delivered may be fraught with subtle hostility or rejection, thereby negatively affecting the quality of the relationship. These issues may be of particular salience with adolescent populations because adolescents are frequently described by researchers and clinicians as more challenging to engage, more resistant, less motivated, less adherent, and more likely to drop out of treatment than adult clients (De Los Reyes & Kazdin, 2004; Oetzel & Scherer, 2003; although see Garland, Lewczyk-Boxmeyer, Gabayan, & Hawley, 2004, for contradictory empirical findings).

Encouraging clinicians to pay attention to the therapeutic relationship, as obvious as this may sound, might be particularly relevant within the current climate of mental health service delivery. Based in part on the substantial contribution made by the American Psychological Association's (APA's) Division 12 (Society of Clinical Psychology) Task Force on Empirically Supported Treatments (Chambless & Hollon, 1998; Nathan & Gorman, 2002; Ollendick & King, 2004), considerable emphasis is currently placed on the application of techniques that have been shown to be effective for particular problems. Such emphasis, in our view, is not problematic per se, as long as it is not at the expense of an appropriate recognition of the therapeutic importance of relationship variables (Castonguay, Boswell, Constantino, Goldfried, & Hill, in press).

Fortunately, task forces recently launched by APA have helped the field recognize (and make use of) the therapeutic value of relational factors, such as the alliance. Sponsored by APA Division 29 (Psychotherapy), the first of these was aimed at identifying specific relationship factors that can be viewed as empirically supported (Norcross, 2002). Initiated by Division 12 and the North American Society for Psychotherapy Research, a more recent task force has delineated 61 empirically anchored principles of change based on the individual and interactive impact of the treatment, relationship, and individual participant factors (Castonguay & Beutler, 2006).

A second clinical implication that one should derive from the established reliability and validity of the alliance construct is that clinicians should routinely assess the quality of their relationship with their clients. Given that clinicians now have at their disposal a number of instruments to measure relationship quality, it would be regrettable for the assessment of the working alliance to be restricted to research projects. That being said, we are certainly aware of the reluctance and difficulties that might be involved with using such instruments in one's day-to-day practice.

To start with, many therapists want to believe that they are keenly aware of what is taking place in their sessions and that given this high level of insight, they might not be inclined to assume that a scale (especially one that was originally constructed for research purposes) could inform them when something has gone amiss in the therapy relationship. We would all like to think that our astute clinical disposition, based on years of intensive training, has prepared us well enough to identify and respond to emergent problems in the relationship. However, research findings have shown that even when therapists are trained with the main intent of recognizing and resolving negative interpersonal dynamics occurring in the room, this by no means guarantees the absence of any negative and interfering interpersonal process. For example, Henry et al. (1993) demonstrated that training therapists to pay particular attention to interpersonal dynamics taking place within the sessions did not improve the quality of the alliance. In fact, the number of hostile and complex messages actually increased significantly after training. These findings suggest that despite intensive training and good clinical dispositions, experienced therapists remain vulnerable to negative interpersonal processes throughout treatment. Thus, they clearly highlight the need to measure the alliance in one's practice.

Moreover, even if therapists are not necessarily engaging in negative interpersonal dynamics, they might still be failing to implement positive ones. The fact is, therapists are not always empathetically attuned to their clients (Burns & Auerbach, 1996). Because most therapists are highly invested in seeing themselves as empathic, it is unlikely that they are always aware when they lack empathy in a given moment and, thus, measuring the therapeutic relationship from differing perspectives seems highly indicated. For example, by using both the therapist and the client versions of an alliance measure after a session, the therapist might notice a large discrepancy with regard to how he or she is viewing the collaborative pursuit of therapy goals and how the client perceives the same dimensions of their engagement. With this information, the therapist can then use the beginning of the next session to address this discrepancy and its possible impediment to therapeutic progress.

A second source of reluctance for measuring the alliance in the day-to-day practice of therapy is likely related to the issue of time involved in the repeated administration of any instrument. However, one of the benefits of the array of alliance instruments is that some have been adapted to be very brief in nature. For example, the brief version of the adult WAI is made up of only 12 items and can be completed easily in just a few minutes. Moreover, this version has been shown to be highly correlated with the original 36-item, psychometrically sound version (Tracey & Kokotovic, 1989).

Even if a measurement system is not used in its entirety or rated exactly as intended, the items or concepts of the instruments can be used in several beneficial ways. With regard to training, for example, a supervisor could use the interpersonal principles underlying the SASB (e.g., complex communications, hostile control) without necessarily formally coding the sessions. Knowledge of this system might be enough to provide helpful heuristics to inexperienced therapists regarding subtle yet significant mistakes they should avoid committing. The same could be said of a supervisor completing the observer form of an alliance scale, such as the brief WAI, and then using this assessment to highlight for his or her supervisee processes needing attention (e.g., acknowledging the lack of a mirroring response, which could then be explored with a client in the next session to rebuild or enhance the relationship quality). Another benefit of the informal use of alliance rating systems is to become increasingly cognizant of differing items and subscales so that in the practice of therapy, one may be better able to catch themselves "online" when engaging in a process known to be detrimental to the therapeutic course or observing a client action known to be the same. For example, knowledge of the WAI might help a therapist to better recognize the detrimental effect of a client failing to agree with a particular task in session (e.g., failing to see the benefit of or buy into the rationale of a two-chair technique in humanistic psychotherapy).

As previously mentioned, research has revealed that the alliance is especially good at predicting outcomes when the client measures it and when it is assessed early in treatment. An obvious implication of this empirical finding is that if a therapist cannot afford to measure the alliance on a consistent basis, he or she should at least measure it at or near the outset of therapy and continue to do so, of course, if the assessment reveals an impaired relationship. Another clear implication is that if there are inconsistencies between the client and therapist ratings of the alliance (and this is likely to occur given the low correlation between these two sources of measurement; Horvath & Bedi, 2002; Shirk & Karver, 2003), then the therapist should put more faith in the client's view and attend to the discrepancy. In sum, the strongest predictive validity of the client's assessment of the relationship, coupled with the relatively modest correlation between client and therapist perspectives, suggests that clinicians should monitor the alliance with standardized scales, even when they believe strongly that they are empathic by nature and by training.

CLIENT CHARACTERISTICS AND THE WORKING ALLIANCE

A large number of studies have addressed whether particular characteristics of clients might facilitate or interfere with the establishment and maintenance of a good alliance. Among these characteristics are demographic variables, expectancies, mental health variables, and intrapsychic and interpersonal variables.

Demographic Variables

Consistent with their main effect on psychotherapy outcomes (Cooper, 2008), most demographic characteristics (e.g., age, gender) have not consistently predicted alliance quality for adults. However, there has been some evidence that it may be harder to establish a working alliance with those clients who are less educated (e.g., Marmar et al., 1989) and less psychologically minded or inclined (Orlinsky et al., 1994). These findings suggest the importance of fully assessing clients' academic history and their ability to engage around psychological themes as forecasts for potential alliance–engagement problems. For adolescents, such assessment should include current scholastic performance, even if not part of the presenting concerns. Furthermore, to the extent that younger clients may be less psychologically inclined than adults, it may be helpful for therapists working with adolescents to check in periodically to ensure that they understand the treatment rationale. Empirically, cognitive developmental level has been found to predict positive psychotherapy outcomes in child and adolescent samples (Durlak, Furhman, & Lampman, 1991; Weisz & Hawley, 2002), although alliance as a mediator of this process has yet to be examined.

Although main effects of demographic variables on alliance quality are infrequent, studies with adults have suggested that a match between therapists and clients on age, religious beliefs, and values is associated with better alliance quality (e.g., Hersoug et al., 2001; Luborsky et al., 1983). Findings related to ethnic similarity between client and therapist have been mixed. For example, Farsimadan, Draghi-Lorenz, and Ellis (2007) found that clients in matched dyads reported a stronger early bond with their therapists than did clients in nonmatched dyads. Furthermore, alliance quality mediated the association between ethnic matching and treatment outcome. However, other studies have failed to demonstrate a significant link between client–therapist ethnic similarity and outcome (e.g., Ricker, Nystul, & Waldo, 1999). Such mixed findings suggest that similarity on cultural values and beliefs might be more relevant for alliance development than ethnic matching per se (Farsimadan et al., 2007).

In adolescent treatments, gender matching effects have been found for substance abusers, with girls showing higher alliance and retention when matched with a female therapist and boys showing particularly low alliance and high dropout rates with female therapists (Wintersteen, Mensinger, & Diamond, 2005). These findings might point to an inherent lack of credibility that a "mismatched" therapist has in the eyes of his or her client. Thus, dissimilarity on gender or perhaps other constructs such as ethnicity, religious beliefs, values, and age (the latter of which is, of course, inherent to psychotherapy with adolescents) should prompt therapists to explore directly and early any client concerns with or ambivalences about such dissimilarities. By privileging and validating the client's experiences, the therapist might be able to instill greater confidence in the therapeutic relationship despite participant differences (see Hilsenroth & Cromer, 2007). At the least, the client might be able to agree to the notion that the therapist can understand his or her perspective on life. Without such a basic agreement, continuing treatment might prove fruitless. The same might be said for parent–therapist similarity in parenting programs because some research has demonstrated that parent–therapist match on both ethnicity and socioeconomic status is related to better alliance specifically (e.g., Orrell-Valente, Pinderhughes, Valente, Laird, & Conduct Problems Prevention Research Group, 1999) and, to a lesser extent, engagement more broadly defined (e.g., retention, attendance; Dumas, Moreland, Gitter, Pearl, & Nordstrom, 2006).

We are not suggesting, however, that a lack of a match on these variables or reluctance to accept a particular treatment rationale necessarily means that the relationship has to be severed. In fact, this may present an opportunity for the therapist to model compromising behavior and to engage the client in discussing the process of therapy from an open, understanding, and affiliative stance. Such behavior may have therapeutic value on its own to the extent that a client is not used to having his or her views addressed with such respect and regard. In fact, findings from a small sample of adolescents in treatment have supported these assertions, with therapist efforts to create an authoritative relationship and to promote adolescent autonomy (by behaving as a resource rather than as an authority figure, allowing adolescents to take the lead in discussions, promoting safety for adolescents to express negative emotion toward them, and apologizing for and exploring alliance ruptures) predicting better alliance quality (Church, 1994).

Expectancies

There are also clinical implications of incongruence between client expectations and the treatment rationale and goals. For example, Elkin et al. (1999) found that patient–treatment fit significantly predicted alliance quality in treatment for depression. They defined *patient–treatment fit* as congruence between clients' assignment to a treatment (e.g., cognitive therapy, psychodynamic–interpersonal therapy, antidepressant medication) and their predilection for that therapy. Predilection was captured by the client's view of what causes depression and what ameliorates it (e.g., cognitive restructuring, insight, biological effects of medication). The implication of this finding for adult treatment is clear because it suggests that ascertaining clients' perceptions of their difficulties and their assumptions about the change mechanisms is indicated (especially early in treatment before a negative alliance develops or clients terminate prematurely). When working with adolescents, this focus may also be useful to address clients' attitudes toward taking medications, being observed in school, and seeing a therapist on a weekly basis. If an adolescent client does not at least partially buy into the potential helpfulness of such treatment elements, then pursuing him or her without addressing the client's concerns is likely to alienate the adolescent from the treatment process, if not drive him or her away altogether. This is particularly salient in light of findings of poor convergence between adolescent, caregiver, and therapist goals (Garland et al., 2004).

More general treatment expectancies, or the notion that one believes he or she will improve, are also associated with adaptive processes and outcomes (Arnkoff, Glass, & Shapiro, 2002; Greenberg, Constantino, & Bruce, 2006). For example, clients' outcome expectations are positively associated with alliance quality across various treatments for various conditions (e.g., Connolly Gibbons et al., 2003; Constantino, Arnow, Blasey, & Agras, 2005). Furthermore, the alliance has been shown to mediate the expectation–outcome link (e.g., Abouguendia, Joyce, Piper, & Ogrodniczuk, 2004; Constantino, Klecak, et al., 2008; Meyer et al., 2002), suggesting that clients who have positive outcome expectations will be more likely to engage in a collaborative working relationship with their therapists, which will in turn promote improvement. Such findings have been couched in terms of goal theories, reflecting the notion that people will work toward a goal provided they expect it is attainable (Austin & Vancouver, 1996; Carver & Scheier, 1998). Without this expectation, people will become highly discouraged and disengage from their goal pursuit. Thus, therapists should spend sufficient time instilling in their clients a sense of hope and positive expectation because such expectancy arousal might be one of the strongest elements of change (Constantino & DeGeorge, 2008; Greenberg et al., 2006; Kirsch, 1990).

Mental Health

Numerous findings in the adult literature have suggested that poorer client mental health is a moderately strong, albeit not entirely consistent, predictor of worse alliance quality (e.g., Gaston & Marmar, 1994; Hersoug, Monsen, et al., 2002; Raue, Castonguay, & Goldfried, 1993; Zuroff et al., 2000). For children and adolescents, there is some suggestion that the type of mental health difficulties may moderate the alliance–outcome association, with a stronger predictive relationship found for externalizing as opposed to internalizing problems (Shirk & Karver, 2003).

In addition to general mental health and symptom level, client avoidance and defensiveness with regard to addressing, dealing with, and working through presenting problems have also been shown to relate negatively to alliance quality in adult treatments (e.g., Gaston, Marmar, Thompson, & Gallagher, 1988). Moreover, a lack of emotional involvement in the treatment process has been shown to be inversely related to the alliance (e.g., Randeau & Wampold, 1991; Sexton, Hembre, & Kvarne, 1996). To the extent that younger clients may have difficulty opening up to or emotionally connecting with adults, these findings may have relevance for the treatment of adolescent problems. At a minimum, these findings can serve as a reminder of potential barriers that avoidance and defensiveness can impose on the change process.

Although the findings on symptom severity, hopelessness, and defensiveness highlight potential barriers to alliance establishment, they do not suggest unequivocally that an alliance is doomed from the start. In fact, even clients diagnosed with borderline personality disorder, a condition marked by severe relational deficits and primitive defense manifestations, have been shown to be able to engage in a quality therapeutic relationship, as rated by clients and therapists (e.g., Gunderson, Najavits, Leonhard, Sullivan, & Sabo, 1997). Moreover, Hersoug, Sexton, and Hoglend (2002) found that overall defensiveness did not predict alliance development in brief dynamic psychotherapy. What the findings on the mental health variables described earlier do suggest is that such factors might pose a particular type of challenge to the establishment of a good alliance, and thus it is incumbent on the therapist to address this relational process.

Intrapsychic and Interpersonal Variables

Research has also uncovered several intrapsychic and interpersonal characteristics of clients that affect their relationship with their therapist. For example, Paivio and Bahr (1998) measured the relation between client introject (Sullivan's [1953] conceptual notion that people tend to treat themselves as they have been treated by important people in their past) and the working alliance in experiential therapy. They found that adult clients who were self-loathing and self-rejecting had a more difficult time establishing a good therapeutic alliance than clients who were more self-loving and self-accepting. On the basis of these results, Paivio and Bahr recommended that therapists emphasize the assessment of clients' self-conceptions. An early assessment of a client's introject may help the therapist recognize maladaptive patterns in the client's relations with self and others and to conceptualize therapeutic goals in terms of necessary shifts to more adaptive ways of treating him- or herself and other people. It seems reasonable to assume that this recommendation applies equally as well to the treatment of adolescents, although the assessment methods might differ depending on various factors, such as age and level of development. The same could be said with respect to perfectionism. Similar to the concept of introjection, *perfectionism* refers to specific, maladaptive views of self and others. A high level of perfectionism, like self-hostility, has been found to relate negatively to alliance quality with adult clients (e.g., Rector, Zuroff, & Segal, 1999; Zuroff et al., 2000).

Several adult studies have also shown that clients' interpersonal problems influence alliance development in different ways. Overall distress from interpersonal interactions tends to be negatively related to alliance quality across various treatments and conditions (e.g., Beretta et al., 2005; Connolly Gibbons et al., 2003; Constantino & Smith-Hansen, 2008). At a more specified level, interpersonal problems of an overly friendly nature tend to be positively associated with the alliance (e.g., Beretta et al., 2005; Muran, Segal, Samstag, & Crawford, 1994; Nevo, 2002; Puschner, Bauer, Horowitz, & Kordy, 2005), whereas interpersonal problems of a too hostile nature tend to be negatively associated with the alliance (e.g., Paivio & Bahr, 1998; Puschner et al., 2005; Saunders, 2001). At the level of interpersonal control, findings are mixed, with some studies showing that submissiveness is positively related to the alliance (e.g., Muran et al., 1994) and others demonstrating that submissiveness is negatively related to the alliance (e.g., Paivio & Bahr, 1998) or that dominance is positively linked (Nevo, 2002). Still other adult studies have examined correlates of alliance trajectories. Beretta et al. (2005) found that clients with stably low alliance levels over time reported more problems with coldness and social inhibition and fewer problems related to excessive affiliation relative to clients who reported stably high or gradually improving alliance levels over time. Stiles et al. (2004) found that clients who evidenced high variability and negative slope in their alliance patterns reported more interpersonal problems of an overly involved, or intrusive, type relative to clients who evidenced more favorable alliance patterns. Constantino and Smith-Hansen (2008) found that the least favorable alliance trajectory group (low and stable) included clients who reported less overly affiliative and more hostile–dominant interpersonal problems than clients in the high and improving alliance trajectory group. For adolescents, there has been limited research in this area; however, in one study, pretreatment interpersonal problems were found to be the best predictor of alliance formation in maltreated adolescents (Eltz, Shirk, & Sarlin, 1995). Moreover, parental interpersonal relatedness has been found to predict caregiver–therapist alliance in the treatment of oppositional youth (Kazdin & Whitley, 2006).

In addition to general interpersonal deficits or excesses, clients who possess poor object relations or have experienced negative (e.g., hostile) early relationships with their parents have been shown to have difficulty forming affiliative relationships with their therapist (e.g., Goldman & Anderson, 2007; Hilliard, Henry, & Strupp, 2000; Kokotovic & Tracey, 1990; Piper et al., 1991; Ryan & Cicchetti, 1985). Attachment style also has an impact on the alliance, with those clients with fearful or preoccupied attachment styles having more difficulty establishing or maintaining a good alliance than clients with secure attachment styles (e.g., Eames & Roth, 2000; Goldman & Anderson, 2007). These interpersonal findings are not surprising given that the client–therapist alliance is likely to involve the same core social skills that were learned (or failed to be learned or modeled) in the family of origin. To the extent possible, it may be particularly important for the treatment of an adolescent to include family interviewing or observation during at least the early stages of treatment in an attempt to better understand how the client relates to important others. Not only will this information and observation provide the therapist with some insight into how the client may interact with him or her, but it may also shed light on central therapeutic goals (e.g., altering communication patterns within a client's family of origin or current living environment).

Whether the therapist is able to observe firsthand the client interacting with his or her early caregiver, the findings described earlier clearly suggest that some clients will recapitulate certain ways of relating with others that can hinder treatment success. Interpersonal theorists (e.g., Benjamin, 1984; Kiesler, 1996) have delineated a number of principles that can help the therapist identify and respond to maladaptive interpersonal strategies frequently imported into the therapy room. The principle of complementarity, for example, states that behaviors represent stable dyadic relations that can be either positive or negative in nature. On the dimension of affiliation, hostility draws for hostility and friendliness for friendliness. On the dimension of inter-dependence, attempting to control someone draws for that person to submit, whereas granting someone autonomy pulls for that person to take it and separate. Somewhat obviously, then, therapists need to be aware of how they are being drawn, or invited, to interact. Engaging in stable, negative complementary interactions will bode poorly for the development or maintenance of a good therapeutic relationship (Safran, 1998). When such exchanges are occurring, it becomes incumbent on the therapist to recognize the pattern and to strive to intervene with a more adaptive interpersonal response, which may then in turn invite the more adaptive and affiliative response from the client. This movement toward a more adaptive dyadic engagement by providing an opposite response to the complement is known as *antithesis* in interpersonal language (e.g., Benjamin, 1984).

It is important to note that alliances with clients who have predisposing characteristics to alliance troubles are not the only ones that go sour. As any practitioner can attest, alliance problems can take place with any client and at any time. The important point is that alliance problems have tended to be more frequent and problematic with certain clients. However, even if ruptures occur, all is not lost in terms of therapeutic gain. As Safran and colleagues (e.g., Safran & Muran, 2000; Safran & Segal 1990) have argued, problems in the alliance are often events ripe for corrective relational and emotional experiences. Furthermore, research has shown that even when certain client characteristics (e.g., interpersonal problems) have a negative influence on early alliance development, the relationship can withstand such problems, grow in a more adaptive direction, and prosper (e.g., Constantino & Smith-Hansen, 2008). As we elaborate in the next section, the clinical priority appears to be to address any alliance problems in a manner that will allow the therapy to continue and that fosters the most relevant change in the client.

THERAPISTS' ACTIONS AND THE WORKING ALLIANCE

Although clients have an impact on the development and trajectory of the working alliance, so too do their therapists (Luborsky, 1994). Although research in this area is less abundant, it has begun to provide some information regarding the therapist's contribution to the development of the alliance, its deterioration, and its repair.

Development of the Alliance

Therapists differ with regard to their ability to establish a positive working alliance with their clients (Baldwin, Wampold, & Imel, 2007). Consistent with this truism, research has uncovered several general therapist attributes and behaviors that have a positive influence on alliance quality. As per Ackerman and Hilsenroth's (2003) review across heterogeneous psychotherapies, the attributes include warmth, interest, respectfulness, flexibility, openness, honesty, trustworthiness, and confidence, and the behaviors include exploration, reflection, accurate interpretation, facilitation of affect expression, and attending to clients' experience. Other alliance-facilitating therapist attributes include involvement, support, empathy, acceptance, and patience (e.g., Lietaer, 1990, 1992; Luborsky, Crits-Christoph, Mintz, & Auerbach, 1988; Watson & Greenberg, 1994). From an interpersonal perspective that frames the alliance as the moment-to-moment interpersonal process within the patient–therapist dyad, Henry and colleagues' work has suggested that positive alliances are marked by therapist behavior that is affiliative, guiding, autonomy granting, and devoid of hostile control (see Constantino, 2000; Henry & Strupp, 1994).

Several specific and innovative strategies for fostering quality alliances have also been developed and tested, at least preliminarily. These strategies differentially address the alliance from its very first step (i.e., the assessment phase) to the psychotherapy alliance proper. As Hilsenroth and Cromer (2007) argued, "Careful awareness of the therapeutic relationship as early as possible in treatment (i.e., initial interview, psychological assessment, first session) may well offer patients the best opportunity for development of a positive therapeutic relationship across the treatment process" (p. 217). Following this logic, clinicians and researchers have more frequently viewed initial assessments as a first, yet crucial, step in the development of a working alliance. For example, Finn and Tonsager (1992, 1997) developed the therapeutic model of assessment (TMA) that integrates elements of the client–therapist relationship that have more traditionally been reserved for subsequent therapy. In particular, TMA encourages assessors to commit strongly to the development of empathic connections with their clients, to work collaboratively with their clients toward establishing assessment and treatment goals, and to share and process their assessment results openly. Typically involving three sessions, the third of which centers on feedback, a TMA fulfills traditional information-gathering functions but also calls for more therapeutic processes such as exploration of, discussion around, and empathic response to current distress; identification of cyclical relational themes; facilitation and processing of client affect and experience; and in-session process commentary and inquiry.

In a study comparing TMA and a traditional information-gathering approach to assessment, Ackerman, Hilsenroth, Baity, and Blagys (2000) found that TMA clients reported better alliances and were also less likely to terminate before treatment proper than information-gathering patients. Furthermore, the assessment alliance (as measured after the feedback session) was positively associated with the treatment alliance (as measured after the third or fourth treatment session), thus supporting the lasting therapeutic impact of using a more therapeutically oriented assessment approach. Additional analyses revealed a positive association between perceived depth of the session and alliance quality among TMA clients, suggesting that clients formed better working alliances when they experienced the assessment as full and powerful and reported gaining insight into important personal conflicts and maladaptive patterns. Assessment length and perceived smoothness were unrelated to alliance quality.

Ackerman et al. (2000) discussed their findings in the context of a theoretical framework involving self, social, and interpersonal psychology. Specifically, they argued that the relational benefits of the TMA, relative to information gathering, might be the result of greater awareness of and initial response to clients' self-verification needs. According to Swann's (1983, 1996) self-verification theory, people (including those with negative self-concepts) are motivated to receive self-consistent feedback because it provides them with a sense of psychological control, coherence, prediction, and competence in at least one crucial domain—that is, knowing oneself. Purportedly, the epistemic security that arises from such consistent feedback protects individuals from the angst that would accompany feeling as though they did not know themselves.

As De La Ronde and Swann (1993) argued, working toward changing an individual's self-views first requires that therapists foster their clients' sense of control and predictability by providing them with accurate and verifying feedback. Failing to do so runs the risk of rendering the therapy exchange unproductive or anxiety ridden or leading to the dissolution of the relationship altogether (Pinel & Constantino, 2003). Thus, as underscored in the TMA model, it may be important to first provide clients with veridical assessment feedback that closely matches their own preconceptions (Finn & Tonsager, 1997). Furthermore, an optimal dose of verification may allow the client to experience the therapist as an understanding and credible helper. As Linehan (1997) noted, "Therapeutic shrewdness increases the client's trust that the real problems will be taken care of" (p. 182). This problem validation, in turn, may promote greater faith in any new, adaptive, and positive information that a therapist may subsequently present in the service of change.

Of course, psychosocial therapies are generally geared toward helping clients change their negative self-conceptions (e.g., J. S. Beck, 1995; Silberschatz, 2005), disembed from maladaptive interpersonal patterns (e.g., Benjamin, 1984; Keisler, 1983, 1988; Silberschatz, 2005), or both. However, therapists who provide discrepant information or engage in novel interactions too quickly may threaten the very working alliance that will help promote the desired changes (Constantino, 2002). Although TMA assessment is rather brief, it may set the stage for clients to begin entertaining alternate ways of perceiving themselves and others, but only after a meaningful dose of verification meets an inherent self-striving, fosters relationship integration, and establishes a condition under which change can be tolerated (Pinel & Constantino, 2003). The benefits of this condition may endure even beyond the early treatment alliance. In a follow-up study, Hilsenroth, Peters, and Ackerman (2004) found that TMA clients maintained high-quality alliances from assessment through late treatment.

Focused on the therapy alliance, Crits-Christoph et al. (2006) examined the preliminary efficacy of a 16-session alliance-fostering therapy that included strategies culled from the expansive literature and organized around Bordin's (1979) tripartite alliance model (i.e., agreement on goals, agreement on tasks, and bond). In particular, five trainees treated three separate cases before, during, and after the alliance training. Although the small sample precluded statistical significance, moderate to large effect sizes were observed for higher client-rated alliance from pre- to posttraining. In another study, Hilsenroth, Ackerman, Clemence, Strassle, and Handler (2002) administered a structured clinical training to 13 advanced doctoral students in clinical psychology. The training included TMA strategies and strategies for building rapport, developing collaboration, making empathic connections, responding to emergent client needs, socializing clients to the treatment, and exploring clients' relational problems, including as they manifest in the client–therapist exchange. Comparing a group of 15 doctoral students delivering treatment as usual (and receiving supervision as usual) with a group of matched clients, the structured clinical training therapists produced higher alliance ratings after the fourth session. In light of these findings, it is clear that therapists can have a positive impact on the development and evolution of the alliance, which is encouraging considering the clinical importance of the client–therapist relationship. Of course, there is the converse scenario in which therapist attributes or behaviors can have a negative impact on the alliance.

Worsening of the Alliance

In a separate review across heterogeneous psychotherapies, Ackerman and Hilsenroth (2001) found that multiple therapist qualities and behaviors had a detrimental influence on the alliance. The qualities included rigidity, criticalness, distance, distractedness, uncertainty, and tenseness, and the behaviors included overstructuring of the session, overuse of transference interpretations, inappropriate self-disclosure, and inappropriate use of silence. Emerging adolescent and youth research in this area has pointed to negative therapist behaviors such as pushing the client to talk, being overly formal, or overly emphasizing shared experiences (Creed & Kendall, 2005) and therapist "lapse" behaviors (misunderstanding, failure to acknowledge emotion, criticism, and too much emphasis on the details of the situation or in recalling information from previous sessions) as contributing to negative alliance (Karver et al., 2008).

Regarding rigidity, several studies have underscored the disruptive nature of adhering rigidly to theory-prescribed techniques. For example, in a study of cognitive therapy for depression, Castonguay, Goldfried, Wiser, Raue, and Hayes (1996) found that therapists' persistent use of cognitive strategies when encountering alliance tensions may actually have exacerbated such tensions, or ruptures, rather than abated them. As revealed through descriptive analyses, when clients expressed doubt about their therapist's ability to help or the utility of the cognitive approach, some therapists responded by attempting to convince clients of the merits of cognitive therapy or by treating the clients' concerns as evidence of a distorted cognition on which they could work. This perseverative adherence to the treatment model did not appear to validate clients' momentary concerns (often relational in nature) and seemed to create a vicious cycle of miscoordination, misattunement, and alliance rupture.

Similar to the vicious cycle observed by Castonguay et al. (1996), Piper et al. (1999) found that therapists' rigid use of transference interpretations to address client resistance in psychodynamic psychotherapy was associated with increased client resistance and reduced client engagement, which in turn prompted more therapist transference interpretations, and so forth. In another study on psychodynamic therapy, Schut et al. (2005) found that a higher concentration of interpretations not only related negatively with outcome but also corresponded to disaffiliative processes before and during interpretations. As they noted, the "results suggest that therapists who persisted with interpretations had more hostile interactions with patients and had patients who reacted with less warmth than therapists who used interpretations more judiciously" (Schut et al., 2005, p. 494). Henry et al. (1993) also found that therapists' rigid adherence to time-limited dynamic psychotherapy was associated with decreased levels of therapist approval, support, and optimism and greater authoritarian and defensive behavior. Ironically, the therapists in this study underwent training in time-limited dynamic psychotherapy that specifically emphasized the recognition of and response to negative interpersonal process. For the practicing clinician, the implication of these process findings should be clear. No matter what type of treatment and irrespective of the presenting problem and population, it is important to avoid perseverating in the application of prescribed techniques without insight into the interpersonal dynamics that are at play. Doing so may be at the expense of the alliance, treatment outcome, or both.

Further analyses of the time-limited dynamic psychotherapy data indicated that therapists' interpersonal histories and self-conceptions also had a bearing on the quality of the relational process between client and therapist. Hilliard et al. (2000) found that therapists' negative perceptions of their own relationship with their parents during childhood predicted poorer interpersonal process in session. Furthermore, Henry, Schacht, and Strupp (1990) found that therapists with more hostile introjects engaged in three times more disaffiliative communications with their clients than therapists with self-affiliative introjects. As Henry and Strupp (1994) cogently discussed, such results suggest that the way therapists are treated by their parents during childhood affects their self-concept, the ways they treat their clients, and ultimately the outcome of therapy. As should not be surprising to any clinician, it is not just the client's relational patterns that make up the therapy session but rather the integration of two individuals' (or more in group, family, and couple's therapy) life histories, introject states, pervasive manners of relating, and overall disposition. Therefore, it appears important that a clinician have an optimal level of insight into his or her ways of relating to self and others because the preceding findings have illustrated the potential impact that such processes can have on the course and nature of therapy.

Resolution of Alliance Ruptures

Although therapists can contribute to problems in the therapeutic relationship, clinical practice and emerging research evidence inform us that they can also take steps to repair such problems. For example, David Burns (1990; Burns & Auerbach, 1996), a leader in cognitive therapy, has argued for using several listening techniques to address a client's negative reaction to the therapy, to the therapeutic relationship, or both. The first involves the therapist warmly inviting the client to discuss his or her subjective experiences. The intent of this listening technique is to foster a safe space for the client to disclose openly any negative thoughts or emotions resulting from perceived therapist failures to be empathetic or attentive to the client's needs. Without such gentle probing, the therapist's assessment of the client's affective state may be purely speculative and possibly incorrect. Burns and Auerbach (1996) encouraged therapists to check in regularly on the emotional status of their clients because this focus should help the therapist better understand the client's subjective experience and trigger an accurate expression of empathy for the client's difficulties (including difficulties related to the treatment or the therapist). As Squier (1990) noted, for empathy to have a beneficial impact, it needs to be consistent with what the client is actually perceiving and feeling.

Drawing on Rogerian (1951) theory, Burns (1990; Burns & Auerbach, 1996) advanced a second therapist listening technique of *empathetic expression*. This technique involves both the rephrasing of the client's words to demonstrate that the therapist is attuned to the client's disclosures (i.e., thought empathy) and the therapist's expression of feelings that he or she thinks the client must be experiencing on the basis of the client's disclosures (i.e., feeling empathy). According to Burns, the therapist's acknowledgment of and inquiry into the client's negative feelings are likely to promote the client's feeling validated, understood, and respected (all of which should have a positive impact on the therapeutic alliance and treatment process). Developmental theory has suggested that such attunement may be particularly important in working with adolescents given the primacy of their working through developmental phases of intimacy and autonomy (Steinberg, 2005).

As the third listening technique, Burns (1990; Burns & Auerbach, 1996) advanced *disarming*. This powerful technique reflects the therapist's explicit validation of the client's negative feelings or criticisms toward him or her or the treatment. Even if the client's criticisms seem exaggerated, distorted, unreasonable, or unfair, the therapist is encouraged to recognize explicitly some truth in the client's disclosures. By doing so, the therapist imparts the message that the client's feelings are valid and respected and that the therapist is willing to take at least partial blame for any relationship difficulties or treatment missteps. According to Burns, therapists virtually always play a role in alliance problems, even if they are working very hard to be technically sound and emotionally sensitive. Although some therapists may find it difficult or embarrassing to admit contributions to the client's negative experience in therapy, the cost of not doing so may well be even more distressing. For example, when clients express that therapy (or the therapist) has not been helpful, the first reaction of many therapists is to point out that the client's situation is not that problematic and that more progress has been made than it might appear. However, many clients perceive such a reaction as defensive and possibly even blaming. This perception would only confirm the client's feelings that the therapist is not being helpful, increase the client's frustration toward the therapist or therapy, or both. Clearly, this negative cycle is not likely to bode well for therapeutic improvement.

As per Burns's (1990; Burns & Auerbach, 1996) disarming strategy, a more therapeutically fruitful approach would involve the therapist accepting some blame for the therapeutic impasse. Such an intervention is likely to create a sense of shared experience between two fallible individuals, as opposed to imposing an invalidating (and invalid) expression that I (the therapist) am right and you (the client) are wrong. Burns and Auerbach (1996) suggested that in response to the client's expression of dissatisfaction, the therapist say something to the effect of,

> You know, what you're saying is important, and I agree with you. I can see from your depression and anxiety scores that you've been extremely upset in the past several weeks. I've also noticed some tension in our relationship, and I'm concerned that recently I haven't done a good job of helping you or understanding how you feel. I can imagine you may be feeling quite discouraged and angry with me. Am I reading you right? I'd like to hear more about how you feel. (p. 154)

According to Burns and Auerbach (1996), this acknowledgment of at least some degree of therapist letdown is likely to disarm the client's antagonism or anger and restore the relationship to one in which each member feels as though he or she is working in a collaborative manner with another. Moreover, by avoiding a blaming or defensive stance, the therapist has disrupted the cycle of negative interpersonal behavior whereby blame heightens client hostility, which then increases the likelihood of a hostile response on the part of the therapist, which invites further defensiveness and blame, and so forth. As we have discussed earlier, research has suggested that therapist defensiveness and hostility can be detrimental to the process and outcome of therapy, whereas the affiliative encouragement of client disclosures is likely to lead to a more productive treatment course.

Although Burns's (1990; Burns & Auerbach, 1996) discussion of listening skills has focused primarily on cognitive therapy, his insightful clinical recommendations are relevant to all psychotherapies. In fact, disarming in many ways parallels the interpersonal principle of antithesis discussed earlier (Benjamin, 1984). According to interpersonal theorists, antithesis reflects a behavior in which one would engage if one were attempting to get the other interactant to behave in a way that is opposite of his or her current interpersonal stance. As Burns and Auerbach (1996) noted, "It may be very difficult for any therapist to resist a difficult patient's subtle but forceful invitation to engage in an adversarial relationship" (p. 151). Cognitive and interpersonal therapists alike (and therapists of all orientations, for that matter) have worked with such clients—those, for example, who sulk and withdraw from therapy because they feel it is not helping and that their therapist has somehow failed them. The interpersonal invitation to the therapist in such instances would be to respond by blaming the client for his or her limited gain because of poor engagement in the treatment process. If a therapist adopts a blaming stance, however, he or she is likely to invite further client withdrawal and sulking, thereby reinforcing a cycle of adversarial dialogue. However, if a therapist acts in an antithetical manner (i.e., doing the opposite of blaming, which in interpersonal terms can be construed as affirming or understanding the client's stance), then it would in turn invite a more adaptive response from the client. That is, if a therapist affirms and validates the client's negative emotions, this transitive interpersonal act on the part of the therapist would then invite the client's intransitive complement of being affirmed and understood, which is to disclose and express one's feelings.

As Benjamin (1984) noted, antithetical behavior invites maximal change and can go a long way toward disrupting a client's maladaptive behavioral cycles. Also, in the example just mentioned, getting a client to disclose and express his or her feelings has much more therapeutic value than continuing the cycle of blame, hostility, and withdrawal. The end result, similar to a therapist who uses Burns's (1990; Burns & Auerbach, 1996) disarming technique in the service of repairing a rupture, is likely to be a return to a stable therapeutic relationship in which the client and therapist work optimally in a collaborative manner toward the goals of treatment.

Jeremy Safran and his colleagues (e.g., Safran et al., 1990; Safran & Muran, 2000; Safran, Muran, Samstag, & Stevens, 2002; Safran & Segal, 1990) have also developed strategies to repair alliance ruptures. These authors placed a premium on therapists being able to adopt a participant–observer stance— that is, remaining engaged in the treatment while being simultaneously attentive to potential problems in the relationship (Sullivan, 1953). Safran and colleagues have also emphasized the importance of therapists exploring their own contributions to the relational strain. Although these authors recognize that clients also contribute to these difficulties, they have argued that the therapist's focus on his or her responsibility should be the starting point for rupture resolution. Echoing Rogers's (1961) words, openness to one's experience leads to another person being open to his or her own experience. During this resolution stage, Safran and colleagues recommended that therapists use empathetic communication skills to help their clients identify and describe their momentary relational experiences. This use of empathy and the therapist's openness to admitting potential mistakes or empathetic failures are similar to Burns's (Burns, 1990; Burns & Auerbach, 1996) notions of thought and feeling empathy and disarming described earlier. The hope is that by acknowledging their own role in the alliance rupture, therapists can engage their clients more therapeutically in the exploration of the clients' contributions to the relationship difficulties (e.g., the client's submissive behaviors inviting therapist's controlling interventions, the client's hostile utterances inviting either subtle or explicit reciprocal therapist hostility). Moreover, to the extent that the therapist can facilitate client openness and momentary processing of the relationship, treatment might then be able to focus on how the relational problems that are occurring in the therapeutic relationship may be core maladaptive patterns linked with relational disturbances outside of therapy.

The listening strategies described by Burns and colleagues (Burns, 1990; Burns & Auerbach, 1996) and Safran and colleagues (e.g., Safran & Muran, 2000; Safran & Segal, 1990) might be particularly relevant to the treatment of adolescents. Because of the importance of modeling as a learning process in adolescence, the therapist's demonstration of openness and willingness to admit mistakes or empathetic failures might go far in helping to shape an adolescent's ways of interacting with others. Adolescence, perhaps more than any period in one's life, is a time when poor ways of interacting with others are either further ingrained in the individual or altered as a result of adaptive encounters with others (e.g., peers, teachers, therapists).

The alliance rupture–resolution techniques just described have begun to receive empirical support in adult treatments. The findings of a number of studies conducted by Safran and colleagues (e.g., Muran et al., 2009; Safran et al., 1990, 1994; Safran & Muran, 1996) have suggested that the exploration of the experience of both therapist and client in therapy does facilitate the resolution of alliance ruptures and contribute to better treatment outcomes. These researchers have also developed brief relational therapy (Safran & Muran, 2000), based on the rupture–resolution principles described earlier. Across two recent clinical trials, brief relational therapy had lower dropout rates than short-term psychodynamic and cognitive–behavioral therapies, thus underscoring the potential value of interpersonal rupture–repair strategies for promoting prolonged treatment engagement (Muran, Safran, Samstag, & Winston, 2005; Safran, Muran, Samstag, & Winston, 2005).

Investigators have also begun to examine whether the rupture–repair strategies developed by Burns (1990; Burns & Auerbach, 1996) and Safran and colleagues (e.g., Safran & Muran, 2000; Safran & Segal, 1990) can be effectively assimilated into a "pure-form" therapy to improve that therapy's effectiveness. Castonguay et al. (2004) developed an integrative cognitive therapy (ICT) for adult depression that incorporates these strategies within traditional cognitive therapy (CT; A. T. Beck, Rush, Shaw, & Emery, 1979; J. S. Beck, 1995). Specifically, ICT therapists are trained to break momentarily from traditional CT when faced with markers of an alliance rupture. Instead of increasing their reliance on the cognitive model and its corresponding techniques (a strategy that may exacerbate rather than resolve relational difficulties; Castonguay et al., 1996), ICT therapists use the aforementioned humanistic and interpersonal strategies for addressing alliance ruptures (i.e., gently inquiring about the relational problems and the client's related feelings, empathizing with the client's stated and likely felt experience related to the alliance rupture, and recognizing and processing the therapist's own contribution to the relational strain). Once the relationship difficulties have been explored and adequately resolved, ICT therapists resume traditional CT techniques.

Across two pilot ICT studies, the findings have been promising (albeit preliminary). Castonguay et al. (2004) found that client improvement was significantly greater in ICT than in a waiting-list control condition, with an effect size for the main depression measure that was more than twice that those of other studies comparing CT to waiting-list or placebo control groups. Using an additive design, Constantino, Marnell, et al. (2008) found that depressed patients receiving ICT evidenced greater posttreatment improvement and more clinically significant change than patients receiving CT proper. ICT patients also had higher alliance and empathy scores across the course of treatment than CT patients.

The same techniques designed to repair alliance ruptures have also been included in a treatment for generalized anxiety disorder that augments cognitive–behavioral therapy with an interpersonal–emotional-processing therapy (Newman, Castonguay, Borkovec & Molnar, 2004). In a preliminary feasibility trial, clients receiving both cognitive–behavioral therapy and interpersonal–emotion-processing therapy demonstrated significant anxiety reduction at posttreatment and durability of gains at 1-year follow-up. Furthermore, clients evidenced clinically significant improvement on target generalized anxiety disorder symptoms and interpersonal functioning, with larger effect sizes than traditional cognitive–behavioral therapy–only treatments (Newman, Castonguay, Borkovec, Nordberg, & Fisher, 2008).

Summary

As documented in this section, therapists should perceive some client characteristics as red flags for the possible development of problems in the therapeutic relationship. It should also be clear, however, that therapists can, by what they do and who they are, interfere with the alliance quality. As Safran et al. (1990) argued, an alliance rupture should be viewed as an interpersonal process and thus, by definition, involves client and therapist contributions. What then are the clinical implications of this later collection of findings related to the therapist's role in the course of the therapeutic relationship?

One finding is that therapists who tend to treat themselves in a hostile manner are at a greater risk of being hostile toward their clients than are those therapists who possess an affiliative introject (Henry et al., 1993). This suggests that these "at-risk" therapists (and by no means only they) should attempt to maintain a participant–observer role in therapy. This engaged observer stance allows therapists to distance themselves from and to become aware of their potentially negative reactions toward clients without disengaging from the collaborative treatment effort. Because this is not an easy task, supervision (including close scrutiny of videotapes) may be indicated for those therapists who tend to treat themselves harshly. The importance of the participant–observer stance (and of supervision to foster it) is further supported by the fact that only a small number of hostile or disaffiliative therapist behaviors can have a significantly negative impact on the course and outcome of treatment (Henry et al., 1993).

Therapists should also keep in mind that some technical strategies, despite being prescribed by one's theoretical orientation, might have a negative impact on the client–therapist relationship when used in inappropriate interpersonal contexts (e.g., when a client has negative feelings related to the therapist, the treatment, or both). Although many techniques (e.g., examining the link between thoughts and emotions, transference interpretations) may be helpful in a variety of clinical situations, they may prove ineffectual if used too rigidly in the context of alliance ruptures or struggles for control of the therapy process (e.g., Castonguay et al., 1996; Piper et al., 1999; Schut et al., 2005).

Although additional research is required before definitive statements can be made, a number of therapeutic interventions may well have a positive impact on the resolution of alliance ruptures. When faced with a problem in the alliance, therapists should first avoid perseverating. They should stop using the techniques in which they are engaged and, instead, reflect on their own experience of what is occurring in the room. Although this step in and of itself is not likely to resolve the rupture, it may well be a crucial step in preventing or disrupting a potentially toxic cycle of interpersonal exchanges. As a second step, therapists are advised to apply listening and communication procedures described by Burns (e.g., Burns, 1990; Burns & Auerbach, 1996), Safran (e.g., Safran & Muran, 2000; Safran & Segal, 1990), and other psychotherapy researchers and practitioners (i.e., inviting clients to discuss their here-and-now experience of the relationship and the treatment itself, exploring and empathizing with clients' emotional disclosures, sharing one's own experience of the interaction and process of therapy, and, above all, taking responsibility for one's own role in the alliance strain). As Binder and Strupp (1997) posited, such strategies are best captured by Kiesler's (1996) notion of metacommunication.

It is also important to keep in mind that alliance ruptures, despite their inherently disaffiliative nature, are not to be avoided at all costs. Change in psychotherapy is a difficult process, and client resistance to, or ambivalence about, change is to be expected. As mentioned earlier, even if clients seeks improvement, any change in how they view themselves and their world is likely to cultivate anxiety and possible feelings of uncontrollability (e.g., Andrews, 1991; Safran, 1998; Sullivan, 1953). Thus, reluctance to change and concomitant relational impasses are likely to occur. Furthermore, the interpersonal dispositions of some clients might invite disruptive and maladaptive responses from their therapists, which can in turn contribute to relational strain. However, with the appropriate response to such strain can come the awareness of and eventual modification of pervasive, maladaptive interpersonal processes. The key, in our view, is to maintain a participant–observer stance and to aim for what Linehan (1993) eloquently described as a balance between change (or challenge) and acceptance (or validation).

CONCLUDING THOUGHTS

Catalyzed by the APA Division 12 Task Force on Empirically Supported Treatments (Chambless & Hollon, 1998), the field has placed considerable emphasis (in terms of research and training priority) on techniques of intervention. The findings described in this chapter, however, suggest that prescribed techniques are not the only variables responsible for change. These findings also suggest that the field is currently moving in a promising direction by paying greater attention to relationship variables. This shift can be seen in the implementation of two recent APA task forces. As mentioned, Division 29 created one of these with the aim of identifying empirically supported relationship variables (Norcross, 2002). Sponsored by Division 12 and the North American Society for Psychotherapy Research, the other delineated effective principles of change on the basis of variables related to technical, relational, and participant factors (Castonguay & Beutler, 2006).

Although the field as a whole is paying more attention to the contribution of relationship variables (the working alliance being chief among them), it is also important to recognize that researchers interested in children and adolescents have yet to devote as much attention to these factors as have researchers interested in adults. In fact, not too long ago in a survey of more than 200 treatment studies (with children, adolescents, or both as the clinical populations) conducted between 1970 and 1988, Kazdin, Bass, et al. (1990) found that only 2.7% of these studies addressed the relationship between process variables (such as the alliance) and outcome. Fortunately, psychotherapy process research, and more specifically the study of the therapeutic alliance, with children and adolescents has been exponentially increasing in recent years, and the field now has several meta-analyses, reviews, and theoretical road maps to guide further practice and research in this area (e.g., Karver et al., 2006, 2008; Kazdin & Nock, 2003; Shirk & Karver, 2003; Weisz & Hawley, 2002). Furthermore, the increased investigation of process variables such as the alliance might not only increase our understanding of why psychotherapy with adolescents either works or fails to work, but it would also help to further solidify the bridge between clinicians and researchers.

REFERENCES

Abouguendia, M., Joyce, A., Piper, W., & Ogrodniczuk, J. (2004). Alliance as a mediator of expectancy effects in short-term group psychotherapy. *Group Dynamics: Theory, Research, and Practice, 8*, 3–12. doi:10.1037/1089-2699.8.1.3

Ackerman, S. J., & Hilsenroth, M. J. (2001). A review of therapist characteristics and techniques negatively impacting the therapeutic alliance. *Psychotherapy: Theory, Research, Practice, Training, 38*, 171–185.

Ackerman, S. J., & Hilsenroth, M. J. (2003). A review of therapist characteristics and techniques positively influencing the therapeutic alliance. *Clinical Psychology Review, 23*, 1–33. doi:10.1016/S0272-7358(02)00146-0

Ackerman, S. J., Hilsenroth, M. J., Baity, M. R., & Blagys, M. D. (2000). Interaction of therapeutic process and alliance during psychological assessment. *Journal of Personality Assessment, 75*, 82–109. doi:10.1207/S15327752JPA7501_7

Alexander, L. B., & Luborsky, L. (1986). The Penn Helping Alliance Scales. In L. S. Greenberg & W. M. Pinsof (Eds.), *The psychotherapeutic process: A research handbook* (pp. 325–366). New York, NY: Guilford Press.

Andrews, J. D. W. (1991). *The active self in psychotherapy: An integration of therapeutic styles.* Boston, MA: Allyn & Bacon.

Arnkoff, D. B., Glass, C. R., & Shapiro, S. J. (2002). Expectations and preferences.. In J. Norcross (Ed.), *Psychotherapy relationships that work: Therapist contributions and responsiveness to patients* (pp. 335–356). New York, NY: Oxford University Press.

Austin, J. T., & Vancouver, J. B. (1996). Goal constructs in psychology: Structure, process and content. *Psychological Bulletin, 120*, 338–375. doi:10.1037/0033-2909.120.3.338

Bachelor, A. (1991). Comparison and relationship to outcome of diverse dimensions of the helping alliance as seen by client and therapist. *Psychotherapy: Theory, Research, Practice, Training, 28*, 534–549.

Baldwin, S. A., Wampold, B. E., & Imel, Z. E. (2007). Untangling the alliance–outcome correlation: Exploring the relative importance of therapist and patient variability in the alliance. *Journal of Consulting and Clinical Psychology, 75*, 842–852. doi:10.1037/0022-006X.75.6.842

Barber, J. P., Connolly, M. B., Crits-Christoph, P., Gladis, L., & Siqueland, L. (2000). Alliance predicts patients' outcome beyond in-treatment change in symptoms. *Journal of Consulting and Clinical Psychology, 68*, 1027–1032. doi:10.1037/0022-006X.68.6.1027

Beck, A. T., Rush, A. J., Shaw, B. F., & Emery, G. (1979). *Cognitive therapy of depression.* New York, NY: Guilford Press.

Beck, J. S. (1995). *Cognitive therapy: Basics and beyond.* New York, NY: Guilford Press.

Benjamin, L. S. (1974). Structural analysis of social behavior. *Psychological Review, 81*, 392–425. doi:10.1037/h0037024

Benjamin, L. S. (1984). Principles of prediction using structural analysis of social behavior. In R. A. Zucker, J. Aranoff, & A. J. Rabin (Eds.), *Personality and the prediction of behavior* (pp. 121–173). New York, NY: Academic Press.

Benjamin, L. S. (1996). Introduction to the special section on structural analysis of social behavior. *Journal of Consulting and Clinical Psychology, 64*, 1203–1212. doi:10.1037/0022-006X.64.6.1203

Beretta, V., de Roten, Y., Stigler, M., Fischer, M., Despland, J., & Drapeau, M. (2005). The influence of patient's interpersonal schemas on early alliance building. *Swiss Journal of Psychology/Schweizerische Zeitschrift für Psychologie/Revue Suisse de Psychologie, 64*, 13–20.

Binder, J. L., & Strupp, H. H. (1997). "Negative process": A recurrently discovered and underestimated facet of therapeutic process and outcome in the individual psychotherapy of adults. *Clinical Psychology: Science and Practice, 4*, 121–139.

Bordin, E. S. (1979). The generalizability of the psychoanalytic concept of the working alliance. *Psychotherapy, 16*, 252–260. doi:10.1037/h0085885

Burns, D. D. (1990). *The feeling good handbook.* New York, NY: Plume.

Burns, D. D., & Auerbach, A. (1996). Therapeutic empathy in cognitive-behavioral therapy: Does it really make a difference? In P. M. Salkovskis (Ed.), *Frontiers of cognitive therapy* (pp. 135–164). New York, NY: Guilford Press.

Carver, C. S., & Scheier, M. (1998). *On the self-regulation of behavior.* New York, NY: Cambridge University Press.

Castonguay, L. G., & Beutler, L. E. (2006). *Principles of therapeutic change that work.* New York, NY: Oxford University Press.

Castonguay, L. G., Boswell, J. F., Constantino, M. J., Goldfried, M. R., & Hill, C. E. (in press). Training implications of harmful effects of psychological treatments. *American Psychologist.*

Castonguay, L. G., Constantino, M. J., & Holtforth, M. G. (2006). The working alliance: Where are we and where should we go? *Psychotherapy: Theory, Research, Practice, Training, 43*, 271–279.

Castonguay, L. G., Constantino, M. J., Przeworksi, A., Newman, M. G., & Borkovec, T. D. (2008, June). *Alliance, therapist adherence, therapist competence, and client receptivity: New analyses on change processes in CBT for generalized anxiety disorder.* Paper presented at the 39th annual meeting of the Society for Psychotherapy Research, Barcelona, Spain.

Castonguay, L. G., Goldfried, M. R., Wiser, S., Raue, P. J., & Hayes, A. M. (1996). Predicting the effect of cognitive therapy for depression: A study of unique and common factors. *Journal of Consulting and Clinical Psychology, 64*, 497–504. doi:10.1037/0022-006X.64.3.497

Castonguay, L. G., Norberg, S. S., Schut, A. J., & Constantino, M. J. (in press). Psychotherapy research. In I. Weiner, W. E. Craighead, & C. B. Nemeroff (Eds.), *Encyclopedia of psychology and neuroscience* (4th ed., pp. –). New York, NY: Wiley.

Castonguay, L. G., Schut, A. J., Aikins, D., Constantino, M. J., Laurenceau, J. P., Bologh, L., & Burns, D. D. (2004). Repairing alliance ruptures in cognitive therapy: A preliminary investigation of an integrative therapy for depression. *Journal of Psychotherapy Integration, 14*, 4–20. doi:10.1037/1053-0479.14.1.4

Chambless, D. K., & Hollon, S. D. (1998). Defining empirically supported therapies. *Journal of Consulting and Clinical Psychology, 66*, 7–18. doi:10.1037/0022-006X.66.1.7

Church, E. (1994). The role of autonomy in adolescent psychotherapy. *Psychotherapy: Theory, Research, Practice, Training, 31*, 101–108.

Connolly Gibbons, M. B., Crits-Christoph, P., de la Cruz, C., Barber, J. P., Siqueland, L., & Gladis, M. (2003). Pretreatment expectations, interpersonal functioning, and symptoms in the prediction of the therapeutic alliance across supportive-expressive psychotherapy and cognitive therapy. *Psychotherapy Research, 13*, 59–76. doi:10.1093/ptr/kpg007

Constantino, M. J. (2000). Interpersonal process in psychotherapy through the lens of the structural analysis of social behavior. *Applied & Preventive Psychology, 9*, 153–172. doi:10.1016/S0962-1849(05)80002-2

Constantino, M. J. (2002). *Interpersonal/intrapsychic process in psychotherapy: The impact of self-verification strivings on the working alliance*. Unpublished doctoral dissertation, Pennsylvania State University, University Park.

Constantino, M. J., Arnow, B. A., Blasey, C., & Agras, W. S. (2005). The association between patient characteristics and the therapeutic alliance in cognitive–behavioral and interpersonal therapy for bulimia nervosa. *Journal of Consulting and Clinical Psychology, 73*, 203–211. doi:10.1037/0022-006X.73.2.203

Constantino, M. J., Castonguay, M. G., & Schut, A. J. (2002). *The working alliance: A flagship for the scientist-practitioner model in psychotherapy*. In G. S. Tryon (Ed.), *Counseling based on process research: Applying what we know* (pp. 81–131). Boston, MA: Allyn & Bacon.

Constantino, M. J., & DeGeorge, J. (2008, March). Believing is seeing: Clinical implications of research on patient expectations. *Psychotherapy E-News*. Retrieved from http://www.divisionofpsychotherapy.org/ PsychotherapyENews/NewsUCanUse/NUCU5.pdf

Constantino, M. J., Klecak. A., Castonguay, L. G., Manning, M. A., Newman, M. G., & Borkovec, T. D. (2008). *Patient expectations, therapeutic alliance, and outcome in cognitive-behavioral therapy for generalized anxiety disorder: Analyzing a mediational pathway*. Manuscript in preparation.

Constantino, M. J., Marnell, M., Haile, A. J., Kanther-Sista, S. N., Wolman, K., Zappert, L., & Arnow, B. A. (2008). Integrative cognitive therapy for depression: A randomized pilot comparison. *Psychotherapy: Theory, Research, Practice, Training, 45*, 122–134.

Constantino, M., & Smith-Hansen, L. (2008). Patient interpersonal factors and the therapeutic alliance in two treatments for bulimia nervosa. *Psychotherapy Research, 18*, 683–698. doi:10.1080/10503300802183702

Cooper, M. (2008). *Essential research findings in counselling and psychotherapy: The facts are friendly*. London, England: Sage.

Creed, T. A., & Kendall, P. C. (2005). Therapist alliance-building behavior within a cognitive–behavioral treatment for anxiety in youth. *Journal of Consulting and Clinical Psychology, 73*, 498–505. doi:10.1037/0022-006X.73.3.498

Crits-Christoph, P., Gibbons, B. C., Crits-Cristoph, K., Narducci, J., Schamberger, M., & Gallop, R. (2006). Can therapists be trained to improve their alliances? A preliminary study of alliance-fostering psychotherapy. *Psychotherapy Research, 16*, 268–281. doi:10.1080/10503300500268557

de La Ronde, C., & Swann, W. B., Jr. (1993). Caught in the crossfire: Positivity and self-verification strivings among people with low self-esteem. In R. F. Baumeister (Ed.), *Self-esteem: The puzzle of low self regard* (pp. 147–165). New York, NY: Plenum Press.

De Los Reyes, A., & Kazdin, A. E. (2004). Measuring informant discrepancies in clinical child research. *Psychological Assessment, 16*, 330–334. doi:10.1037/1040-3590.16.3.330

DiGiuseppe, R., Linscott, J., & Jilton, R. (1996). Developing the therapeutic alliance in child-adolescent psychotherapy. *Applied and Preventive Psychology, 5,* 85–100. doi:10.1016/S0962-1849(96)80002-3

Dumas, J. E., Moreland, A. D., Gitter, A. H., Pearl, A. M., & Nordstrom, A. H. (2006). Engaging parents in preventive parenting groups: Do ethnic, socioeconomic, and belief match between parents and group leaders matter? *Health Education & Behavior, 35,* 619–633. doi:10.1177/1090198106291374

Durlak, J. A., Fuhrman, T., & Lampman, C. (1991). Effectiveness of cognitive-behavior therapy for maladapting children: A meta-analysis. *Psychological Bulletin, 110,* 204–214. doi:10.1037/0033-2909.110.2.204

Eames, V., & Roth, A. (2000). Patient attachment orientation and the early working alliance: A study of patient and therapist reports of alliance quality and ruptures. *Psychotherapy Research, 10,* 421–434. doi:10.1093/ptr/10.4.421

Elkin, I., Yamaguchi, J. L., Arnkoff, D. B., Glass, C. R., Sotsky, S. M., & Krupnick, J. L. (1999). "Patient-treatment fit" and early engagement in therapy. *Psychotherapy Research, 9,* 437–451. doi:10.1093/ptr/9.4.437

Elvins, R., & Green, J. (2008). The conceptualization and measurement of therapeutic alliance: An empirical review. *Clinical Psychology Review, 28,* 1167–1187. doi:10.1016/j.cpr.2008.04.002

Eltz, M. J., Shirk, S. R., & Sarlin, N. (1995). Alliance formation and treatment outcome among maltreated adolescents. *Child Abuse & Neglect, 19,* 419–431. doi:10.1016/0145-2134(95)00008-V

Farsimadan, F., Draghi-Lorenz, R., & Ellis, J. (2007). Process and outcome of therapy in ethnically similar and dissimilar therapeutic dyads. *Psychotherapy Research, 17,* 567–575. doi:10.1080/10503300601139996

Faw, L., Hogue, A., Johnson, S., Diamond, G. M., & Liddle, H. A. (2005). The Adolescent Therapeutic Alliance Scale (ATAS): Initial psychometrics and prediction of outcome in family-based substance abuse prevention counseling. *Psychotherapy Research, 15,* 141–154.

Finn, S. E., & Tonsager, M. E. (1992). The therapeutic effects of providing MMPI-2 feedback to college students awaiting psychotherapy. *Psychological Assessment, 4,* 278–287. doi:10.1037/1040-3590.4.3.278

Finn, S. E., & Tonsager, M. E. (1997). Information-gathering and therapeutic models of assessment: Complementary paradigms. *Psychological Assessment, 9,* 374–385. doi:10.1037/1040-3590.9.4.374

Fitzpatrick, M. R., & Irannejad, S. (2008). Adolescent readiness for change and working alliance in counseling. *Journal of Counseling and Development, 86,* 438–445.

Florsheim, P., Shotorbani, S., Guest-Warnick, G., Barratt, T., & Hwang, W. (2000). Role of the working alliance in the treatment of delinquent boys in community-based programs. *Journal of Clinical Child Psychology, 29,* 94–107. doi:10.1207/S15374424jccp2901_10

Freedheim, D. K., & Russ, S. K. (1983). Psychotherapy with children. In C. E. Walter & M. C. Roberts (Eds.), *Handbook of child psychology* (pp. 978–994). New York, NY: Wiley.

Garcia, J. A., & Weisz, J. R. (2002). When youth mental health care stops: Therapeutic relationship problems and other reasons for ending youth outpatient treatment. *Journal of Consulting and Clinical Psychology, 70,* 439–443. doi:10.1037/0022-006X.70.2.439

Garland, A. F., Lewczyk-Boxmeyer, C. M., Gabayan, E. N., & Hawley, K. M. (2004). Multiple stakeholder agreement on desired outcomes for adolescents' mental health services. *Psychiatric Services, 55,* 671–676. doi:10.1176/appi.ps.55.6.671

Gaston, L., & Marmar, C. R. (1994). The California Psychotherapy Alliance Scales. In A. O. Horvath & L. S. Greenberg (Eds.), *The working alliance: Theory, research and practice* (pp. 85–108). New York, NY: Wiley.

Gaston, L., Marmar, C., Thompson, L. W., & Gallagher, D. (1988). Relation of patient pre-treatment characteristics to the therapeutic alliance in diverse psychotherapies. *Journal of Consulting and Clinical Psychology, 56*, 483–489. doi:10.1037/0022-006X.56.4.483

Goldman, G. A., & Anderson, T. (2007). Quality of object relations and security of attachment as predictors of early therapeutic alliance. *Journal of Counseling Psychology, 54*, 111–117. doi:10.1037/0022-0167.54.2.111

Gomes-Schwartz, B. (1978). Effective ingredients in psychotherapy: Prediction of outcome from process variables. *Journal of Consulting and Clinical Psychology, 46*, 1023–1035. doi:10.1037/0022-006X.46.5.1023

Greenberg, R. P., Constantino, M. J., & Bruce, N. (2006). Are patient expectations still relevant for psychotherapy process and outcome? *Clinical Psychology Review, 26*, 657–678. doi:10.1016/j.cpr.2005.03.002

Gunderson, J. G., Najavits, L. M., Leonhard, C., Sullivan, C. N., & Sabo, A. N. (1997). Ontogeny of the therapeutic alliance in borderline patients. *Psychotherapy Research, 7*, 301–309.

Hartley, D. E., & Strupp, H. H. (1983). The therapeutic alliance: Its relationship to outcome in brief psychotherapy. In J. Masling (Ed.), *Empirical studies in analytic theories* (pp. 1–37). Hillside, NJ: Erlbaum.

Hatcher, R. L. (1999). Therapists' views of treatment alliance and collaboration in therapy. *Psychotherapy Research, 9*, 405–423. doi:10.1093/ptr/9.4.405

Hatcher, R. L., & Barends, A. W. (1996). Patients' view of the alliance in psychotherapy: Exploratory factor analysis of three alliance measures. *Journal of Consulting and Clinical Psychology, 64*, 1326–1336. doi:10.1037/0022-006X.64.6.1326

Hatcher, R. L., Barends, A. W., Hansell, J., & Gutfreund, M. J. (1995). Patients' and therapists' shared and unique views of the therapeutic alliance: An investigation using confirmatory factory analysis in a nested design. *Psychoanalytic Quarterly, 63*, 636–643.

Hawley, K. M., & Garland, A. F. (2008). Working alliance in adolescent outpatient therapy: Youth, parent and therapist reports and associations with therapy outcomes. *Child and Youth Care Forum, 37*, 59–74. doi:10.1007/s10566-008-9050-x

Hawley, K. M., & Weisz, J. R. (2005). Youth versus parent working alliance in usual clinical care: Distinctive associations with retention, satisfaction, and treatment outcome. *Journal of Clinical Child and Adolescent Psychology, 34*, 117–128. doi:10.1207/s15374424jccp3401_11

Henry, W. P., Schacht, T. E., & Strupp, H. H. (1986). Structural analysis of social behavior: Application to a study of interpersonal process in differential psychotherapeutic outcome. *Journal of Consulting and Clinical Psychology, 54*, 27–31. doi:10.1037/0022-006X.54.1.27

Henry, W. P., Schacht, T. E., & Strupp, H. H. (1990). Patient and therapist introject, inter-personal process and differential psychotherapy outcome. *Journal of Consulting and Clinical Psychology, 58*, 768–774. doi:10.1037/0022-006X.58.6.768

Henry, W. P., & Strupp, H. H. (1994). The therapeutic alliance as interpersonal process. In A. O. Horvath & L. S. Greenberg (Eds.), *The working alliance: Theory, research and practice* (pp. 51–84). New York, NY: Wiley.

Henry, W. P., Strupp, H. H., Butler, S. F., Schacht, T. E., & Binder, J. L. (1993). The effects of training in time-limited dynamic psychotherapy: Changes in therapist behavior. *Journal of Consulting and Clinical Psychology, 61*, 434–440. doi:10.1037/0022-006X.61.3.434

Hersoug, A. G., Hoglend, P., Monsen, J. T., & Havik, O. E. (2001). Quality of working alliance in psychotherapy: Therapist variables and patient/therapist similarity as predictors. *Journal of Psychotherapy Process and Research, 10*, 205–216.

Hersoug, A. G., Monsen, J. T., Havik, O. E., & Hoglend, P. (2002). Quality of early working alliance in psychotherapy: Diagnoses, relationship and intrapsychic variables as predictors. *Psychotherapy and Psychosomatics, 71*, 18–27. doi:10.1159/000049340

Hersoug, A. G., Sexton, H. C., & Hoglend, P. (2002). Contribution of defensive functioning to the quality of working alliance and psychotherapy outcome. *American Journal of Psychotherapy, 56*, 539–554.

Hill, C. E., & Knox, S. (2009). Processing the therapeutic relationship. *Psychotherapy Research, 19*, 13–29.

Hilliard, R. B., Henry, W. P., & Strupp, H. H. (2000). An interpersonal model of psychotherapy: Linking patient and therapist developmental history, therapeutic process and types of outcome. *Journal of Consulting and Clinical Psychology, 68*, 125–133.

Hilsenroth, M., Ackerman, S., Clemence, A., Strassle, C., & Handler, L. (2002). Effects of structured clinician training on patient and therapist perspectives of alliance early in psychotherapy. *Psychotherapy: Theory, Research, Practice, Training, 39*, 309–323.

Hilsenroth, M. J., & Cromer, T. D. (2007). Clinical interventions related to alliance during the initial interview and psychological assessment. *Psychotherapy: Theory, Research, Practice, Training, 44*, 205–218.

Hilsenroth, M., Peters, E., & Ackerman, S. (2004). The development of therapeutic alliance during psychological assessment: Patient and therapist perspectives across treatment. *Journal of Personality Assessment, 83*, 332–344.

Horvath, A. O., & Bedi, R. P. (2002). The alliance. In J. C. Norcross (Ed.), *Psychotherapy relationships that work: Therapist contributions and responsiveness to patients* (pp. 37–69). New York, NY: Oxford University Press.

Horvath, A. O., & Greenberg, L. S. (1986). Development of the working alliance inventory. In L. S. Greenberg & W. M. Pinsoff (Eds.), *The psychotherapeutic process: A research handbook* (pp. 529–556). New York, NY: Guilford Press.

Horvath, A. O., & Greenberg, L. S. (1989). Development and validation of the Working Alliance Inventory (WAI). *Journal of Counseling Psychology, 36*, 223–233.

Horvath, A. O., & Greenberg, L. S. (1994). *The working alliance: Theory, research, and practice*. New York, NY: Wiley.

Humphrey, L. L. (1989). Observed family interactions among subtypes of eating disorders using structural analysis of social behavior. *Journal of Consulting and Clinical Psychology, 57*, 206–214.

Karver, M. S., Handelsman, J. B., Fields, S., & Bickman, L. (2005). A theoretical model of common process factors in youth and family therapy. *Mental Health Services Research, 7*, 35–51.

Karver, M. S., Handelsman, J. B., Fields, S., & Bickman, L. (2006). Meta-analysis of therapeutic relationship variables in youth and family therapy: The evidence for different relationship variables in the child and adolescent treatment outcome literature. *Clinical Psychology Review, 26*, 50–65.

Karver, M., Shirk, S., Handelsman, J. B., Fields, S., Crisp, H., Gudmundsen, G., & McMakin, D. (2008). Relationship processes in youth psychotherapy: Measuring alliance, alliance-building behaviors, and client involvement. *Journal of Emotional and Behavioral Disorders, 16*, 15–28.

Kazdin, A. E., Bass, D., Ayers, W. A., Rodgers, A. (1990). Empirical and clinical focus of child and adolescent psychotherapy research. *Journal of Consulting and Clinical Psychology, 58*, 729–740.

Kazdin, A. E., & Nock, M. K. (2003). Delineating mechanisms of change in child and adolescent therapy: Methodological issues and research recommendations. *Journal of Child Psychology and Psychiatry, 44*, 1116–29.

Kazdin, A. E., Siegel, T. C., & Bass, D. (1990). Drawing on clinical practice to inform research on child and adolescent psychotherapy: Survey of practitioners. *Professional Psychology: Research and Practice, 21*, 189–198.

Kazdin, A. E., & Whitley, M. K. (2006). Pretreatment social relations, therapeutic alliance, and improvements in parenting practices in parent management training. *Journal of Consulting and Clinical Psychology, 74*, 345–355.

Kiesler, D. J. (1983). The 1982 interpersonal circle: A taxonomy for complementarity in human transactions. *Psychological Review, 90*, 185–214.

Kiesler, D. J. (1988). *Therapeutic metacommunication: Therapists' impact disclosures as feedback in psychotherapy*. Palo Alto, CA: Consulting Psychologists Press.

Kiesler, D. J. (1996). *Contemporary interpersonal theory and research: Personality psychopathology and psychotherapy*. New York, NY: Wiley.

Kirsch, I. (1990). *Changing expectations: A key to effective psychotherapy*. Pacific Grove, CA: Brooks/Cole.

Klein, D. N., Santiago, N. J., Vivian, D., Arnow, B. A., Blalock, J. A., Dunner, D. L., . . . Keller, M. B. (2004). Cognitive–behavioral analysis system of psychotherapy as a maintenance treatment for chronic depression. *Journal of Consulting and Clinical Psychology, 72*, 681–688.

Kokotovic, A. M., & Tracey, T. J. (1990). Working alliance in early phase of counseling. *Journal of Counseling Psychology, 37*, 16–21.

Kroll, L., & Green, J. (1997). The therapeutic alliance in child inpatient treatment: Development and initial validation of a Family Engagement Questionnaire. *Clinical Child Psychology and Psychiatry, 2*, 431–47.

Levinson, L. H. (1973). Communication with an adolescent in psychotherapy. *Social Casework, 54*, 480–488.

Lietaer, G. (1990). The client-centered approach after the Wisconsin project: A personal view on its evolution. In G. Lietaer, J. Rombauts, & R. Van Balen (Eds.), *Client-centered and experiential psychotherapy in the nineties* (pp. 19–45). Leuven, Belgium: Leuven University Press.

Lietaer, G. (1992). Helping and hindering processes in client-centered/experiential psychotherapy: A content analysis of client and therapist postsession perceptions. In S. G. Toukmanian & D.L. Rennie (Eds.), *Psychotherapy process research: Paradigmatic and narrative approaches* (pp. 134–162). Thousand Oaks, CA: Sage.

Linehan, M. M. (1993). *Cognitive-behavioral treatment of borderline personality disorder*. New York, NY: Guilford Press.

Linehan, M. M. (1997). Self-verification and drug abusers: Implications for treatment. *Psychological Science, 8*, 181–183.

Luborsky, L. (1976). Helping alliances in psychotherapy. In J. L. Cleghorn (Ed.), *Successful psychotherapy* (pp. 92–116) New York, NY: Brunner/Mazel.

Luborsky, L. (1994). Therapeutic alliances as predictors of psychotherapy outcomes: Factors explaining the predictive success. In A.O. Horvath & L. S. Greenberg (Eds.), *The working alliance: Theory, research and practice* (pp. 38–50). New York, NY: Wiley.

Luborsky, L., Crits-Christoph, P., Alexander, L., Margolis, M., & Cohen, M. (1983). Two helping alliance methods for predicting outcomes of psychotherapy: A counting signs vs. a global rating method. *Journal of Nervous and Mental Disease, 171*, 480–491.

Luborsky, L., Crits-Christoph, P., Mintz, J., & Auerbach, A. (1988). *Who will benefit from psychotherapy? Predicting therapeutic outcome*. New York, NY: Basic Books.

Marmar, C. R., Weiss, D. S., & Gaston, L. (1989). Toward the validation of the California Psychotherapy Alliance Rating System. *Psychological Assessment, 1*, 46–52.

Martin, D. J., Garske, J. P., & Davis, M. K. (2000). Relation of the therapeutic alliance with outcome and other variables: A meta-analytic review. *Journal of Consulting and Clinical Psychology, 68*, 438–450.

Marziali, E. (1984). Prediction of outcome of brief psychotherapy from therapist interpretive interventions. *Archives of General Psychiatry, 41,* 301–305.

Meyer, B., Pilkonis, P. A., Krupnick, J. L., Egan, M. K., Simmens, S. J., & Sotsky, S. M. (2002). Treatment expectancies, patient alliance and outcome: Further analyses from the National Institute of Mental Health Treatment of Depression Collaborative Research Program. *Journal of Consulting and Clinical Psychology, 70,* 1051–1055.

Moras, K., & Strupp, H. H. (1982). Pretherapy interpersonal relations, patients' alliance, and outcome in brief therapy. *Archives of General Psychiatry, 39,* 405–409.

Morris, R. J., & Nicholson, J. (1993). The therapeutic relationship in child and adolescent psychotherapy: Research issues and trends. In T. R. Kratchowill & R. J. Morris (Eds.), *Handbook of psychotherapy with children and adolescents* (pp. 405–425). Needham Heights, MA: Allyn & Bacon.

Muran, J. C., Safran, J. D., Gorman, B. S., Eubanks-Carter, C., Winston, A., & Samstag, L. W. (2009). The relationship of early alliance ruptures and their resolution to process and outcome in three time-limited psychotherapies for personality disorders. *Psychotherapy: Theory, Research, Practice, Training, 46,* 233–248.

Muran, J., Safran, J., Samstag, L., & Winston, A. (2005). Evaluating an alliance-focused treatment for personality disorders. *Psychotherapy: Theory, Research, Practice, Training, 42,* 532–545.

Muran, J. C., Segal, Z. V., Samstag, L. W., & Crawford, C. (1994). Patient pretreatment interpersonal problems and therapeutic alliance in short-term cognitive therapy. *Journal of Consulting and Clinical Psychology, 62,* 185–190.

Nathan, P. E., & Gorman, J. M. (2002). *A guide to treatments that work* (2nd ed.) New York, NY: Oxford University Press.

Nevo, R. (2002). Interpersonal problems as they affect the development of therapeutic alliance and group climate in group psychotherapy for women survivors of childhood sexual abuse (Doctoral dissertation, Pacific Graduate School of Psychology, 2002). *Dissertation Abstracts International, 63,* 3-B.

Newman, M. G., Castonguay, L. G., Borkovec, T. D., & Molnar, C. (2004). Integrative therapy for generalized anxiety disorder. In R. G. Heimberg, C. L. Turk, & D. S. Mennin (Eds.), *Generalized anxiety disorder: Advances in research and practice.* New York, NY: Guilford Press.

Newman, M. G., Castonguay, L. G., Borkovec, T. D., Nordberg, S. S., & Fisher, A. J. (2008). An open trial of integrative therapy for generalized anxiety disorder. *Psychotherapy: Theory, Research, Practice, Training, 45,* 135–147.

Norcross, J. C. (Ed.). (2002). *Psychotherapy relationships that work: Therapist contributions and responsiveness to patients.* New York, NY: Oxford University Press.

Oetzel, K. B., & Scherer, D. G. (2003). Therapeutic engagement with adolescents in psychotherapy. *Psychotherapy: Theory, Research, Practice, Training, 40,* 215–225.

Ollendick, T. H., & King, N. J. (2004). Empirically supported treatments for children and adolescents: Advances toward evidence-based practice. In P. M. Barrett & T. H. Ollendick (Eds.), *Handbook of interventions that work with children and adolescents: Prevention and treatment* (pp. 3–25). New York, NY: Wiley.

O'Malley, S. S., Suh, C. S., & Strupp, H. H. (1983). The Vanderbilt Psychotherapy Process Scale: A report on the scale development and a process–outcome study. *Journal of Consulting and Clinical Psychology, 51,* 581–586.

Orlinsky, D. E., Grawe, K., & Parks, B. K. (1994). Process and outcome in psychotherapy— Noch einmal. In A. E. Bergin & S. L. Garfield (Eds.), *Handbook of psychotherapy and behavior change* (4th ed. pp. 270–336). New York, NY: Wiley.

Orlinsky, D. E., & Howard, K. I. (1987). A generic model of psychotherapy. *Journal of Integrative and Eclectic Psychotherapy, 6,* 6–27.

Orlinsky, D. E., Rønnestad, M. H., & Willutzki, U. (2004). Fifty years of process-outcome research: Continuity and change. In M. J. Lambert (Ed.), *Bergin and Garfield's handbook of psychotherapy and behavior change* (5th ed., pp. 307–390). New York, NY: Wiley.

Orrell-Valente, J. K., Pinderhughes, E. E., Valente, E., Laird, R. D., & Conduct Problems Prevention Research Group. (1999). If it's offered, will they come? Influences on parent's participation in a community-based conduct problems prevention program. *American Journal of Community Psychology, 27,* 753–783.

Paivio, S.C., & Bahr, L. M. (1998). Interpersonal problems, working alliance and outcome in short-term experiential therapy. *Psychotherapy Research, 8,* 392–407.

Pinel, E. C., & Constantino, M. J. (2003). Putting self-psychology to good use: When social psychologists and clinical psychologists unite. *Journal of Psychotherapy Integration, 13,* 9–32.

Piper, W. E., Azim, H. F. A., Joyce, A. S., McCallum, M., Nixon, G. W. H., & Segal, P. S. (1991). Quality of object relations vs. interpersonal functioning as a predictor of therapeutic alliance and psychotherapy outcome. *Journal of Nervous and Mental Disease, 179,* 432–438.

Piper, W. E., Joyce, A. S., Rosie, J. S., Ogrodniczuk, J. S., McCallum, M., O'Kelly, J. G., & Steinberg, P. I. (1999). Prediction of dropping out in time-limited, interpretive individual psychotherapy. *Psychotherapy: Theory, Research, Practice, Training, 36,* 114–122.

Puschner, B., Bauer, S., Horowitz, L. M., & Kordy, H. (2005). The relationship between interpersonal problems and the helping alliance. *Journal of Clinical Psychology, 61,* 415–419.

Randeau, S. G., & Wampold, B. E. (1991). Relationship of power and involvement to working alliance: A multiple-case sequential analysis of brief therapy. *Journal of Counseling Psychology, 38,* 107–114.

Raue, P. J., Castonguay, L. G., & Goldfried, M. R. (1993). The working alliance: A comparison of two therapies. *Psychotherapy Research, 3,* 197–207.

Rector, N. A., Zuroff, D. C., & Segal, Z. V. (1999). Cognitive change and the therapeutic alliance: The role of technical and non-technical factors in cognitive therapy. *Psychotherapy, 36,* 320–328.

Ricker, M., Nystul, M., & Waldo, M. (1999). Counselors' and clients' ethnic similarity and therapeutic alliance in time-limited outcomes of counseling. *Psychological Reports, 84,* 674–676.

Rogers, C. R. (1951). *Client-centered therapy.* Boston, MA: Houghton Mifflin.

Rogers, C. R. (1961). *On becoming a person.* Boston, MA: Houghton-Mifflin

Ryan, E. R., & Cicchetti, D. V. (1985). Predicting quality of alliance in the initial psychotherapy interview. *Journal of Nervous and Mental Disease, 173,* 717–723.

Safran, J. D. (1998). *Widening the scope of cognitive therapy.* Northvale, NJ: Jason Aronson.

Safran, J. D., Crocker, P., McMain, S., & Murray, P. (1990). The therapeutic alliance rupture as a therapy event for empirical investigation. *Psychotherapy: Theory, Research, Practice, Training, 27* 154–165.

Safran, J. D., & Muran, J. C. (1996). The resolution of ruptures in the therapeutic alliance *Journal of Consulting and Clinical Psychology, 64,* 447–458.

Safran, J. D., & Muran, J. C. (2000). *Negotiating the therapeutic alliance: A relational treatment guide.* New York, NY: Guilford Press.

Safran, J. D., Muran, J. C., & Samstag, L. W. (1994). Resolving therapeutic alliance ruptures: A task analytic investigation. In A.O. Horvath & L. S. Greenberg (Eds.), *The working alliance: Theory, research and practice* (pp. 225–255). New York, NY: Wiley.

Safran, J. D., Muran, J. C., Samstag, L. W., & Stevens, C. (2002). Repairing alliance ruptures. In J. C. Norcross (Ed.), *Psychotherapy relationships that work: Therapists contributions and responsiveness to patients* (pp. 235–254). New York, NY: Oxford University Press.

Safran, J. D., Muran, J. C., Samstag, L. W., & Winston, A. (2005). Evaluating alliance-focused intervention for potential treatment failures: A feasibility study and descriptive analysis. *Psychotherapy: Theory, Research, Practice, Training, 42*, 512–531.

Safran, J. D., & Segal, Z. V. (1990). *Interpersonal process in cognitive therapy.* New York, NY: Basic Books.

Saunders, S. M. (2001). Pre-treatment correlates of therapeutic bond. *Journal of Clinical Psychology, 57*, 1339–1352.

Schut, A. J., Castonguay, L. G., Flanagan, K. M., Yamaski, A. S., Bedick, J. D., Smith, T. L., & Barber, J. P. (2005). Therapist interpretation, patient–therapist interpersonal process, and outcome in psychodynamic psychotherapy for avoidant personality disorder. *Psychotherapy: Theory, Research, Practice, Training, 42*, 494–511.

Sexton, H. C., Hembre, K., & Kvarme, G. (1996). The interaction of the alliance and therapy microprocess: A sequential analysis. *Journal of Consulting and Clinical Psychology, 64*, 471–480.

Shirk, S. R., & Karver, M. (2003). Prediction of treatment outcome from relationship variables in child and adolescent therapy: A meta-analytic review. *Journal of Consulting and Clinical Psychology, 71*, 452–464.

Shirk, S. R., & Russell, R. L. (1996). *Change processes in child psychotherapy: Revitalizing treatment and research.* New York, NY: Guilford Press.

Silberschatz, G. (2005). *Transformative relationships: The control mastery theory of psychotherapy.* New York, NY: Routledge.

Squier, R. W. (1990). A model of empathic understanding and adherence to treatment regimens in practitioner-patient relationships. *Social Science and Medicine, 30*, 325– 339.

Steinberg, L. (2005). *Adolescence* (7th ed.). New York, NY: McGraw-Hill.

Stiles, W. B., Agnew-Davies, R., Hardy, G. E., Barkham, M., & Shapiro, D. A. (1998). Relations of the alliance with psychotherapy outcome: Findings in the second Sheffield psychotherapy project. *Journal of Consulting and Clinical Psychology, 66*, 791–802.

Stiles, W. B., Glick, M. J., Osatuke, K., Hardy, G. E., Shapiro, D. A., Agnew-Davies, R., . . . Barkham, M. (2004). Patterns of alliance development and the rupture-repair hypothesis: Are productive relationships U-shaped or V-shaped? *Journal of Counseling Psychology, 51*, 81–92.

Strupp, H. H. (1993). The Vanderbilt psychotherapy studies: Synopsis. *Journal of Consulting and Clinical Psychology, 61*, 431–433.

Sullivan, H. S. (1953). *The interpersonal theory of psychiatry.* New York, NY: Norton.

Swann, W. B., Jr. (1983). Self-verification: Bringing social reality into harmony with the self. In J. Suls & A.G. Greenwald (Eds.), *Psychological perspectives on the self* (Vol. 2, pp. 33–66). Hillsdale, NJ: Erlbaum.

Swann, W. B., Jr. (1996). *Self-traps: The elusive quest for higher self-esteem.* New York, NY: Freeman.

Tichenor, V., & Hill, C. E. (1989). A comparison of six measures of working alliance. *Psychotherapy: Theory, Research and Practice, 26*, 195–199.

Tracey, T. J., & Kokotovic, A. (1989). Factor structure of the Working Alliance Inventory *Psychological Assessment, 1*, 207–210.

Watson, J. C., & Greenberg, L. S. (1994). The alliance in experiential therapy: Enacting the relationship conditions. In A. O. Horvath & L. S. Greenberg (Eds.), *The working alliance: Theory, research, and practice* (pp. 153–172). Oxford, England: Wiley.

Weisz, J. R., & Hawley, K. M. (2002). Developmental factors in the treatment of adolescents. *Journal of Consulting and Clinical Psychology, 70,* 21–43.

Wintersteen, M. B., Mensinger, J. L., & Diamond, G. S. (2005). Do gender and racial differences between patient and therapist affect therapeutic alliance and treatment retention in adolescents? *Professional Psychology: Research and Practice, 36,* 400– 408.

Ybrandt, H. (2008). The relation between self-concept and social functioning in adolescence. *Journal of Adolescence, 31,* 1–16.

Zack, S. E., Castonguay, L. G., & Boswell, J. F. (2007). Youth working alliance: A core clinical construct in need of empirical maturity. *Harvard Review of Psychiatry, 15,* 278–88.

Zuroff, D. C., Blatt, S. J., Sotsky, S. M., Krupnick, J. L., Martin, D. J., Sanislow, C. A., & Simmens, S. (2000). Relation of therapeutic alliance and perfectionism to outcome in brief outpatient treatment of depression. *Journal of Consulting and Clinical Psychology, 68,* 114–124.

2

THE ALLIANCE IN ADOLESCENT THERAPY: CONCEPTUAL, OPERATIONAL, AND PREDICTIVE ISSUES

STEPHEN R. SHIRK, NICOLE E. CAPORINO, AND MARC S. KARVER

The adult psychotherapy literature has shown the therapeutic alliance to be one of the best process predictors of treatment outcome (Horvath & Luborsky, 1993; Martin, Garske, & Davis, 2000). Two meta-analytic reviews of alliance–outcome relations have revealed moderate, but consistent, predictive relationships across types of treatments, disorders, and outcomes (Horvath & Symonds, 1991; Martin et al., 2000). Because of its reliable association with outcome, the alliance has been advanced as the pivotal common factor across diverse, efficacious psychotherapies (Safran & Muran, 1995).

The therapeutic alliance has been a focal construct in the adolescent psychotherapy literature for some time (A. Freud, 1946; Meeks, 1971). Adolescents have long been regarded as among the most challenging patients to engage in therapy (Meeks, 1971). Although there are numerous explanations for this clinical phenomenon, one of the most common involves the collision of therapy processes with one of the central tasks of adolescent development, namely, the press toward increasing autonomy. In this context, adolescents are often reluctant to rely on adult figures, including therapists, for guidance, direction, or help with problems. The task is further complicated by the fact that adolescents are often referred by others who may have a very different agenda for therapy than the adolescent's (DiGiuseppe,

Linscott, & Jilton, 1996). Conflicts around problem definition and the goals of treatment are hallmarks of alliance difficulties (Bordin, 1979). Given the challenges of alliance formation with adolescents, a wide range of clinical approaches emphasize the importance of the therapy relationship in the treatment of adolescents (Brendt & Poling, 1997; Meeks, 1971; Mufson, Moreau, Weissman, & Klerman, 1993).

Research on the therapeutic alliance in adolescent treatment is in an emergent state and pales in comparison with research with adults. In their meta-analysis of relationship predictors of child and adolescent outcomes, Shirk and Karver (2003) found only a handful of studies on alliance with adolescents. In fact, only one study in this sample would have met criteria for inclusion in the adult meta-analyses, largely because alliance was rarely measured before outcome. As our review shows, research on the alliance in adolescent treatment has grown in recent years to a point where a meta-analysis is now feasible. Yet, despite this growth, it is not clear that the field has reached consensus about the nature of the adolescent alliance or the best way to measure it.

The major aims of this chapter are (a) to explicate the conceptual underpinnings of the alliance in adolescent treatment, (b) to review existing measures of the therapeutic alliance used with adolescents, (c) to evaluate the extant research literature on alliance–outcome relations with adolescent samples, and (d) to provide some guidelines for future research on the therapeutic alliance in adolescent treatment.

MODELS OF THE ALLIANCE IN ADOLESCENT TREATMENT

In the adult psychotherapy literature, the alliance has been conceptualized as a collaborative working relationship with a positive affective valence (Bordin, 1979; Horvath & Symonds, 1991). Although the alliance is often viewed as a unitary construct, for some time researchers have proposed that the alliance consists of multiple, interrelated dimensions (Bordin, 1979; L. Luborsky, 1976). Bordin's (1979) reformulation of the working alliance as a multidimensional construct has provided a useful framework for recent research on alliance–outcome relations. According to Bordin, the alliance involves three components: (a) *bonds*, or the emotional relationship between patient and therapist; (b) *tasks*, or collaboration with therapeutic activities; and (c) *goals*, or agreements about the aims or expected outcomes of therapy. For Bordin, the alliance was both a facilitator of collaborative work and a change mechanism itself. Measures of the alliance in the adult literature vary in terms of the specific dimensions they purport to assess, but virtually all instruments appear to tap both the emotional quality of the relationship and aspects of treatment collaboration or involvement (Martin et al., 2000).

Research on the alliance in child and adolescent treatment has borrowed heavily from the adult literature. For example, in an early effort to assess the alliance in child treatment, Shirk and Saiz (1992) developed a measure based on the distinction between the affective and working components of the relationship. Because this measure was first used in the context of psychodynamic treatment, agreement on goals was not considered because such agreements are less explicit in this form of child therapy compared with behavioral and cognitive–behavioral treatments. Results from this initial investigation revealed that therapy bond was associated with treatment collaboration, in this case, talking about feelings and problems, but neither the emotional component of the relationship nor the task component predicted treatment outcome, in large part because of a restricted range of outcomes (Shirk & Saiz, 1992). Consistent with Bordin's (1979) hypothesis, the emotional bond appeared to facilitate task collaboration; however, given the concurrent measurement of alliance components, direction of effect could not be inferred.

Similarly, in their research on alliance–outcome relations in the treatment of abused adolescents, Eltz, Shirk, and Sarlin (1995) drew on L. Luborsky's (1976) distinction between two aspects of the patient's experience of the therapist, namely, as a helpful person and as a collaborator in the tasks of treatment. To this end, these investigators modified the Penn Helping Alliance Questionnaire (HaQ) for use with adolescents and found that changes in the alliance over the course of treatment predicted treatment improvement for both maltreated and nonmaltreated adolescents.

Along similar lines, DiGiuseppe et al. (1996) modified the Working Alliance Inventory (WAI; Horvath & Greenberg, 1989) for use with adolescents. This scale was explicitly designed to measure Bordin's (1979) three components of the working alliance. Results obtained with an adolescent treatment sample interestingly yielded one large factor that accounted for most of the variance. It is possible, as DiGiuseppe et al. noted, that aspects of alliance are not well differentiated by adolescents, at least along the dimensions proposed by Bordin.

As these studies have illustrated, conceptualizations of the therapeutic alliance in adolescence have been "downloaded" from the adult literature. Like adult alliance models, perspectives on the alliance in adolescence appear to differ in terms of their relative emphasis on the emotional quality or the contractual nature of the therapy relationship.

ADOLESCENT ALLIANCE: ATTACHMENT OR AGREEMENT?

Shirk and colleagues (Shirk, Gudmundsen, Kaplinski, & McMakin, 2008; Shirk & Russell, 1996; Shirk & Saiz, 1992) have underscored the importance of the adolescent's experience of the therapist as reliable, dependable, and responsive as the foundation for treatment collaboration. Drawing on attachment theory (Bowlby, 1988), this approach emphasizes the importance of a secure base for treatment involvement. The therapy bond is analogous to an attachment relationship insofar as it allows the adolescent to feel safe in exploring the highly emotional developmental challenges of adolescence. Moreover, the therapist represents a sensitive and responsive individual to whom the adolescent can turn for safety and protection in times of distress. As has been demonstrated in the literature on the development of close relationships in adolescence, adolescents develop attachments to friends, romantic partners, and other significant adults (Furman, Simon, Shaffer, & Bouchey, 2002). To the degree that the therapist is viewed as a reliable person who can be helpful in times of distress, a therapeutic bond is attained. The bond facilitates treatment involvement, and the formation of such a bond can be a change process in its own right (Shirk & Russell, 1996).

In contrast, DiGiuseppe et al. (1996) have criticized this perspective for failing to acknowledge social contractual features of the therapeutic alliance. As they have noted, "Traditional theories of child and adolescent psychotherapy appear to have overly focused on the *bond* [italics added] as necessary and sufficient for change" (p. 87). From this perspective, the central component of the alliance, especially with adolescents, consists of agreements regarding treatment goals and the methods for accomplishing the agreed-on goals. According to DiGiuseppe et al., the fact that adolescents are typically referred by others makes the establishment of agreements both difficult and essential for treatment collaboration. Without soliciting the adolescent's input, a clinician is likely to pursue goals identified by the referring party. In the absence of an explicit agreement with the adolescent about the aims and methods of therapy, the clinician might have a positive therapy relationship with him or her but not a working alliance.

Given the different emphases, these two approaches also differ in terms of therapeutic strategies for promoting alliance formation. Insofar as the alliance represents a secure base for therapeutic activities (Bowlby, 1988), one of the most important early tasks for the therapist is to respond sensitively to the adolescent's emotional expressions. In one study, Karver et al. (2008) found that failure to attend to adolescents' emotional expressions was associated with poorer subsequent alliances. More recently, Russell, Shirk, and Jungbluth (2008) discovered that therapists who elicit adolescent experiences and then integrate them with the treatment model show more positive subsequent alliances than therapists who do not. Similarly, Diamond, Liddle, Hogue, and Dakof (1999) found that therapists who closely attended to adolescents' experience in initial sessions secured more positive alliances by the third session. Taken together, these emerging results suggest that therapists should take time to understand the adolescent's experience and situation before launching into other therapy tasks.

Consistent with the emphasis on the contractual nature of the alliance, DiGiuseppe et al. (1996) proposed that formulating explicit treatment goals and providing the adolescent with a clear picture of why he or she is in therapy are essential for alliance formation. In fact, they contended that reflective techniques, although useful with younger children, may be experienced as manipulative by adolescents. In this connection, they hypothesized that early active interventions may be experienced as caring by adolescents. Again, results obtained by Diamond et al. (1999) support the importance of formulating goals. Adolescents with improved alliances at the third session had therapists who were more likely to focus on clarifying goals in initial sessions than did adolescents with unimproved alliances.

It is quite likely that both components of the alliance and alliance formation are important for understanding the engagement process with adolescents. In fact, Shirk and Karver (2006) advanced a process model that integrates these components by placing them in a temporal sequence. In this model, three core constructs are distinguished: engagement, alliance, and involvement. *Engagement* refers to therapist behaviors and strategies that promote alliance, involvement, and treatment continuation. For example, therapist efforts to attend to and validate adolescent experience or attempts to formulate treatment goals represent early engagement strategies. *Involvement* goes well beyond mere attendance and refers to the adolescent's level of participation in therapy "work."[1] For example, cognitive–behavioral therapists often teach problem-solving skills as part of treatment, and involvement would be gauged by the adolescent's active participation in or resistance to specific therapy tasks. As this example implies, the concept of involvement is contingent on the specification of therapy tasks, typically outlined in the treatment manual and viewed as the critical change processes in therapy. *Alliance*, then, refers to the adolescent's experience of the therapist as someone who can be counted on for help in overcoming problems or distress (Shirk & Karver, 2006). In this respect, the alliance involves experiencing the therapist as being on your side or on the same team. The prototypic, but rarely declared, cognition for the adolescent, then, would be "I feel comfortable working with you to reach our goals." Viewed from this experiential perspective, the alliance captures the adolescent's views on bond, collaborative work, and goal agreement.

According to Shirk and Karver (2006), early interactions between therapist and adolescent contribute to the development of an alliance that,

---

[1]Note that some authors have used the term *engagement* to refer to the construct identified by Shirk and Karver (2006) as client involvement. To maintain consistency throughout the chapter, we substitute *involvement* for the term *engagement* when the reference is to client participation in therapy tasks.

in turn, catalyzes treatment involvement (i.e., active participation in the tasks of therapy). In this model, the alliance is both an experiential and a motivational construct. A strong positive alliance is considered to be essential for active involvement in sessions, especially when involvement is demanding—for example, when participating in exposures or constructing a trauma narrative. It is hypothesized that the degree to which an adolescent feels he or she can count on or trust the therapist and believe that the therapist is offering an approach that can help to accomplish the adolescent's goals will translate into overcoming avoidance and working through challenging treatment tasks.

Essentially, then, this process model distinguishes among the dimensions outlined by Bordin (1979)—that is, bond, tasks, and goals—but does so by placing them in a process sequence. Moreover, the varied components of this process may require different methods of assessment. For example, therapist engagement strategies are likely to be most accurately evaluated through direct observation, whereas the patient's experience of the alliance might be best assessed through patient self-report. Given that youth are unlikely to be fully aware of the specific tasks of therapy, level of therapy involvement might be best assessed from therapist or observer perspectives, although in their sample of depressed adolescents Shirk et al. (2008) found that both therapist and adolescent ratings of early task collaboration were significantly associated with observer ratings of therapy involvement.

In summary, research on the adolescent alliance has drawn heavily from the adult psychotherapy literature. Specifically, Bordin's (1979) transtheoretical model, with its emphasis on bond, tasks, and goals, has shaped prevailing views of the adolescent alliance. Recently, a process model that distinguishes among engagement, alliance, and treatment involvement has been advanced as a framework for understanding associations among therapy processes and their direct and indirect links with outcome (Shirk & Karver, 2006). At the center of this model is the therapeutic alliance, framed as a consequence of engagement processes and an antecedent of treatment involvement.

MEASURES OF THE ALLIANCE IN ADOLESCENT TREATMENT

To evaluate the current state of research on the alliance in adolescent treatment, we conducted a comprehensive search of the literature using PsycINFO. The first step in locating the relevant literature involved searching keywords pertaining to process research in adolescent treatment. The second step involved reading through abstracts and narrowing the focus to articles that appeared to measure the adolescent–therapist treatment alliance. While reading these articles, we identified additional articles for retrieval. References from previous reviews of child process research were searched as well. On the basis of this procedure, it is likely that we completed a comprehensive search and that this review includes most existing measures of the alliance with adolescents. This review focuses on measures that have been used in adolescent treatment studies after 1999; measures used in earlier studies are presented but not reviewed in detail. Psychometric characteristics and conceptual underpinnings of each measure are presented. Instruments are grouped by source of measurement, participant measures (reports from adolescent, therapist, parent, or program staff), and observational measures.

Participant Measures

Consistent with the adult literature on the alliance, a number of self- and therapist report measures have been developed and examined with adolescent clients. In fact, the most widely used measures of alliance are downward extensions of scales originally developed for use with adults. Recently, however, there has been some focus on developing an alliance scale specifically tailored to the developmental level of adolescents.

Working Alliance Inventory

The WAI (Horvath and Greenberg, 1989) consists of 36 items rated on a 7-point Likert-type scale. It is available in several versions: adolescent self-report, therapist report, and rating of psychotherapy sessions by observers. Adolescent and therapist report versions also come in a short form (WAI–S), which consists of only 12 items. The WAI measures the quality of the therapeutic relationship across three subscales: Bonds, Tasks, and Goals. The final item pool for the measure was generated on the basis of careful content analysis of Bordin's (1979) model followed by expert ratings of degree of fit between items and Bordin's definition of the working alliance.

The measure was designed for use with adult clients but has been modified for use with adolescents in seven studies (Dennis, Ives, White, & Muck, 2008; Fitzpatrick & Irannejad, 2008; Florsheim, Shotorbani, Guest-Warnick, Barratt, & Hwang, 2000; Glueckauf, Fritz, et al., 2002; Glueckauf, Liss, et al., 2002; Tetzlaff et al., 2005; Linscott, DiGiuseppe, & Jilton, 1993). Florsheim et al. (2000) created the modified WAI by replacing "therapist" with "program staff person" and "therapy" with "program." Glueckauf, Fritz, et al. (2002; Glueckauf, Liss, et al., 2002) modified the wording of the items to fit the multiclient context of family therapy and to ensure that the measure could be understood at a third-grade reading level. Fitzpatrick and Irannejad (2008), Tetzlaff et al. (2005), and Dennis, Ives, White, and Muck (2008) adapted the WAI–S for use with adolescents by rewording some items without changing their content. Linscott et al. (1993) made more substantial modifications to the long form of the WAI by rewriting all of the items and altering their content to fit adolescent treatment in addition to simplifying language to reduce reading demands. The resulting measure, referred to as the Adolescent WAI, preserves the subscale structure of the adult version.

The WAI as it is used with adolescents may represent a significant departure from the adult scale. Although Horvath (1994) confirmed the three-factor structure with adults, analyses of the structure of the Adolescent WAI yielded one large first factor rather than three. Three other factors were present, but they did not consistently represent any content area and accounted for small amounts of variance. Similar findings have been reported for the WAI–S. As Linscott et al. (1993) observed, it is possible that adolescent clients do not distinguish different components of the therapy relationship. Instead, the alliance may reflect a global evaluation of the relationship as positive or negative.

Internal consistency estimates for adolescent and therapist report versions of the long form of the WAI are acceptable and range from .83 to .96. Modified versions of the long form also have acceptable levels of internal consistency, with alphas ranging from .81 to .96. Only one study reported on the internal consistency of the observer-rated version of the WAI. Alphas ranged from .75 to .98; however, these estimates were cal-culated using data on alliances with adolescents and parents (as opposed to adolescents only). Internal consistency has been demonstrated for the WAI–S in seven studies, with alphas ranging from .89 to .97 for adolescent and therapist versions.

Test–retest reliability was reported for Florsheim et al.'s (2000) modifi-cation of the full WAI. After 10 weeks of treatment, correlations for the scales ranged from .66 to .70. Hawley and Garland (2008) reported that scores on the WAI–S administered 1 month after intake correlated .67 with scores at 6 months. Such stability is impressive given the duration of intensive treatment. Of course, it is debatable whether alliance scores should show high levels of stability across the course of treatment. Research with adults has shown both cross-session variability (Safran & Muran, 1995) and relative stability after the early sessions of therapy (Horvath & Luborsky, 1993).

Cross-informant agreement has been examined in several studies. Correlations between adolescents' and therapists' ratings on the long form of the WAI ranged from .39 to .57 in a study conducted in an inpatient setting. For the modified WAI, cross-informant agreement between adolescent and staff ratings ranged from as low as $r = .07$ to $r = .22$. Correlations between client and therapist scores on the subscales and full-scale Adolescent WAI were higher, with an average of .40. Two studies in the substance abuse literature examined cross-informant agreement using the WAI–S. Auerbach, May,

Stevens, and Kiesler (2008) reported correlations between client and counselor scores that ranged from .07 to .28, with higher scores based on client report. Diamond et al. (2006) reported that total WAI–S scores were correlated .50; however, only 47% of the sample completed the measure. Thus, it appears that cross-informant agreement has varied considerably across studies regardless of which form of the WAI was used, whether it was modified, and the population of adolescents sampled.

In the adult literature, the WAI has been shown to correlate with several other alliance measures beyond the .5 cutoff for acceptable convergent validity. In the adolescent literature, correlations with subscales of the Context Specific Therapeutic Alliance Scale have ranged from .19 to .59; the total scale correlated .46 with the WAI (Sapyta, Karver, & Bickman, 1999). Also, correlations of a magnitude above .5 have been reported for the WAI and three of four subscales of the Stages of Change Scale. In support of the convergent validity of the WAI–S, correlations between counselor ratings and scores on the Client Affiliation axis of the Impact Message Inventory-Circumplex, a measure of dyadic interactions in psychotherapy, ranged from .62 to .70; also, Counselor Affiliation scores were correlated .58 with adolescent scores on the Bond subscale of the WAI–S. In another study, the correlation between the adolescent report WAI–S and ratings made by observers using the Alliance Observation Coding System was .85.

Few studies have reported on divergent validity or discriminant validity. Tetzlaff et al. (2005) found that scores on the WAI–S and a measure of treatment satisfaction were only moderately positively correlated ($r = .36$), suggesting that alliance and satisfaction are empirically distinct constructs. Florsheim et al. (2000) reported that the modified WAI successfully discriminated between treatment completers and youth who ran away from the program. The WAI does not appear to be developmentally biased; one study showed that there were no differences in age between good and poor working alliance groups, which were determined by a median split. Cultural sensitivity has not been evaluated.

Penn Helping Alliance Scales

The Penn Helping Alliance Scales (PHAS; Alexander & Luborsky, 1986) consist of 11 items rated on a 6-point Likert-type scale. There are several versions: adolescent self-report, counselor report, and rating of psychotherapy sessions by trained observers. The PHAS measure the emotional relationship and mutual involvement between the adolescent client and the therapist (Alexander & Luborsky, 1986). The Penn HaQ method assesses the client's perspective and is supposed to ascertain the client's view of the therapist's degree of helpfulness and sense of collaboration between client and therapist. The therapist version, the Penn Therapist Facilitating Behavior Questionnaire method, is meant to parallel the client version and measures the degree to which the therapist feels he or she is helping the client.

The PHAS aim to assess two types of alliance. The Type 1 alliance focuses on the client's experience of the therapist as warm, supportive, and helpful. The Type 2 alliance focuses on the client's sense of working together with the therapist toward treatment goals. The Type 1 alliance is meant to reflect the psychoanalytic focus on the client's affective bond with the therapist, but it has been pointed out that the measure has been used successfully with clients receiving adult cognitive–behavioral therapy (Cecero, Fenton, Frankforter, Nich, & Carroll, 2001). The Type 2 alliance is based on Bordin's (1979) definition of the alliance as mutual agreement between client and therapist on tasks and goals. It is interesting that the items were not derived from the theory but were based on observed differences between the sessions with the most versus the least improved adult patients in the Penn Psychotherapy Project sample (L. Luborsky, 2000).

Although the PHAS were designed for use with adult clients, the original scales have been used with adolescents in three studies (Eltz et al., 1995; R. D. Smith, 1999; Zaitsoff, Doyle, Hoste, & le Grange, 2008). The HaQ was modified for use with adolescents in a fourth study (Holmqvist, Hill, & Lang, 2007) by deleting one item and changing the rating scale to include 10 response options instead of six. Only one of the studies reported test–retest reliability, which was unacceptably low at .45 for adolescent and therapist report. However, one might expect relatively low stability given that assessments were made early in treatment and at termination. Thus, alliance scores were subject to variability as a result of both time and the impact of inpatient treatment. Internal consistency was acceptable at .92 for adolescent and therapist reports. Cross-informant agreement between adolescent and counselor ratings has ranged across studies from as low as 0 to .40 for the original version of the measure and .09 to .45 for the modified version. Interrater reliability between similar informants has not been assessed with adolescent clients.

Some evidence has been found for the convergent validity of the PHAS as determined by correlations with the Menninger Collaboration Scale (MCS; J. G. Allen, Deering, Buskirk, & Coyne, 1988), with coefficients ranging from 0 to .76 depending on time of measurement and the informant for each measure. In addition, adolescents' scores on the HaQ have been found to be correlated .50 with the observer ratings of the emotional connection with the therapist in family therapy (Friedlander et al., 2006), as determined using the System for Observing Family Therapy Alliances (Friedlander, Escudero, & Heatherington, 2001). Scores on a modified version of the HaQ were found to be related to various dimensions of a relationship measure, the Feeling Checklist, with correlation coefficients ranging from −.11 to .66 (Holmqvist et al., 2007). Also, scores on this modified version of the HaQ were significantly associated with clinician ratings of adolescents' perception of the helpfulness of the treatment model, which were based on a qualitative interview; correlation coefficients ranged from .44 (Type 2 alliance–collaboration) to .55 (total). There is some question as to the acceptability of this measure's divergent validity because it has been found to correlate as highly as −.26 with IQ. In support of the discriminant validity, scores on the PHAS have discriminated significantly between and among groups expected to differ on therapeutic alliance: maltreated versus nonmaltreated adolescents and groups showing low or moderate versus high levels of change on several outcome measures.

The adolescent report does not appear to be developmentally biased because it correlates between .09 and .13 with age; however, the therapist report has been found to correlate as highly as .32 with client age. There does not appear to be evidence of cultural bias because no differences between racial or ethnic groups have been found. There may be some gender bias with the measure given that female adolescents showed more positive ratings than male adolescents (Sarlin, 1992), although it may be the case that female adolescents form more positive alliances than their male counterparts.

Therapeutic Alliance Scale for Adolescents

The Therapeutic Alliance Scale for Adolescents (TASA; Shirk, 2003) consists of 12 items rated on a 6-point Likert-type scale. The TASA comes in adolescent and therapist versions. It is an upward extension of the Therapeutic Alliance Scale for Children (Shirk & Saiz, 1992) and measures the emotional bond between client and therapist as well as the level of task collaboration. Item content is consistent across adolescent and therapist scales, but the therapist ratings refer to the adolescent's experience.

Internal consistency was acceptable, with alphas of .86 for the adolescent version and .85 for the therapist version. Four-week test–retest reliabilities were .53 and .40 for the adolescent and therapist versions, respectively. For both versions of the scale, the Bond and Collaboration subscales were highly correlated ($rs = .76$ and $.73$, respectively), suggesting a single alliance dimension–collaborative bond. Concurrent validity is supported by reliable associations between both therapist and adolescent scores on the TASA and observer-rated treatment collaboration. Both therapist- and adolescent-rated alliance were significantly associated with an observational measure of alliance based on the Vanderbilt Psychotherapy Process Scale (VPPS; O'Malley, Suh, & Strupp, 1983). There was greater convergence between therapist ratings and observer ratings than between adolescent ratings and observer ratings.

Shirk et al. (2008) found that adolescent-reported alliance was significantly associated with change in depressive symptoms in cognitive–behavioral therapy. Therapist ratings were in the predicted direction but did not attain statistical significance.

Working Relationship Scale

The Working Relationship Scale (WRS; Bickman et al., 2004; Doucette, 2004), which has also been referred to as the Therapeutic Alliance Scale, has its origins in a large item pool developed by Sapyta et al. (1999). Items were drawn from 10 domains presumed to be potentially important for a good adolescent therapeutic alliance. These domains included openness–truthfulness; supportive caring; security, stability, and continuity; non-judgmental attitude; bond; clarity of helper; goals; perceptiveness of helper; rules; and conflict. On the basis of exploration of the child mental health services literature, the therapeutic alliance literature, discussion with experts, and the clinical experience of the authors of the measure, 114 items were generated for this measure. The item pool was reduced by item analysis of data collected from adolescents and ratings of clarity and relevance by samples of counselor–helpers.

Variations of the WRS consist of 30 to 32 statements that are rated on a 4-point Likert-type scale (Bickman et al., 2004; Handwerk et al., 2008). The WRS was developed using item response theory to address concerns that classical test theory methods applied to data collected from relatively small samples could limit generalizability and obscure multidimensional patterns. Items on the WRS tap into three domains: mutuality–empathic qualities of the relationship, collaboration or "working rapport," and attitudes toward treatment setting or resistance. It is recommended that the Resistance subscale be considered separately.

One study has reported on the psychometric properties of the WRS administered to a sample of adolescents and clinicians in residential care. Internal consistency was excellent at .95, and the average weekly test–retest reliability across the first 10 sessions was .76. The correlation between youth- and clinician-rated alliance was low at the beginning of therapy ($r = .34$) and declined somewhat by the end of therapy ($r = .24$). Research is needed to establish the validity of the WRS for use with adolescents.

Other Participant Measures

A number of other adolescent alliance scales were developed or adapted for a specific study and have not subsequently been used. Adaptations of both the WAI and the PHAS have been used in treatment studies. Two studies combined items from the WAI with items from other instruments to measure adolescents' treatment involvement (Hawke, Hennen, & Gallione, 2005; B. D. Smith, Duffee, Steinke, Haung, & Larkin, 2008). In the first study (Hawke et al., 2005), factor analyses were conducted on a combined item pool formed from scales that had been used in the adult literature: the WAI, the Treatment Participation scale of the Client Evaluation of Self and Treatment Scales, and a five-item Counselor Rapport measure from the Drug Abuse Treatment Outcome Study. The resulting 13-item measure has three subscales: Therapeutic Involvement (referred to by the authors as engagement), Counselor Rapport, and Working Alliance. Reliability was acceptable, with alphas for the scales ranging from .84 to .94, but research examining the validity of this measure is needed. In the second study (Smith et al., 2008), a 17-item Involvement scale was formed by combining items from the WAI with items from the University of Rhode Island Change Assessment Scale (McConnaughy, Prochaska, & Velicer, 1983). Data on the reliability and validity of this measure were not reported.

Similarly, Gavin, Wamboldt, Sorokin, Levy, and Wamboldt (1999) adapted the PHAS to assess alliance between adolescent and physician in the context of asthma treatment. Alliance is assessed from physician, parent, and adolescent perspective. Test–retest reliability has not been reported, but internal consistency was quite good across reporters and ranged from .77 to .95. Mixed results were obtained for associations between alliance ratings and medication adherence.

A number of measures have been developed to assess alliance or collaboration in the context of inpatient treatment. The MCS (J. G. Allen, Deering, Buskirk, & Coyne, 1988) consists of 12 items rated on a 5-point scale with detailed anchors. The MCS was developed to measure inpatient collaboration and active involvement in hospital treatment. It has three factors based on the results of a factor analysis conducted with an adult sample: Goal Orientation, which assesses reflective and purposeful involvement in hospital treatment; Involvement, which assesses communication with staff; and Use of Structure, which assesses the degree to which the treatment regimen is followed. The MCS has a patient version, which is much simpler than the clinician version. Although the scale was originally developed for use with adults, it has been modified for use with adolescents. Findings with inpatient adolescents revealed modest cross-perspective correlations and relatively low test–retest reliability, although ratings were made at admission and discharge. Staff ratings of collaboration were, interestingly, significantly correlated with adolescent IQ, raising some concerns about the validity of the scale. The MCS has been shown to discriminate between patients with poor versus good outcomes, although it should be noted that IQ has also been shown to be a predictor of inpatient outcomes.

J. G. Allen et al. (1988) developed the Therapeutic Alliance Difficulty rating scale to evaluate collaboration–resistance in inpatient adolescent treatment. The Therapeutic Alliance Difficulty scale consists of one item rated on a 5-point scale. It is completed by members of an inpatient mental health treatment team. Test–retest reliability and cross-informant agreement have not been examined with adolescents, and internal consistency reliability is not applicable to a one-item measure. The absence of evidence on cross-informant agreement is troubling given that the final score is the average of team members' ratings. There is some evidence for convergent validity of the Therapeutic Alliance Difficulty scale as reflected by its correlation with the overall Treatment Difficulty Scale ($r = .53$), but one should take into account that a single informant made both ratings and that the Therapeutic Alliance Difficulty scale is part of the broader scale.

A third measure of inpatient alliance–collaboration is the Family Engagement Questionnaire (Kroll & Green, 1997). The Family Engagement Questionnaire consists of 16 items rated on a 4-point scale. The measure is rated by clinicians (e.g., the key nurse and coworking nurse). The Family Engagement Questionnaire was designed to assess the teen's personal and therapeutic relationships with unit staff, involvement in therapeutic activities, and relationships with peers on the unit. Information on test–retest reliability and cross-informant agreement has not been collected. Internal consistency has been highly uneven for the different scales, ranging from −.7 to .87. Inter-rater reliability between similar informants is unacceptably low, especially considering that a weighted kappa was used ($\kappa_w s = .10–.71$ across items). The three subscales correlated .26 to .59 with a four-item structured clinical assessment of involvement. There is evidence that the scale correlates with involvement ratings based on independent clinical interviews, but there is no evidence for the validity of clinician judgments of involvement. Unfortunately, additional research on the scale has not been published.

Finally, Pinsof and Catherall (1986) developed the Family Therapy Alliance Scale for use in family-focused treatment. The Family Therapy Alliance Scale consists of 29 items rated on a 7-point Likert-type scale. It has three subscales: Bonds, Tasks, and Goals. It has been used in two studies to evaluate perceptions of the therapeutic relationship in clients 12 years of age or older who participated in home-based therapy (Johnson, Ketring, Rohacs, & Brewer, 2006; Johnson, Wright, & Ketring, 2002). Although both studies reported on its internal consistency, neither study separated adolescents' data from parents' data in calculating these estimates. Alphas ranged from .90 to .93 for Bonds, from .86 to .92 for Tasks, and from .75 to .86 for Goals. The authors acknowledged that the validity of the Family Therapy Alliance Scale is not well established.

Observational Measures

As in the case of participant measures, the starting point for the development of observational measures of alliance with adolescents has been the adult therapy literature. However, several systems have been developed specifically for the evaluation of alliance in adolescent treatment.

Vanderbilt Therapeutic Alliance Scale

The Vanderbilt Therapeutic Alliance Scale (VTAS; Hartley & Strupp, 1983) is a 44-item observational measure that uses a 6-point Likert-type scale. The VTAS was designed to measure the strength of the therapeutic alliance in individual therapy from the perspective of expert clinical raters. The full scale has three subscales: Therapist Contribution, Patient Contribution, and Therapist–Client Interaction. According to Henry and Strupp (1994), VTAS items were drawn from the theoretical and research work of Bordin (1979), Greenson (1965), Langs (1976), and L. Luborsky (1976). Diamond et al. (1999) eliminated the Therapist Contribution subscale in their study of adolescent treatment, thereby reducing the measure to 26 items sometimes referred to as the Vanderbilt Therapeutic Alliance Scale—Revised (VTAS–R). Because Diamond et al. defined the therapeutic alliance as collaboration between client and therapist and not as therapist technique, Therapist Contribution items were excluded. Their view of the alliance as collaboration is consistent with research indicating that patient involvement in treatment is a reliable predictor of outcome (Tryon & Winograd, 2002). Other researchers have removed individual items because of poor interrater reliability; thus, the VTAS has consisted of from 23 to 26 items depending on the study.

Factor analyses of the VTAS (and VTAS–R) have been conducted in several studies that sampled adolescents, resulting in a couple of different short forms of the measure. One study reported two factors: Bond and Agreement on Goals–Tasks. Two studies reported single-factor solutions (Hogue, Dauber, Stambaugh, Cecero, & Liddle, 2006; Shelef & Diamond, 2008). In the first study (Hogue et al., 2006), a short form consisting of items with the six highest loadings was determined to measure client and therapist efforts to work collaboratively, client identification with the therapy, and client honesty and participation in treatment. In the second study (Shelef & Diamond, 2008), five of the 15 items that loaded on the single factor were selected for a short form on the basis of face validity. Three factors emerged in a study by Robbins, Turner, Alexander, and Perez (2003): Positive Working Relationship, Negative Relationship, and Superficial/Boring Session Interactions. The six-item Positive Working Relationship scale was used to measure the alliance in at least one subsequent study (Flicker, Turner, Waldron, Brody, & Ozechowski, 2008).

With adolescents, estimates of internal consistency have been highly acceptable; alphas have ranged from .93 to .98 across all versions of the VTAS with the exception of the six-item reduced scale developed by Robbins et al. (2003), for which alphas have been slightly more variable (ranging from .79 to .90). The only intraclass correlation coefficient (ICC) reported for this six-item scale was .66. For the five-item version, ICCs were reported for individual items and ranged from .55 to .87. Interrater reliability has been acceptable for the full VTAS (and VTAS–R), with ICCs ranging from .80 to .93 for subscales and the total scale. We note, however, that the full VTAS requires at least 15 hours of coder training.

More research is needed to establish the validity of the VTAS for use with adolescents. Although the VTAS and the WAI were both administered in one study, their correlation ($r = .43$) did not meet the .5 standard for establishing convergent validity. The five-item version of the VTAS, however, has been found to correlate highly ($r = .94$) with the other 18 items that make up the VTAS–R. There is some concern about discriminant validity because it has been reported in several studies that scores on the VTAS did not differentiate between adolescents who completed treatment and those who dropped out. However, a study (Robbins et al., 2006) that used the six-item version of the VTAS developed by Robbins et al. (2003) found that the change in alliance scores from the first to the second session discriminated between these two groups. Other studies (Robbins et al., 2008) that used the same measure have shown that imbalances between the adolescent–therapist alliance and the parent–therapist alliance were related to dropout.

The VTAS has been used with African American, Hispanic, and non-Hispanic White adolescents. Although Hogue et al. (2006) found no differences in alliance by race or ethnicity using their six-item version of the VTAS, Shelef, Diamond, Diamond, and Liddle (2005) found that scores on their five-item version were significantly higher for non-Hispanic White adolescents than for African American adolescents. Scores did not, however, differ significantly by age. No other studies have provided information related to the developmental sensitivity of the VTAS.

Overall Adolescent Engagement Scale

The Overall Adolescent Engagement Scale (OAES; Jackson-Gilfort, Liddle, Tejeda, & Dakof, 2001) is a 21-item observational measure of adolescent involvement in treatment. The instrument is used to rate segments of recorded therapy sessions. The OAES uses three subscales of the VPPS (O'Malley, Suh, & Strupp, 1983): the Patient Participation scale, the Patient Exploration scale, and the Patient Hostility scale. The three scales are used to measure adolescent involvement in treatment, that is, the extent to which the adolescent participated in therapy, examined his or her feelings and experiences during sessions, and expressed hostility in sessions. The VPPS is based on Henry and Strupp's (1994) formulation of alliance processes. According to this perspective, the therapist offers supportive conditions analogous to a good parent. The therapist is warm, responsive, and empathic. Through experiencing the therapist in a positive manner, patients come to identify with the therapist and engage in the process of exploration prompted by the therapist. In essence, the therapist-offered conditions provide leverage for patient participation and exploration. Involvement in the tasks of therapy hinges on a positive experience of and identification with the therapist.

The VPPS was derived from the Therapy Session Report (Orlinsky & Howard, 1967) but does not include dimensions that tap outcomes. The measure was designed for use with adult patients but has been modified for use with adolescents (Jackson-Gilfort et al., 2001). Test–retest reliability and cross-informant agreement have not been examined with adolescents. Internal consistency of the OAES was acceptable, with alphas ranging from .84 to .95 across scales and the total score. All raters in the study by Jackson-Gilfort et al. (2001) were trained to an interrater reliability standard of an ICC of .80. However, actual reliability from the study data was not reported. No information has been collected on the convergent, divergent, or discriminant validity of the OAES. In addition, no information is available on developmental sensitivity. The OAES has been used with African American male adolescents in Jackson-Gilfort et al. (2001), a study discussing cultural themes and impact on involvement. The discussion of some themes did lead to higher involvement in the following session, but no attempt was made in this study to relate involvement to the relationship measure.

Adolescent Therapeutic Alliance Scale

The Adolescent Therapeutic Alliance Scale (ATAS; Faw, Hogue, Johnson, Diamond, & Liddle, 2005) consists of 14 items, each rated on a 6-point scale, that assess the therapeutic alliance in both family and individual therapy with adolescents. The ATAS grew out of the VTAS and is consistent with Bordin's (1979) conceptualization of the alliance as consisting of bond and agreement on the goals and tasks of therapy. VTAS items that tap therapist contributions to the alliance were excluded because of lack of variability in observer ratings and low reliability and predictive power. Client contribution items from the VTAS were revised to make the scale developmentally appropriate for clients across the adolescent age span and applicable to a variety of intervention types, including prevention.

Although the ATAS includes separate Patient Contribution and Patient–Therapist Contribution subscales, results of an exploratory factor analysis indicated that the ATAS is unidimensional, with item loadings ranging from .40 to .90. Convergent validity was established using therapist and observer ratings of treatment engagement; correlations ranged from .31 to .70. Internal consistency was high at .90, and interrater reliability was acceptable, with an ICC of .74 for the total score. Developmental and cultural sensitivity were not evaluated.

Alliance Observation Coding System

The Alliance Observation Coding System (Karver, Shirk, Day, Fields, & Handelsman, 2003) is an observer measure that involves rating the therapeutic alliance across 10 categories: feeling advocated for, comfort in talking, receptive to feedback, feeling understood, valuing therapist–therapy, positive affect toward the therapist, feeling comforted after distress, synchrony, negative reactions, and interrupts therapist. After rating these categories, observers code intensely positive and negative responses made by the adolescent, his or her level of personal disclosure, dominance of conversation by client or therapist, and global alliance. Ratings are made on a 5-point scale. An advantage of the Alliance Observation Coding System is that it was designed by considering adolescent development and typical adolescent emotional and cognitive responses to a therapist as opposed to adapting adult therapeutic alliance coding systems.

Internal consistency was very high at .92. Interrater agreement was also high, with an ICC of .84. In support of convergent validity, the Alliance Observation Coding System ratings correlated significantly with adolescent report of the alliance during the third session using the WAI–S ($r = .85$).

Other Adolescent–Therapist Relationship Measures

From the early 1980s to the present, there has been an increase in the design of therapeutic alliance measures, and more specifically in measures that have been used with adolescent populations. Before this period, research on the relationship in adolescent treatment tended to use more general relationship measures or measures that focused on the qualities of the clinician. These measures included the following: the Barrett-Lennard Relationship Inventory (Barrett-Lennard, 1962), considered the pioneer instrument for patient and therapist judgments of the therapeutic relationship (M. R. Luborsky, 1994) and used with adolescents in seven studies (Hansen, Zimpfer, & Easterling, 1967; Joseph,1997; Lanning & Lemons, 1974; Maurer & Tindall, 1983; McNally & Drummond, 1973; Sandhu, Reeves, & Portes, 1993; Selfridge & Vander Kolk, 1976); the Carkhuff's scales (Carkhuff, 1969), used with adolescents in two studies (Joseph, 1997; McNally & Drummond, 1973); the Counselor Rating Form (Barak & LaCrosse, 1975; Corrigan & Schmidt,

1983), used with adolescents in three studies (Blankenship, Eels, Calozzi, Perry, & Barnes, 1998; Hagborg, 1991; Sandhu et al., 1993); the Origin Climate Questionnaire (De Charms, 1976), used with adolescents in Taylor, Adelman, and Kaser-Boyd (1986); the Personal and Professional Therapist Qualities and Characteristic Rating Form modified (Hatfield, 1983); the Leathers Nonverbal Feedback Rating Instrument (Leathers, 1978), used with adolescents in Sandhu et al. (1993); the Feeling Word Checklist (Holmqvist & Armelius, 1994), used with adolescents in Holmqvist et al. (2007); the Impact Message Inventory-Circumplex (Kiesler, 1996), used with adolescents in Auerbach et al. (2008); and the Client–Therapist Relationship Scale (Noser & Bickman, 2000), which is a derivative of a satisfaction questionnaire. As this list of instruments indicates, there is substantial variability in the types of measures used to assess the relationship in adolescent therapy.

Summary

Our review has revealed increasing interest in assessing relational processes in adolescent treatment over the past 10 years. There has been some movement away from measurement of general relationship characteristics toward the assessment of the therapy alliance, typically operationalized as some combination of relational comfort–conflict, task or goal agreement, and collaborative involvement in therapy tasks. Even with this increased focus, a diverse collection of instruments has emerged, and the field has yet to converge on the use of a measure or set of measures. Most of these instruments have been used in a limited number of studies, and their psychometric properties are preliminary, at best. Moreover, many of the instruments have been developed for use with specific populations such as psychiatric inpatients, incarcerated youth, or adolescents with specific medical problems. Given the paucity of data on measurement properties, it is not clear whether the use of measures developed for specific populations in specific settings can be validly generalized to other samples and other types of treatment. Thus, investigators are cautioned in their choice of extant alliance measures for adolescents: Look before you leap! Given the limited data on most of these measures, investigators should pilot the selected measure(s) with their population and type of treatment before proceeding with the full study.

Although participant measures of the alliance were prominent in adolescent research, a number of promising observational measures have emerged over the past 10 years. At least two of these instruments have been adapted from the VPSS, and both have shown promise with adolescents. Similarly, the most widely used participant measure to this point, the WAI, represents an adaptation of the original adult alliance scale. It is noteworthy that factor analyses of this measure have failed to produce the familiar three-factor solution of bond, task, and goals found with adults. It may be the case that the adolescent alliance is a unitary construct that reflects a collaborative bond between teen and therapist. Similar results have been obtained with the TASA (Shirk et al., 2008) and with a number of the observational measures as well. It is possible that what has been called the alliance with adolescents refers to a relatively global positive–negative relationship dimension that is reflected across bond, tasks, and goals. Alternatively, it may be profitable to attempt to distinguish broad dimensions such as relationship and work, as obtained in factor analyses of child therapy (Estrada & Russell, 1999). The first dimension refers to the quality of the emotional connection between child and therapist and the second to the actual level of involvement in treatment tasks (as opposed to agreements on tasks). Although Estrada and Russell (1999) extracted these dimensions from observational data, it is possible that relationship as an experiential construct might best be assessed by participant report and work by observational ratings.

No study has administered a battery of alliance measures as has been done with adults (Tichenor & Hill, 1989); consequently, it is difficult to know whether varied measures are essentially tapping the same core construct or whether sets of measures might actually fall into meaningful clusters that assess different aspects of the alliance. Such a study would require a relatively large sample of adolescent patients, and it is not certain that one could combine samples of youth receiving different forms of therapy. In brief, the alliance as a unitary or multidimensional construct might depend on the type of therapy delivered and the specific clinical population receiving the treatment. Nevertheless, current results found using measures with multiple dimensions do not point to clearly distinguishable factors.

Of course, the importance of the therapeutic alliance in adolescent treatment rests on the construct's predictive association with outcomes or with variables such as attendance and involvement that presumably mediate outcomes. Thus, predictive validity represents one of the critical validity criteria for any measure of the alliance in adolescent treatment. In the next section, we examine the limited set of studies that have evaluated associations between the adolescent alliance and treatment outcomes.

ALLIANCE–OUTCOME RELATIONS IN ADOLESCENT THERAPY

The clinical literature has underscored the importance of the therapeutic alliance for successful treatment of adolescents (DiGiuseppe et al., 1996; Meeks, 1971). From this vantage point, the alliance is hypothesized to be a robust predictor of treatment outcomes. To evaluate the evidence for this frequently cited clinical observation, we conducted an extensive literature search to locate empirical studies of alliance–outcome relations in adolescent treatment.

We used several search methods to identify relevant studies. First, we conducted a literature review using the following databases: PsycINFO, Medline, and Dissertation Abstracts. Second, we examined studies that were included in two previous reviews of child treatment process and outcome research (Russell & Shirk, 1998; Weisz, Huey, & Weersing, 1998). Third, we included relevant studies included in meta-analyses by Shirk and Karver (2003) and Karver, Handelsman, Fields, and Bickman (2006). On the basis of these search strategies, we identified 29 studies that examined associations between relationship variables and treatment outcomes among youth ages 13 to 18. The reviewed studies all included a quantitative measure of association between alliance and outcome, included more than 10 participants, and involved actual treatment (i.e., were not analogue studies). Studies included in this review are listed in Table 2.1 (http://pubs.apa.org/books/supp/elusive/).

To evaluate the studies with a common metric, we used the product–moment correlation as the effect size estimate. Before all computations involving correlation coefficients, we converted the r values to Fisher's Z equivalents to control for the bias of the r distribution. To find the overall alliance to outcome relationship, we weighted the effect size in proportion to the number of participants in the study. In most of the studies, more than one alliance–outcome association was reported. To offset any bias that might follow from one study contributing more effect sizes than another, we computed the mean effect size for each study. Both weighted effect sizes and mean correlations for each study are presented in Table 2.1 (http://pubs.apa.org/books/supp/elusive/).

To maintain consistency with alliance–outcome estimates in the adult therapy literature, we applied three more inclusion criteria. First, a putative measure of alliance rather than general relationship measures such as therapist warmth or empathy needed to be included. Second, modality of treatment was restricted to individual therapy but could involve any approach, for example, cognitive–behavioral or psychodynamic. Third, associations between alliance and outcome were limited to prospective relations as opposed to concurrent measurements; alliance needed to be assessed before outcomes. When these additional criteria were applied, seven studies—Auerbach et al. (2008), Eltz et al. (1995), Handwerk et al. (2008), Hogue et al. (2006), Karver et al. (2008), Shirk et al. (2008), and Zaitsoff et al. (2008)—were identified. Although the number of studies is quite limited, this sample represents a sevenfold increase since the Shirk and Karver meta-analysis published in 2003.

Thus, our first conclusion is that the alliance, although deemed clinically important for adolescent treatment, remains understudied. Three studies have evaluated the alliance in cognitive–behavioral therapy. The other studies involved psychodynamic therapy, nondirective supportive therapy, and variations of treatment as usual. Two samples included substance-abusing youth, two included depressed adolescents, two involved mixed samples in residential or inpatient treatment, and one included adolescents with bulimia. On average, sample sizes have been small (mean $N = 45$). In terms of alliance measures, only the WAI–S has been used in more than one study. Thus, this sample of adolescent alliance studies involving individual therapy with a prospective design includes a variety of participant and observational measures completed in quite varied forms of therapy. Only adolescents with substance abuse problems or depression have been examined in more than one study.

Effect sizes in this sample ranged from −.02 to .53 with a mean effect size of .21, quite comparable to results obtained with adults. From a "box score" perspective, three of the studies yielded small to moderate effects (Eltz et al., 1995; Handwerk et al., 2008; Shirk et al., 2008), one produced a large effect (Zaitsoff et al., 2008), and three resulted in null or very small effects (Auerbach et al., 2008; Hogue et al., 2006; Karver et al., 2008). Two of the three studies with the smallest effects involved treatment of adolescent substance abuse, and the third involved adolescents ascertained in the emergency room after a suicide attempt, a group that likely included a significant number of substance-abusing teens. The two studies yielding the largest effect sizes both used variations of the PHAS. The only observational measure to yield a moderate effect was the WRS.

To evaluate the current results relative to effect sizes obtained in treatment–control comparisons, we converted the average r to the effect size d. When converted, the d for the current sample of adolescent alliance studies was 0.41. According to Cohen (1992), this estimate represents a medium effect. For purposes of comparison, average effect sizes (ds) for treatment–control comparisons in the child and adolescent literature hover around 0.7 (Weisz, Weiss, Han, Granger, & Morton, 1995). More important, comparisons between research treatments and active controls have produced smaller effects. For example, comparisons of evidence-based treatments with treatment as usual have yielded an average effect size of .30 (Weisz, Jensen-Doss, & Hawley, 2006).

In addition to individual therapy, family therapy is often used in the treatment of adolescents. In fact, we identified seven additional studies examining alliance–outcome relations in family therapy with a prospective design (Diamond, Siqueland, & Diamond, 2003; Faw et al., 2005; Hogue et al., 2006; Pereira, Lock, & Oggins, 2006; Shelef et al., 2005; Shelef & Diamond, 2008; Zaitsoff et al., 2008). Like the individual therapy studies, this sample involved a variety of adolescent problems including substance abuse, bulimia, and depression. Multidimensional family therapy was the most common form of family therapy, and it was delivered in four studies of substance use or abuse. In comparison to the studies of individual therapy, observational measures of the alliance were more likely to be used (in six of the seven studies). Again, sample sizes were relatively small (mean $N = 43$).

Effect sizes for the sample of family therapy studies ranged from −.22 to .26 with an average effect of .07. Two of the studies did not provide enough information to estimate the correlation between alliance and outcome, and in keeping with convention, effect sizes were estimated to be 0 when results were reported as nonsignificant. This approach to estimation could bias the overall effect in such a small sample of studies, so we recomputed effect sizes after excluding these two studies. The resulting effect size estimate is .11, still quite small.

It would be premature to conclude that the alliance is less important in family therapy than in individual therapy because of notable differences in study samples. First, four of seven studies of family therapy involved the treatment of substance use or abuse, whereas only two individual studies focused on this population and together yielded an average effect of .05. It is possible that the alliance is less predictive in the treatment of substance abuse than of other disorders, or possibly more difficult to assess with substance-using teens. Alternatively, method of assessment might explain the difference in effect sizes because five of the six studies of adolescent substance use or abuse used observational measures of alliance. Thus, method of assessment is confounded with type of disorder. In this connection, it is noteworthy that observational measures in individual and family therapy yielded an average effect size of .10, whereas participant measures produced an average effect of .25. It is likely that the simplest explanation for the apparent difference in magnitude of association between alliance and outcome across individual and family therapy studies is that it is the result of differences in method of alliance assessment.

Most measures of adolescent alliance have each been used in one prospective study, including the Alliance Observation Coding System, ATAS, TASA, and WRS. Two of these scales—TASA and WRS—significantly predicted outcomes, thereby providing preliminary evidence for their predictive validity. Three scales were used in multiple studies—variations of the WAI, the PHAS, and the VTAS. Interestingly, none of these scales were developed specifically for use with adolescents. Across prospective studies, the average correlation between alliance and outcome was .13 for the WAI scales, .27 for the PHAS, and .04 for the VTAS. Although correlations varied across studies and measures within studies, only the PHAS showed a moderate predictive relationship with outcomes. The average predictive correlation for the VTAS, an observational measure, is quite low and raises some concern about its predictive validity. However, it could be argued that predictive validity should be assessed with more proximal outcomes such as level of in-session involvement or treatment continuation. On the basis of current findings, then, no alliance instrument has emerged as the clear choice for research with adolescents. Investigators are advised to review existing evidence for each scale as well as the context in which it has been used to select the most appropriate measure.

Summary

Although there has been an increase in the number of studies that prospectively evaluate alliance–outcome relations in adolescence, this literature pales in comparison to that of research with adults. Nevertheless, results with adolescent samples have indicated that associations between alliance and outcome are quite comparable to those obtained with adults in individual therapy. Effects obtained from family therapy studies are somewhat smaller, possibly owing to the more frequent use of observational measures in family therapy than in individual therapy.

There are notable limitations in the existing research. First, almost half of the studies involve treatments of no known efficacy. If treatments fail to produce reliable change or fail to create substantial variations in outcomes, there is little for the alliance to predict. Although our review suggests an increase in the number of studies of evidence-based treatments compared with earlier reviews (e.g., Shirk & Karver, 2003), the contribution of the alliance to outcome in many evidence-based treatments has not been examined. Similarly, adolescents with a variety of disorders are conspicuously missing from the current sample of studies, for example, adolescents with social phobia, obsessive–compulsive disorder, generalized anxiety disorder, posttraumatic stress disorder, bipolar disorder, and conduct disorder. At this point, it is impossible to know whether the contribution of alliance to outcome is comparable across disorders or varies with type of adolescent problem.

Observational measures of alliance are increasingly being used, and at this point, they appear to yield relatively small associations with outcome. An early meta-analysis by Horvath and Symonds (1991) of alliance–outcome associations in adult therapy suggested that patient reports yield larger correlations than observer reports; however, a more recent meta-analytic review of adult therapy did not reveal differences related to alliance source (Martin et al., 2000). It is possible that the apparent difference between participant and observer reports with adolescents represents a developmental difference from adult treatment, but given the small number of studies, this finding must be viewed as preliminary. A clearer picture will emerge when variance attributable to shared source across alliance and outcome measures is evaluated. Most existing studies have used only one alliance measure, so direct comparisons are quite limited.

In terms of predictive validity, measures that have been used in multiple predictive studies have yielded small to virtually nonexistent associations with treatment outcome, raising some concern about their predictive validity. A number of participant measures used in single studies have fared better, but clearly more research is needed to establish their predictive validity.

CONCLUSION: IMPROVING RESEARCH ON THE ALLIANCE IN ADOLESCENT THERAPY

Our review of the alliance in adolescent therapy revealed a number of trends. First, investigators have borrowed heavily from the adult therapy literature in their conceptualization of the alliance. Bordin's (1979) trans-theoretical model has been highly influential, with some researchers emphasizing the bond component of the alliance and others focusing on agreements about treatment tasks and goals. Emerging evidence from both participant and observer ratings of alliance has suggested that these dimensions are highly related and that the adolescent alliance might best be viewed as a unitary construct: collaborative bond. Research is needed to determine whether distinct facets of the alliance are more strongly associated with outcomes than others, but at present overall strength of collaborative bond appears to be the most parsimonious approach.

Second, quite a number of alliance scales have been adapted or developed for use with adolescents. Many of these instruments have been used in only one study, and psychometric data are preliminary or limited for a number of the newer scales. The most widely used measure of alliance in adolescent therapy has been the WAI and variations of it. Originally developed for use with adults, this scale has been adapted, modified, or shortened for use with adolescents. Results with adolescents indicate good test–retest reliability and very good internal consistency, especially for the short form of the scale. Moreover, there is some evidence of moderate cross-informant agreement and significant association with an alternative measure of alliance. Although correlations with outcomes have varied across studies, the average predictive correlation is quite small.

Another measurement trend involves the emergence of observer rating scales for the adolescent alliance. Again, most of these instruments have been used in only one study. One exception is the VTAS, which has been used in four studies, including three prospective studies. We should note, however, that the VTAS has been modified and shortened on the basis of factor analyses and that psychometric properties vary across versions of the scale. Predictive validity is uncertain because associations with outcome are quite negligible.

A third trend involves an increase in the number of studies that examined prospective relations between alliance and outcome. Although the number is still quite small, results have suggested small to medium effects that are quite comparable to findings with adults. There appears to be substantial variation in effects across studies, but low numbers make this difficult to test. Some of this variation appears to be attributable to method of assessment, with participant measures yielding larger effects than observational instruments. At this point, however, we have insufficient data to determine the relative contribution of alliance to outcome in different types of treatments or disorders. In this connection, the relatively smaller association between alliance and outcome in family therapy cannot be separated from the potential effect of sample differences in individual and family therapy studies.

A number of important issues need to be addressed in adolescent alliance measurement research. First, investigators must reevaluate the nature of the alliance construct in adolescent treatment. Most researchers have adopted the prevailing adult conceptualization and then adapted measures from the adult literature. However, this measurement scheme has several unresolved limitations. One major limitation is that of ceiling effects. In the adult treatment process literature, the meta-analysis by Tryon, Blackwell, and Hammel (2008) demonstrated that participants using adult alliance measures typically use only the top 20% of available rating points. Hughes and Kendall (2007) suggested that the same problem occurs in youth reports of the therapeutic alliance. Moreover, research has not confirmed the theorized factor structure of youth alliance measures. Although agreements and attachments may be important components of the alliance at any age, some consideration should be given to other dimensions that might be particularly salient to adolescents. One potential candidate involves the degree to which therapists facilitate adolescent autonomy, a central task of this developmental period. Alternatively, communications between therapist and parent may be more salient to adolescents than to children and may represent a critical aspect of confidence in the therapist.

Also, research to clarify the role of adolescents' perceptions of therapist credibility in relation to the alliance is also needed. The extent to which a therapist is perceived as credible (i.e., having expertise, trustworthy) has been considered to influence client expectations of positive treatment outcomes. This type of cognitive connection with the therapist may be worth assessing separately from emotional bond and client participation in treatment (see Karver et al., 2005). For example, in the case of treatments that involve aversive procedures, such as exposure-based therapies, it might not be unusual for an adolescent to develop a strong emotional bond with the therapist while remaining skeptical of the rationale for participating in the tasks that the therapist proposes. If the adolescent does not feel that participation is worth the effort (i.e., worth tolerating the distress that the task initially induces), he or she may not participate even if he or she likes the therapist. Thus, it may be beneficial to add a credibility dimension to existing alliance models and measures.

Second, the trend toward prospective designs of alliance–outcome relations in treatments of known efficacy must continue. A limited number of evidence-based treatments have been investigated. Of equal importance, the contribution of the alliance to outcome with additional, prevalent adolescent disorders such as social phobia and posttraumatic stress disorder should be pursued. At this point, most prospective studies of the alliance use only one or two points of assessment. This "snapshot" approach to measuring the alliance fails to account for variation in alliance over the course of treatment and introduces error through insufficient sampling. Other research has suggested that the shape of relational processes over time, such as the pattern of resistance (Patterson & Chamberlain, 1994) or pattern of therapist alliance-building interventions (Russell et al., 2008), is a better predictor than single-point or averaged scores. Thus, the magnitude of the association between adolescent alliance and outcome may be obscured by insufficient sampling of alliance strength.

A third issue involves the outcomes predicted by the alliance. It is possible that the alliance is clinically important for reasons other than its modest direct association with posttreatment outcomes. That is, a positive alliance may be critical for treatment continuation, level of in-session involvement, and completion of between-session homework assignments (Shirk & Karver, 2006). Results with children and parents have suggested that treatment dropout is associated with early alliance and therapy relationship problems (Garcia & Weisz, 2002; Hawley & Weisz, 2005; Kazdin, Holland, & Crowley, 1997). In addition, Karver et al. (2008) found that the alliance is associated with in-session treatment participation among depressed adolescents. However, very few studies have examined these associations in the adolescent literature. From this perspective, the alliance attains its importance as an indirect predictor of outcome. In essence, the alliance increases exposure to the active ingredients of therapy by facilitating treatment continuation and active involvement.

In this connection, the magnitude of alliance effects might be more substantial with more proximal outcomes. In prospective studies, a significant amount of time typically separates alliance assessment, often in the early phase of treatment, and treatment outcome. Other factors, including change in the alliance over time, could intervene between initial assessment and subsequent outcome. Two points are worth considering. First, the alliance measured early in treatment might be more predictive of early gains, that is, symptom reduction after a few sessions. Early gains are evident in both the adult and the adolescent treatment literature across types of treatments and disorders (Gaynor, Weersing, & Kolko, 2003; Hardy, Cahill, Stiles, Ispan, Macaskill,

& Barkham, 2005). Subsequent changes in symptoms might be linked to other processes that obscure the early contribution of alliance to posttreatment outcomes. Second, the alliance as a relational process might be more strongly associated with conceptually proximal outcomes, such as change in interpersonal schema or social coping strategies rather than with symptom change. In turn, changes in relational variables could contribute to symptom change, but again, the stronger association would be with relationship variables rather than symptoms per se.

Finally, and perhaps most important, the causal status of the alliance needs to be established. Implicit in most existing research is the view that the alliance promotes, facilitates, or contributes to emotional and behavioral change. This view has been supported by prospective associations between alliance and outcome; alliance measured early in treatment predicts change over the course of therapy. However, prospective results are not sufficient for demonstrating a causal relationship. First, most research on the alliance has measured the alliance after a few sessions. From the perspective of alliance formation, this makes sense; however, it is possible that early alliance is a function of early treatment gains. The alliance, then, is the consequence of improvement rather than its cause. This pivotal question has not been evaluated in the adolescent literature. Even if alliance predicts subsequent outcomes after controlling for early gains, no study of the adolescent alliance has attempted to experimentally manipulate the alliance to demonstrate its causal influence. Until this step is taken, the alliance will remain a predictor but only a potential cause of therapeutic change.

In conclusion, some progress in research on the alliance in adolescent therapy has been made over the past 10 years. Clearly, however, substantial work remains to be done. Although the clinical literature casts the alliance in a starring role in adolescent therapy, current research has yet to determine whether the alliance will play a leading, supporting, or peripheral role in the outcome literature.

REFERENCES

Alexander, L. B., & Luborsky, L. (1986). The Penn Helping Alliance Scales. In E. Leslie, S. Greenberg, & William M. Pinsof (Ed.), *The psychotherapeutic process: A research handbook* (pp. 325–366). New York, NY: Guilford Press.

Allen, J. G., Deering, C. D., Buskirk, J. R., & Coyne, L. (1988). Assessment of therapeutic alliances in the psychiatric hospital milieu. *Psychiatry: Journal for the Study of Interpersonal Processes, 51*, 291–299.

Auerbach, S. M., May, J. C., Stevens, M., & Kiesler, D. J. (2008). The interactive role of working alliance and counselor-client interpersonal behaviors in adolescent substance abuse treatment. *International Journal of Clinical and Health Psychology, 8*, 617–629.

Barak, A., & LaCrosse, M. B. (1975). Multidimensional perception of counselor behavior. *Journal of Counseling Psychology, 22*, 471–476. doi:10.1037/0022-0167.22.6.471

Barrett-Lennard, G. T. (1962). Dimensions of therapist response as causal factors in therapeutic change. *Psychological Monographs, 76*(43, Whole No. 562).

Bickman, L., Vides de Andrade, A. R., Lambert, W., Doucette, A., Sapyta, J., Boyd, A. S., . . . Rauktis, M. B. (2004). Youth therapeutic alliance in intensive treatment settings. *Journal of Behavioral Health Services & Research, 31*, 134–148.

Blankenship, B. L., Eels, G. T., Carlozzi, A. F., Perry, K., & Barnes, L. B. (1998). Adolescent client perceptions and reactions to reframe and symptom prescription techniques. *Journal of Mental Health Counseling, 20*, 172–182.

Bordin, E. S. (1979). The generalizability of the psychoanalytic concept of the working alliance. *Psychotherapy: Theory, Research, and Practice, 16*, 252–260. doi:10.1037/h0085885

Bowlby, J. (1988). *A secure base: Parent–child attachment and healthy human development.* New York, NY: Basic Books.

Brendt, D. A., & Poling, K. (1997). *Cognitive therapy treatment manual for depressed and suicidal youth.* Pittsburgh, PA: University of Pittsburgh.

Carkhuff, R. R. (1969). Helper communication as a function of helpee affect and content. *Journal of Counseling Psychology, 16*(2, Pt.1), 126–131. doi:10.1037/h0027200

Cecero, J. J., Fenton, L. R., Frankforter, T. L., Nich, C., & Carroll, K. M. (2001). Focus on therapeutic alliance: The psychometric properties of six measures across three treatments. *Psychotherapy: Theory, Research, Practice, Training, 38*, 1–11.

Cohen, J. (1992). A power primer. *Psychological Bulletin, 112*, 155–159. doi:10.1037/0033-2909. 112.1.155

Colson, D. B., Cornsweet, C., Murphy, T., O'Malley, F., Hyland, P. S., McParland, M., & Coyne, L. (1991). Perceived treatment difficulty and therapeutic alliance on an adolescent psychiatric hospital unit. *American Journal of Orthopsychiatry, 61*, 221–229. doi:10.1037/h0079253

Corrigan, J. D., & Schmidt, L. D. (1983). Development and validation of revisions in the Counselor Rating Form. *Journal of Counseling Psychology, 30*, 64–75. doi:10.1037/0022-0167.30.1.64

De Charms, R. (1976). *Enhancing motivation.* New York, NY: Irvington.

Dennis, M. L., Ives, M. L., White, M. K., & Muck, R. D. (2008). The Strengthening Communities for Youth (SCY) initiative: A cluster analysis of the services received, their correlates and how they are associated with outcomes. *Journal of Psychoactive Drugs, 40*, 3–16.

Diamond, G. M., Liddle, H. A., Hogue, A., & Dakof, G. A. (1999). Alliance-building interventions with adolescents in family therapy: A process study. *Psychotherapy, 36*, 355–368. doi:10.1037/h0087729

Diamond, G. S., Liddle, H. A., Wintersteen, M. B., Dennis, M. L., Godley, S. H., & Tims, F. (2006). Early therapeutic alliance as a predictor of treatment outcome for adolescent cannabis users in outpatient treatment. *American Journal on Addictions, 15*, 26–33. doi:10.1080/10550490601003664

Diamond, G., Siqueland, L., & Diamond, G. M. (2003). Attachment-based family therapy for depressed adolescents: Programmatic treatment development. *Clinical Child and Family Psychology Review, 6*, 107–127. doi:10.1023/A:1023782510786

DiGiuseppe, R., Linscott, J., & Jilton, R. (1996). Developing the therapeutic alliance in child-adolescent psychotherapy. *Applied & Preventive Psychology, 5*, 85–100. doi:10.1016/S0962-1849(96)80002-3

Doucette, A. (2004). *Child/Adolescent Measurement System (CAMS): User manual.* Nashville, TN: Author.

Eltz, M. J., Shirk, S. R., & Sarlin, N. (1995). Alliance formation and treatment outcome among maltreated adolescents. *Child Abuse & Neglect, 19,* 419–431. doi:10.1016/0145-2134 (95)00008-V

Estrada, A. U., & Russell, R. L. (1999). The development of the Child Therapy Process Scales (CPSS). *Psychotherapy Research, 9,* 154–166.

Faw, L., Hogue, A., Johnson, S., Diamond, G. M., & Liddle, H. A. (2005). The Adolescent Therapeutic Alliance Scale (ATAS): Initial psychometrics and prediction of outcome in family-based substance abuse prevention counseling. *Psychotherapy Research, 15*(1-2), 141–154. doi:10.1080/10503300512331326994

Fitzpatrick, M. R., & Irannejad, S. (2008). Adolescent readiness for change and the working alliance in counseling. *Journal of Counseling and Development, 86,* 438–445.

Flicker, S. M., Turner, C. W., Waldron, H. B., Brody, J. L., & Ozechowski, T. J. (2008). Ethnic background, therapeutic alliance, and treatment retention in functional family therapy with adolescents who abuse substances. *Journal of Family Psychology, 22,* 167–170. doi:10.1037/0893-3200.22.1.167

Florsheim, P., Shotorbani, S., Guest-Warnick, G., Barratt, T., & Hwang, W. (2000). Role of the working alliance in the treatment of delinquent boys in community-based programs. *Journal of Clinical Child Psychology, 29,* 94–107. doi:10.1207/S15374424jccp2901_10

Friedlander, M. L., Escudero, V., & Heatherington, L. (2001). SOFTA-o for clients. Unpublished measure. (Available at http://www.softasoatif.net)

Friedlander, M. L., Escudero, V., Horvath, A., Heatherington, L., Cabero, A., & Martens, M. P. (2006). System for Observing Family Therapy Alliances: A tool for research and practice. *Journal of Counseling Psychology, 53,* 214–225.

Freud, A. (1946). *The psychoanalytic treatment of children.* New York, NY: International Universities Press.

Furman, W., Simon, V. A., Shaffer, L., & Bouchey, H. A. (2002). Adolescents' working models and styles for relationships with parents, friends, and romantic partners. *Child Development, 73,* 241–255.

Garcia, J. A., & Weisz, J. (2002). When youth mental health care stops: Therapeutic relationship problems and other reasons for ending youth outpatient treatment. *Journal of Consulting and Clinical Psychology, 70,* 439–443. doi:10.1037/0022-006X.70.2.439

Gavin, L. A., Wamboldt, M. Z., Sorokin, N., Levy, S. Y., & Wamboldt, F. S. (1999). Treatment alliance and its association with family functioning, adherence, and medical outcome in adolescents with severe, chronic asthma. *Journal of Pediatric Psychology, 24,* 355–365. doi:10.1093/jpepsy/24.4.355

Gaynor, S. T., Weersing, V. R., & Kolko, D. J. (2003). The prevalence and impact of large sudden improvements during adolescent therapy for depression: A comparison across cognitive–behavioral, family and supportive therapy. *Journal of Consulting and Clinical Psychology, 71,* 386–393. doi:10.1037/0022-006X.71.2.386

Glueckauf, R. L., Fritz, S. P., Ecklunk-Johnson, E. P., Liss, H. J., Dages, P., & Carney, P. (2002). Videoconferencing-based family counseling for rural teenagers with epilepsy: Phase 1 findings. *Rehabilitation Psychology, 47,* 49–72. doi:10.1037/0090-5550.47.1.49

Glueckauf, R. L., Liss, H. J., McQuillen, D. E., Webb, P. M., Dairaghi, J., & Carter, C. B. (2002). Therapeutic alliance in family therapy for adolescents with epilepsy: An exploratory study. *American Journal of Family Therapy, 30,* 125–139. doi:10.1080/019261802753573849

Green, J., Kroll, L., Imrie, D., Frances, F. M., Begum, K., Harrison, L., & Anson, R. (2001). Health gain and outcome predictors during inpatient and related day treatment in child and adolescent psychiatry. *Journal of the American Academy of Child & Adolescent Psychiatry, 40,* 325–332. doi:10.1097/00004583-200103000-00012

Greenson, R. R. (1965). The working alliance and the transference neurosis. *Psychoanalytic Quarterly, 34,* 155–181.

Hagborg, W. J. (1991). Adolescent clients and perceived counselor characteristics: A study of background characteristics, therapeutic progress, psychological distress, and social desirability. *Journal of Clinical Psychology, 47,* 107–113. doi:10.1002/1097-4679(199101) 47:1<107::AID-JCLP2270470118>3.0.CO;2-R

Handwerk, M. L., Huefner, J. C., Ringle, J. L., Howard, B. K., Soper, S. H., Almquist, J. K., . . . Father Flanagan's Boys' Home. (2008). The role of therapeutic alliance in therapy outcomes for youth in residential care. *Residential Treatment for Children & Youth, 25,* 145–165. doi:10.1080/08865710802310152

Hansen, J. C., Zimpfer, D. G., & Easterling, R. E. (1967). A study of the relationships in multiple counseling. *Journal of Educational Research, 60,* 461–463.

Hardy, G. E., Cahill, J., Stiles, W. B., Ispan, C., Macaskill, N., & Barkham, M. (2005). Sudden gains in cognitive therapy for depression: A replication and extension. *Journal of Consulting and Clinical Psychology, 73,* 59–67. doi:10.1037/0022-006X.73.1.59

Hartley, D. E., & Strupp, H. H. (1983). The therapeutic alliance: Its relationship to outcome in brief psychotherapy. In J. Masling (Ed.), *Empirical studies of psychoanalytical theories* (Vol. 1, pp. 1–38). Hillsdale, NJ: Analytical Press.

Hatfield, A. B. (1983). What families want of family therapists. In W. McFarlane (Ed.), *Family therapy in schizophrenia* (pp. 41–65). New York, NY: Guilford Press.

Hawke, J. M., Hennen, J., & Gallione, P. (2005). Correlates of therapeutic involvement among adolescents in residential drug treatment. *American Journal of Drug and Alcohol Abuse, 31,* 163–177. doi:10.1081/ADA-200047913

Hawley, K. M., & Garland, A. F. (2008). Working alliance in adolescent outpatient therapy: Youth, parent and therapist reports and associations with therapy outcomes. *Child and Youth Care Forum, 37,* 59–74. doi:10.1007/s10566-008-9050-x

Hawley, K. M., & Weisz, J. (2005). Youth versus parent working alliance in usual clinical care: Distinctive associations with retention, satisfaction, and treatment outcome. *Journal of Clinical Child and Adolescent Psychology, 34,* 117–128. doi:10.1207/s15374424jccp3401_11

Henry, W. P., & Strupp, H. H. (1994). The therapeutic alliance as interpersonal process. In A. O. Horvath & L. S. Greenberg (Eds.), *The working alliance: Theory, research, and practice* (pp. 51–84). New York, NY: Wiley.

Holmqvist, R., & Armelius, B. A. (1994). Emotional reactions to psychiatric patients. *Acta Psychiatrica Scandinavica, 90,* 204–209. doi:10.1111/j.1600-0447.1994.tb01578.x

Holmqvist, R., Hill, T., & Lang, A. (2007). Treatment alliance in residential treatment of criminal adolescents. *Child and Youth Care Forum, 36,* 163–178. doi:10.1007/ s10566-007-9037-z

Hogue, A., Dauber, S., Stambaugh, L. F., Cecero, J. J., & Liddle, H. A. (2006). Early therapeutic alliance and treatment outcome in individual and family therapy for adolescent behavior problems. *Journal of Consulting and Clinical Psychology, 74,* 121–129. doi:10.1037/ 0022-006X.74.1.121

Horvath, A. O. (1994). Empirical validation of Bordin's pantheoretical model of the alliance: The Working Alliance Inventory perspective. In A. O. Horvath & L. S. Greenberg (Eds.), *The working alliance: Theory, research, and practice* (pp. 109–128). New York, NY: Wiley.

Horvath, A. O., & Greenberg, L. S. (1989). Development and validation of the Working Alliance Inventory. *Journal of Counseling Psychology, 36,* 223–233. doi:10.1037/0022-0167. 36.2.223

Horvath, A. O., & Luborsky, L. (1993). The role of the therapeutic alliance in psychotherapy. *Journal of Consulting and Clinical Psychology, 61,* 561–573. doi:10.1037/0022-006X.61.4.561

Horvath, A. O., & Symonds, B. D. (1991). Relation between working alliance and outcome in psychotherapy: A meta-analysis. *Journal of Counseling Psychology, 38,* 139–149. doi:10.1037/0022-0167.38.2.139

Hughes, A. A., & Kendall, P. C. (2007). Prediction of cognitive behavior treatment outcome for children with anxiety disorders: Therapeutic relationship and homework compliance. *Behavioural and Cognitive Psychotherapy, 35,* 487–494. doi:10.1017/S1352465807003761

Jackson-Gilfort, A., Liddle, H. A., Tejeda, M. J., & Dakof, G. A. (2001). Facilitating engagement of African American male adolescents in family therapy: A cultural theme process study. *Journal of Black Psychology, 27,* 321–340. doi:10.1177/0095798401027003005

Johnson, L. N., Ketring, S. A., Rohacs, J., & Brewer, A. L. (2006). Attachment and the therapeutic alliance in family therapy. *American Journal of Family Therapy, 34,* 205–218. doi:10.1080/01926180500358022

Johnson, L. N., Wright, D. W., & Ketring, S. A. (2002). The therapeutic alliance in home-based family therapy: Is it predictive of outcome? *Journal of Marital and Family Therapy, 28,* 93–102. doi:10.1111/j.1752-0606.2002.tb01177.x

Joseph, S. C. (1997). *Exploration of the therapeutic relationship with families.* Unpublished doctoral dissertation, Wayne State University, Detroit, MI.

Karver, M., Handelsman, J. B., Fields, S., & Bickman, L. (2005). A theoretical model of common process factors in youth and family therapy. *Mental Health Services Research, 7,* 35–51.

Karver, M., Handlesman, J. B., Fields, S., & Bickman, L. (2006). Meta-analysis of therapeutic relationship variables in youth and family therapy: The evidence for different relationship variables in the child and adolescent treatment outcome literature. *Clinical Psychology Review, 26,* 50–65.

Karver, M., Shirk, S., Day, R., Fields, S., & Handelsman, J. (2003). *Rater's manual for the Alliance Observation Coding System.* Unpublished manual, University of South Florida, Tampa.

Karver, M., Shirk, S., Handelsman, J. B., Fields, S., Crisp, H., Gudmundsen, G., & McMakin, D. (2008). Relationship processes in youth psychotherapy: Measuring alliance, alliance-building behaviors, and client involvement. *Journal of Emotional and Behavioral Disorders, 16,* 15–28. doi:10.1177/1063426607312536

Kaufman, N. K., Rohde, P., Seeley, J. R., Clarke, G. N., & Stice, E. (2005). Potential mediators of cognitive–behavioral therapy for adolescents with comorbid major depression and conduct disorder. *Journal of Consulting and Clinical Psychology, 73,* 38–46. doi:10.1037/0022-006X.73.1.38

Kazdin, A. E., Holland, L., & Crowley, M. (1997). Family experience of barriers to treatment and premature termination from child therapy. *Journal of Consulting and Clinical Psychology, 65,* 453–463. doi:10.1037/0022-006X.65.3.453

Kiesler, D. J. (1996). *Contemporary interpersonal theory and research: Personality, psychopathology and psychotherapy.* New York, NY: Wiley.

Kroll, L., & Green, J. (1997). The therapeutic alliance in child inpatient treatment: Development and initial validation of a Family Engagement Questionnaire. *Clinical Child Psychology and Psychiatry, 2,* 431–447. doi:10.1177/1359104597023009

Langs, R. (1976). *The therapeutic interaction* (Vols. 1 & 2). New York, NY: Aronson.

Lanning, W. L., & Lemons, S. L. (1974). Another look at the factor structure of the Barrett-Lennard Relationship Inventory. *Measurement and Evaluation in Guidance, 6,* 228–231.

Leathers, D. G. (1978). *Nonverbal communication systems.* Boston: Allyn & Bacon.

Linscott, J., DiGiuseppe, R., & Jilton, R. (1993, August). *A measure of TA in adolescent psychotherapy.* Poster presented at the 101st Annual Convention of the American Psychological Association, Toronto, Ontario, Canada.

Luborsky, L. (1976). Helping alliances in psychotherapy. In J. Claghorn (Ed.), *Successful psychotherapy* (pp. 92–111). New York, NY: Brunner/Mazel.

Luborsky, L. (2000). A pattern-setting therapeutic alliance study revisited. *Psychotherapy Research, 10,* 17–29. doi:10.1080/713663591

Luborsky, M. R. (1994). The identification and analysis of themes and patterns. In J. F. Gubrium & A. Sankar (Eds.), *Qualitative methods in aging research* (pp. 189–210). Newbury Park, CA: Sage.

Martin, D. J., Garske, J., & Davis, M. (2000). Relation of the therapeutic alliance with outcome and other variables: A meta-analytic review. *Journal of Consulting and Clinical Psychology, 68,* 438–450. doi:10.1037/0022-006X.68.3.438

Maurer, R. E., & Tindall, J. H. (1983). Effect of postural congruence on clients' perception of counselor empathy. *Journal of Counseling Psychology, 30,* 158–163. doi:10.1037/0022-0167.30.2.158

McConnaughy, E. A., Prochaska, J. O., & Velicer, W. F. (1983). Stages of change in psychotherapy: Measurement and sample profiles. *Psychotherapy: Theory, Research, Practice, Training, 20,* 368–375.

McNally, H., & Drummond, R. (1973). Clients' need for social approval and perceptions of counseling relationship and outcomes. *Psychological Reports, 32,* 363–366.

Meeks, J. (1971). *The fragile alliance.* New York, NY: Krieger.

Mufson, L., Moreau, D., Weissman, M., & Klerman, G. (1993). *Interpersonal psychotherapy for depressed adolescents.* New York, NY: Guilford Press.

Noser, K., & Bickman, L. (2000). Quality indicators of children's mental health services: Do they predict improved client outcomes? *Journal of Emotional and Behavioral Disorders, 8,* 9–18. doi:10.1177/106342660000800102

O'Malley, S. S., Suh, C. S., & Strupp, H. H. (1983). The Vanderbilt Psychotherapy Process Scale: A report on the scale development and a process-outcome study. *Journal of Consulting and Clinical Psychology, 51,* 581–586. doi:10.1037/0022-006X.51.4.581

Orlinsky, D. E., & Howard, K. I. (1967). The good therapy hour: Experiential correlates of patients' and therapists' evaluations of therapy sessions. *Archives of General Psychiatry, 16,* 621–632.

Patterson, G. R., & Chamberlain, P. (1994). A functional analysis of resistance during parent training therapy. *Clinical Psychology: Science and Practice, 1,* 53–70.

Pereira, T., Lock, J., & Oggins, J. (2006). Role of therapeutic alliance in family therapy for adolescent anorexia nervosa. *International Journal of Eating Disorders, 39,* 677–684. doi:10.1002/eat.20303

Pinsof, W. M., & Catherall, D. (1986). The integrative psychotherapy alliance: Family, couple and individual therapy scales. *Journal of Marital and Family Therapy, 12,* 137–151. doi:10.1111/j.1752-0606.1986.tb01631.x

Robbins, M. S., Liddle, H. A., Turner, C., Dakof, G., Alexander, J. F., & Kogan, S. (2006). Adolescent and parent therapeutic alliances as predictors of dropout in multidimensional family therapy. *Journal of Family Psychology, 20,* 108–116.

Robbins, M. S., Mayorga, C. C., Mitrani, V. B., Szapocznik, J., Turner, C. W., & Alexander, J. F. (2008). Adolescent and parent alliances with therapists in brief strategic family therapy with drug-using Hispanic adolescents. *Journal of Marital and Family Therapy, 34,* 316–328.

Robbins, M. S., Turner, C. W., Alexander, J. F., & Perez, G. A. (2003). Alliance and dropout in family therapy for adolescents with behavior problems: Individual and systemic effects. *Journal of Family Psychology, 17,* 534–544. doi:10.1037/0893-3200.17.4.534

Russell, R. L., & Shirk, S. R. (1998). Child psychotherapy process research. *Advances in Clinical Child Psychology, 20,* 93–124.

Russell, R. L., Shirk, S. R., & Jungbluth, N. (2008). First-session pathways to the working alliance in cognitive behavioral therapy for adolescent depression. *Psychotherapy Research*, *18*, 15–27.

Safran, J. D., & Muran, J. C. (1995). Resolving therapeutic alliance ruptures: Diversity and integration. *Psychotherapy in Practice*, *1*, 81–92.

Sandhu, D. S., Reeves, T. G., & Portes, P. R. (1993). Cross-cultural counseling and neuro-linguistic mirroring with Native American adolescents. *Journal of Multicultural Counseling and Development*, *21*, 106–118.

Sapyta, J. J., Karver, M. S., & Bickman, L. (1999). Therapeutic alliance: Significance in non-psychotherapy settings. In C.L. Liberton, C. Newman, K. Kutash, & R.M. Friedman (Eds.), *12th Annual Research Conference Proceedings, a system of care for children's mental health: Expanding the research base* (pp.183–186). Tampa: University of South Florida Press.

Sarlin, N. S. (1992). *Working relationships in the treatment of adolescent inpatients: Early treatment predictors and associations with outcome.* Unpublished dissertation, University of Denver, Denver, CO.

Selfridge, F. F., & Vander Kolk, C. (1976). Correlates of counselor self-actualization and client-perceived facilitativeness. *Counselor Education and Supervision*, *15*, 189–194.

Shelef, K., & Diamond, G. M. (2008). Short form of the revised Vanderbilt Therapeutic Alliance Scale: Development, reliability, and validity. *Psychotherapy Research*, *18*, 433–443. doi:10.1080/10503300701810801

Shelef, K., Diamond, G. M., Diamond, G. S., & Liddle, H. A. (2005). Adolescent and parent alliance and treatment outcome in multidimensional family therapy. *Journal of Consulting and Clinical Psychology*, *73*, 689–698. doi:10.1037/0022-006X.73.4.689

Shirk, S. (2003, November). *Relationship processes in youth CBT: Measuring alliance and collaboration.* Paper presented at meeting of the Association for the Advancement of Behavior Therapy, Boston.

Shirk, S. R., Gudmundsen, G., Kaplinski, H. C., & McMakin, D. L. (2008). Alliance and outcome in cognitive-behavioral therapy for adolescent depression. *Journal of Clinical Child and Adolescent Psychology*, *37*, 631–639. doi:10.1080/15374410802148061

Shirk, S. R., & Karver, M. (2003). Prediction of outcome from relationship variables in child psychotherapy: A meta-analytic review. *Journal of Consulting and Clinical Psychology*, *71*, 452–464. doi:10.1037/0022-006X.71.3.452

Shirk, S., & Karver, M. S. (2006). Process issues in cognitive-behavioral therapy for youth. In P. Kendall (Ed.), *Child and adolescent therapy* (3rd ed., pp. 465–491). New York, NY: Guilford Press.

Shirk, S. R., & Russell, R. L. (1996). *Change processes in child psychotherapy: Revitalizing treatment and research.* New York, NY: Guilford Press.

Shirk, S. R., & Saiz, S. (1992). Clinical, empirical, and developmental perspectives on the therapeutic relationship in child psychotherapy. *Development and Psychopathology*, *4*, 713–728. doi:10.1017/S0954579400004946

Smith, B. D., Duffee, D. E., Steinke, C. M., Haung, Y., & Larkin, H. (2008). Outcomes in residential treatment for youth: The role of early engagement. *Children and Youth Services Review*, *30*, 1425–1436. doi:10.1016/j.childyouth.2008.04.010

Smith, R. D. (1999). *Using object relations to predict outcome for adolescents in residential treatment.* Unpublished dissertation, University of Denver, Denver, CO.

Taylor, L., Adelman, H., & Kaser-Boyd, N. (1986). The Origin Climate Questionnaire as a tool for studying psychotherapeutic process. *Journal of Child and Adolescent Psychotherapy*, *3*, 10–16.

Tetzlaff, B. T., Kahn, J. H., Godley, S. H., Godley, M. D., Diamond, G. S., & Funk, R. R. (2005). Working alliance, treatment satisfaction, and patterns of post treatment use among adolescent substance users. *Psychology of Addictive Behaviors, 19*, 199–207. doi:10.1037/0893-164X.19.2.199

Tichenor, V., & Hill, C. E. (1989). A comparison of six measures of working alliance. *Psychotherapy: Theory, Research, Practice, Training, 26*, 195–199.

Tryon, G. S., Blackwell, S. C., & Hammel, E. F. (2008). The magnitude of client and therapist working alliance ratings. *Psychotherapy: Theory, Research, Practice, Training, 45*, 546–551.

Tryon, G. S., & Winograd, G. (2002). Goal consensus and collaboration. In J. C. Norcross (Ed.), *Psychotherapy relationships that work* (pp. 109–125). New York, NY: Oxford University Press.

Weisz, J. R., Huey, S. M., & Weersing, V. R. (1998). Psychotherapy outcome research with children and adolescents: The state of the art. In T. H. Ollendick & R. J. Prinz (Eds.), *Advances in clinical child psychology* (Vol. 20, pp. 49–92). New York, NY: Plenum Press.

Weisz, J. R., Jensen-Doss, A., & Hawley, K. M. (2006). Evidence-based youth psychotherapies versus usual clinical care: A meta-analysis of direct comparisons. *American Psychologist, 61*, 671–689.

Weisz, J. R., Weiss, B., Han, S. S., Granger, D. A., & Morton, T. (1995). Effects of psychotherapy with children and adolescents revisited: A meta-analysis of treatment outcome studies. *Psychological Bulletin, 117*, 450–468.

Zaitsoff, S. L., Doyle, A. C., Hoste, R. R., & le Grange, D. (2008). How do adolescents with bulimia nervosa rate the acceptability and therapeutic relationship in family-based treatment? *International Journal of Eating Disorders, 41*, 390–398. doi:10.1002/eat.20515

3

INVOLVEMENT SHIFTS, ALLIANCE RUPTURES, AND MANAGING ENGAGEMENT OVER THERAPY

BRIAN C. CHU, CYNTHIA SUVEG, TORREY A. CREED,
AND PHILIP C. KENDALL

The ability to identify committed and involved clients has long been important to clinical researchers and practitioners. Regardless of theoretical approach or clinical population, a minimal level of engagement is required for therapy to impart its effects. Research in this area has attempted to uncover factors underlying problems in client engagement and identify therapist techniques that facilitate involvement. To provide recommendations for managing engagement with adolescents in psychotherapy, we review several related literatures, including the psychotherapy process and developmental literatures. We critically evaluate research on client involvement, therapeutic alliance, and treatment attrition to understand who might make the least or most engaged clients. Then, we summarize the rapid changes in social, cognitive, biological, and emotional domains of adolescent development and their potential impact on the engagement process. Throughout, we emphasize the need for ongoing therapist monitoring of the adolescent's motivation and involvement in therapy because these variables are likely to wax and wane during the treatment process.

Portions of this work were supported by National Institutes of Health Grant 64484 awarded to Philip C. Kendall.

One limitation through most of the engagement literature has been its method for assessing involvement, particularly with adolescents who may be changing along biological, cognitive, and social domains during a prescribed course of therapy. Researchers have examined a number of variables to predict potential problems in client engagement, including pretreatment youth and family traits that predict low motivation or attrition from therapy. Researchers have also studied within-session behavior, such as the client's degree of verbal participation or involvement in the therapeutic alliance. Surprisingly, much of this research has settled for measuring client involvement at a single time point in therapy—either at pretreatment or at a single session during therapy. This approach helps simplify data collection and analysis, but this simplification may also limit our understanding of the total engagement process. Clinically, it is easy to note that a client's level of involvement varies over the course of therapy. Changes in engagement may occur with the simple passage of time, in response to specific therapist intervention, or from the client's perception that the treatment is working and so he or she becomes more engaged. Throughout this chapter, we review the literature to highlight the developing process of client engagement. Although the literature often focuses on single time-point assessments, we make a point to integrate the data when possible to make recommendations for how therapists might monitor client involvement at different points in therapy. Special attention is given to research examining critical processes of change over time, including alliance ruptures and negative involvement shifts that describe how a therapist can monitor and intervene with client disengagement throughout therapy. Terminology varies across the literature; as a general principle, terms reported here adhere to those used in the original studies. In general, *engagement* refers more often to within-session behavioral participation or to the factors that affect client attendance, motivation, or adherence. The *alliance* often refers to relationship and affective bonds between client and therapist, whereas *involvement* has been used to refer to any of these constructs.

EARLY PREDICTORS OF ENGAGEMENT

To identify clients with potential engagement problems, investigators have examined pretreatment factors associated with treatment refusal and early dropout. A number of client and ecological factors have been associated with unplanned termination, but relations have not always been in a consistent direction. For example, in time-limited cognitive–behavioral therapy (CBT) for anxious youth, ethnic minority status, single-parent households, and less anxious symptomatology at the start of therapy predicted clients who either refused or terminated treatment early (Kendall & Sugarman, 1997). In a sample of adolescents referred for drug treatment, higher parental reports of youth externalizing symptoms and youth perceptions of family conflict also predicted greater treatment retention. However, other family traits such as income, minority group status, family structure, and parental psychopathology did not (Dakof, Tejeda, & Liddle, 2001). Symptom severity appears to be a predictor of continued attendance, suggesting that parent or youth recognition of a serious problem may be important to consider.

Practical and perceived barriers at the start of treatment also influence a family's decision to initially obtain therapy. Practical obstacles (e.g., transportation, financial burden, scheduling), poor initial therapeutic relationship, and perceptions that treatment is not highly relevant to a child's problem or is too demanding (e.g., time commitment is too great, therapy is emotionally strenuous, homework is too burdensome) are likely to interfere with seeking and remaining in therapy (Kazdin, 1996). Although specific family, parent, and child characteristics do not seem to predict who is more sensitive to perceived barriers, those who do report greater barriers tend to demonstrate poorer attendance in and completion of therapy (Kazdin, Holland, & Crowley, 1997; Kazdin & Wassell, 1999). Perceived barriers have also been linked to poorer treatment outcomes (Allart-van Dam, Hosman, & Keijsers, 2004; Kazdin et al., 1997; Kazdin & Wassell, 1999). The attentive clinician will want to directly assess perceived barriers and provide education about treatment or attempt to collaborate on solutions to real problems that hinder attendance.

Expectations for treatment outcomes and early commitment to therapy also appear important. For example, in a preventive adult depression program, negative outcome expectations and doubts about ability to meet treatment demands predicted poorer outcomes (Allart-van Dam et al., 2004). Positive parental expectations for the youth's potential educational achievement have also been linked to greater treatment retention in adolescent treatment for drug use (Dakof et al., 2001). Thus, client perceptions about usefulness of treatment and the family's expectation that the client can succeed, in general or in therapy, may be important moderators of retention and success. Others have found early client commitment a useful predictor of treatment retention. For instance, a youth's participation in the consenting process and the strength of his or her commitment in early sessions predicts better adjustment in a group treatment, less attrition, and better ultimate outcomes (Adelman, Kaser-Boyd, & Taylor, 1984). In a treatment sample of adult cocaine users, the extent to which clients endorsed the 12-step recovery philosophy and engaged in recommended behaviors predicted better drug use outcomes (Crits-Christoph et al., 2003).

Interviews with clients after termination reinforce the importance of assessing client attitudes toward therapy during treatment. In follow-up interviews of parents who refused treatment or terminated early in CBT for anxiety, 32% responded, "My child did not like the clinic and did not want to go there," and 44% said, "Help was no longer necessary because my child's problem improved" (Kendall & Sugarman, 1997). In another follow-up study of parents who had prematurely terminated therapy in a general community mental health clinic, the most cited reasons for leaving against therapist advice were the therapeutic relationship (e.g., "My child or I didn't like the therapist"), therapist competence (e.g., "Therapist did not seem to be doing the right things"), treatment appropriateness (e.g., "My child's treatment was not clearly explained to me"), and treatment effectiveness (e.g., "I decided going to the clinic would not help my child"; Garcia & Weisz, 2002). Therapist attention to these issues during the treatment process may potentially reduce early therapy termination.

Using broad demographic features like ethnicity and family composition to predict early disengagement or attrition may be helpful in some situations but not all. Initial client symptomatology, perceived barriers, and attitudes toward treatment may serve as more consistent predictors. A client or a parent who acknowledges greater problem severity may be more motivated to commit to therapy than when symptoms are less severe, suggesting that therapists should provide thorough feedback from assessments. Clients also appear sensitive to service barriers like timing of sessions and location of clinic, so the therapist should be prepared to problem solve these issues with clients and also be familiar with local resources that might help. Furthermore, given the importance of the therapeutic relationship and treatment appropriateness to the client, initial therapy sessions may benefit from providing education about the nature of therapy and its documented efficacy (Chambless & Ollendick, 2001). Establishing reasonable expectations about the course of therapy, the timing of expected gains, and the anticipated commitment ("burden") for the client should also help prevent misunderstandings and disappointment later in treatment.

MONITORING INVOLVEMENT DURING THERAPY

Once therapy has started, it continues to be important to monitor client engagement. Research from the psychotherapy process literature has developed systems to observe behaviors that would help distinguish involved from disengaged clients. In therapies using a more psychodynamic or client-centered model, involvement has typically been defined as verbal self-disclosure, initiation of difficult topics, and willingness to engage the therapeutic relationship. Using this definition, greater involvement in adult psychotherapy has consistently demonstrated a positive—albeit moderate—association with therapy progress (e.g., Eugster & Wampold, 1996; Gomes-Schwartz, 1978; O'Malley,

Suh, & Strupp, 1983; Windholz & Silberschatz, 1988) and associated techniques such as the therapeutic alliance (Reandeau & Wampold, 1991; Tryon & Kane, 1995). In youth psychotherapy, where definitions of involvement have often overlapped with the therapeutic alliance, measures of the relationship and affective bond have been linked moderately—although significantly—to outcomes (Karver, Handelsman, Fields, & Bickman, 2006; Shirk & Karver, 2003) and greater behavioral participation (e.g., greater verbal disclosure in dynamic therapy; Shirk & Saiz, 1992).

In behavioral treatment approaches, client involvement tends to focus on evidence of observable client participation, including self-disclosures, homework completion, and actively shaping therapeutic tasks (e.g., asking questions, making suggestions; Braswell, Kendall, Braith, Carey, & Vye, 1985). In adult marriage therapy, couples who helped to build a collaborative set, actively participated in session, and completed homework made the most therapeutic gains (Holtzworth-Munroe, Jacobson, DeKlyen, & Whisman, 1989). In a study of child involvement in cognitive–behavioral treatment for anxiety, ratings of youth self-disclosure, enthusiasm, initiating conversations, and elaborating on therapy lessons predicted positive diagnostic outcomes at posttreatment (Chu & Kendall, 2004). Similarly, a treatment study of self-control therapy (CBT) for youth with impulsivity problems found that frequency of client suggestions to modify therapeutic tasks was correlated with improved teacher ratings of self-control (Braswell et al., 1985). These findings suggest that the involved client who elaborates on therapy topics or tries to adapt tasks to make activities more interesting or relevant is likely to experience better outcomes.

When and How to Assess Change in Therapy

Process research has regrettably based many of its conclusions on single time-point assessments or averaged assessments of client engagement. A large number of studies in the literature have assessed involvement only at a single time point in therapy (e.g., Eugster & Wampold, 1996; Windholz & Silberschatz, 1988). Others that assessed involvement at multiple time points often summed or averaged engagement ratings to calculate an overall score for the case (e.g., Braswell et al., 1985; Gomes-Schwartz, 1978; Holtzworth-Munroe et al., 1989). Although this approach simplifies statistical analyses, and perhaps interpretation, it may conceal important patterns in therapy process and potentially obscure some significant relations.

Recent findings have suggested that assessing involvement at multiple time points and the timing of when a therapy process is assessed may determine its relation to outcomes. For example, in a meta-analysis of the therapeutic relationship and outcomes in youth psychotherapy, alliance was more strongly related to outcomes when assessed in later sessions than earlier ones (Shirk & Karver, 2003). Similarly, in a study of child involvement assessed at multiple time points, ratings of behavioral participation at midtreatment were associated with posttreatment outcomes, but earlier ratings were not (Chu & Kendall, 2004). These findings are in contrast to the findings of a meta-analysis of therapeutic alliance with adults, where the strongest relations between alliance and outcomes occurred by the fourth session (Horvath & Symonds, 1991). In a recent observational study of alliance–outcome relations in CBT for youth, earlier alliance was also found to be more predictive of treatment outcomes than later alliance (Chiu, McLeod, Har, & Wood, 2009). Thus, the implications of similar periodic relationships (e.g., stronger or weaker alliance or engagement at various time points throughout therapy) may vary by the time point at which they are assessed, the clinical population, and the specific construct under study.

In an attempt to identify patterns in involvement–outcomes relations, O'Malley et al. (1983) assessed client involvement during the first three sessions of adult outpatient psychotherapy. Independent judges rated active participation and lack of hostility from audiotaped sessions, and client involvement was generally associated with better overall and target outcomes reported by client, therapist, and independent raters. The investigators also found that the strength and number of significant involvement–outcome relations increased from the first to third sessions. In Session 1, only one of 18 possible involvement–outcome relations was statistically significant, but nine of the 18 relations were significant in the third session. Second-session ratings produced six of 18 significant relations, suggesting that the strength of the association between client involvement and treatment success increased gradually over the first three sessions. Unfortunately, involvement was not assessed beyond the third session in this therapy, which offered a maximum of 25 sessions. Assessing involvement over the rest of therapy may have revealed additional patterns: a continuous growth, a steep initial growth followed by a decline, or multiple peaks and valleys in the strength of relations of involvement and outcomes.

Chu and Kendall (2004) also assessed treatment involvement at multiple times in therapy and conducted preliminary analyses to understand the relationships between shifts in involvement and therapy outcomes. In 16-week time-limited CBT for children with anxiety, child involvement was assessed from the audiotapes of four sessions over the first half of treatment. Child involvement was considered essential in the first half of treatment because it focused on cognitive–educational skills that set the foundation for later in vivo exposures. Involvement, using behavioral indices such as self-disclosure, initiating discussion, elaborating on issues, and demonstrating enthusiasm, was rated in two early sessions (Sessions 2–5) and in two later sessions (Sessions 6–10). A single early involvement score was then calculated by summing the scores from two early sessions, and a later involvement score was calculated by totaling the scores from the two later sessions. Although this data reduction may have limited some analyses, it did provide an indication of child involvement both early and later in therapy, just before the midpoint of treatment.

Even though early and later involvement were highly correlated ($r = .61$), later involvement predicted diagnostic improvement in the child's primary disorder, whereas earlier ratings of involvement did not. Indeed, youth who demonstrated a 10-point advantage in involvement at midtreatment, just before the start of in vivo exposures, were 4 times as likely to be free of their principal anxiety disorder at posttreatment. Later involvement ratings also accounted for 7% of the variance in posttreatment impairment ratings associated with the child's principal diagnosis.

To assess the effect of changes in involvement over time, Chu and Kendall (2004) calculated involvement change scores, subtracting earlier involvement from later involvement, and termed this score *involvement shifts*. In this treatment sample, in which outcomes were generally positive (50.9% reported diagnostic improvement), the overall mean involvement shift was negative (mean shift = -1.81), demonstrating a slight overall trend toward disengagement over therapy. There was also a large range of involvement shifts over therapy (range = -19 to 9), suggesting that the children in this treatment sample had a wide range of experiences. Finally, 11 of the 57 (19%) youth in this sample demonstrated large involvement shifts of 9 points or greater, suggesting a significant proportion of youth in this sample was affected by large negative or positive shifts.

Because earlier analyses identified a 10-point involvement difference as important to clinical outcomes, Chu and Kendall (2004) conducted follow-up analyses of youth who experienced positive and negative involvement shifts of similar magnitude. Of the nine children who experienced large negative shifts, seven (77.8%) still reported their principal anxiety disorder at posttreatment. This was half the success rate of the overall sample. Neither of the two cases with a large positive involvement shift reported their diagnosis at the end of therapy.

Given the overall positive treatment effects of this intervention (see, e.g., Ollendick & King, 2000), involvement was expected to remain either stable or even increase over therapy. Instead, most large shifts occurred in the negative direction, and the majority of these youth did not improve in therapy. This suggests that maintenance of baseline child involvement may be even more important than increasing participation of the already involved child.

Displays of decreased self-disclosure, enthusiasm, engagement with tasks, or increased withdrawal may provide the clinician with meaningful early indications of poorer subsequent outcomes. Although disengagement in any session should alert the therapist to enact reengagement strategies, observing a consistent decline in participation over several sessions may be of particular concern. Similar findings have been found for alliance shifts in CBT for anxious youth (Chiu et al., 2009); thus, further research on the trajectories of involvement and alliance in therapy is warranted.

Alliance as Engagement

Observing the therapeutic alliance is another way that researchers and clinicians have monitored engagement in therapy. The specific roles ascribed to the client and therapist in the working relationship distinguish the alliance from definitions of behavioral engagement. Traditional approaches to the therapeutic relationship have focused on therapist-offered warmth and unconditional regard, but Bordin (1979) reformulated the alliance to focus on three aspects of the working relationship: agreement on overall goals for therapy, agreement on therapeutic tasks to meet those goals, and the affective bond between client and therapist. These three elements have been found to be moderately correlated but distinctive facets of the relationship construct (Estrada & Russell, 1999; Shirk & Karver, 2003; Shirk & Saiz, 1992).

In psychotherapy with adults, alliance has consistently been moderately associated with positive clinical outcomes. In the first major meta-analysis of alliance and treatment outcomes in adult psychotherapy, Horvath and Symonds (1991) found a weighted effect size (ES_w) of .26 between various measures of the therapeutic relationship and treatment outcomes (ESs calculated from paired quantitative data, such as Pearson's r). Such an ES_w suggests that the alliance accounts for 7% of total variance in treatment outcomes. This finding is consistently upheld in the literature, underscoring the alliance as an important therapy process. Client reports of the alliance were the strongest predictors of treatment outcome, followed by therapist and observer report. Martin, Garske, and Davis (2000) subsequently reviewed 79 studies of alliance, including those in the Horvath and Symonds (1991) meta-analysis, and replicated the overall weighted effect size of the relation between alliance and outcome ($ES_w = .23$). In the second analysis, however, alliance–outcome relations did not significantly differ by reporter of alliance, time of alliance assessment, reporter of outcome, type of outcome, or treatment type. The improved quality of the later studies in the Martin et al. (2000) analyses, including those in Horvath and Symonds, suggests that Martin et al.'s findings may be more representative. The consistency in overall positive correlations between alliance and outcome suggests that alliance may be a part of an important therapeutic mediator of change, even if the specific underlying mechanism needs to be determined (Martin et al., 2000).

A strong therapeutic relationship may be particularly important for successful treatment with youth (Luborsky, 1994; Shirk & Karver, 2003; Sommers-Flanagan & Sommers-Flanagan, 1995). Youth do not typically self-refer to treatment; they are typically brought by their parents or referred by their school, the courts, or another social service provider. Matters are further complicated when adolescents are referred for problems that they do not themselves believe exist or have control over (DiGiuseppe, Linscott, & Jilton, 1996; Kazdin, 2004). Assessing and addressing a youth's initial hesitance and building a positive working relationship is key to increasing motivation for therapy, retention in treatment, and positive clinical outcomes.

In the first meta-analysis to examine relationship variables and outcome in youth therapy (Shirk & Karver, 2003), several findings came to light. The small, but positive, effect size (ES = .22) between relationship variables and outcome, across treatment type and theoretical modality, was comparable to that found in the adult literature (Horvath & Symonds, 1991; Martin et al., 2000). The only child characteristic that moderated the association between therapeutic relationship and outcome was the child's presenting problem. The relation between alliance and outcome was not as strong, but still positive, for children with internalizing disorders (e.g., anxiety, depression; $r = .10$, a small effect) versus children with externalizing disorders (e.g., disruptive behaviors; $r = .30$, a medium effect). This does not suggest that the alliance is unimportant with children with internalizing disorders. Instead, it likely highlights a uniquely critical role that interpersonal relations play in fostering motivation for change in youth with behavior problems (Henggeler, Schoenwald, Borduin, Rowland, & Cunningham, 1998). It may be possible that children with internalizing disorders form an alliance more readily with a therapist, such that the range of alliance quality has less impact on outcomes (Shirk & Karver, 2003). Another explanation Shirk and Karver (2003) offered was that therapy with children with externalizing difficulties was more likely to include a parent-training component, which may confound the roles of the youth and parent in the alliance (Shirk & Karver, 2003). These findings have been supported by research specifically with anxious children in which child, parent, and therapist reports of the alliance were found to remain positive even as the child engaged in the challenging exposure sessions in a behavioral treatment for anxiety (Kendall et al., 2009).

Although little research has directly addressed the differential impact of the goal, task, and bond facets of the alliance with youth, a recent study found that a therapist's early collaborative stance (e.g., therapist presented treatment as a team effort) affected later alliance ratings (Creed & Kendall, 2005). In a manual-based treatment for anxious youth, 10 observable therapist behaviors were rated during the first three sessions and correlated with therapist, child, and independent observer ratings of alliance later in therapy. Of the 10 therapist behaviors, "therapist collaborative stance" over the first three sessions positively predicted child and observer ratings of alliance at Session 3, whereas "pushing the child to talk" and "overemphasizing commonalities with the child" negatively predicted child ratings of alliance. None of the early therapist behaviors were significantly related to therapist ratings of alliance at Session 3. Early therapist behaviors were also correlated with later therapist- and client-rated alliance at Session 7. Pushing the child to talk early in therapy was still negatively related to child alliance ratings at Session 7. Therapist alliance ratings were positively predicted by collaboration and negatively predicted by being overly formal. These findings suggest that there may be specific, concrete behaviors that the therapist can use to build the alliance. Early collaborative stance predicted strong alliance both early and later in therapy. In contrast, pushing the child to talk was negatively correlated with alliance both early and later in therapy. Thus, early collaborative stance and pushing the child to talk had fairly enduring effects on later therapy processes. It is difficult to be conclusive given the multiple correlations across different informants, but these results provide initial data that therapist strategies early in therapy may have long-lasting effects. Similar research on therapist flexibility within a CBT protocol (i.e., the degree to which a therapist adapts a session to meet the needs, interests, or abilities of the child) has shown significant relations between a therapist's level of responsiveness and a child's subsequent engagement in therapy (Chu & Kendall, 2009). Future research is needed to further study these empirically supported relationship-building behaviors, and such work will benefit from coding relationship-building strategies at multiple points in therapy.

Collaboration has also shown a consistent association with treatment outcome in the adult literature. In a recent meta-analysis, collaboration was significantly positively related to outcome 89% of the time (Tryon & Winograd, 2002). In another study assessing collaborative goal setting and outcome in cognitive therapy for adult depression, perceived agreement with treatment goals at Session 3 was associated with lower depression symptoms on the Beck Depression Inventory after 20 sessions (Safran & Wallner, 1991). The use of a single assessment of goal agreement limits our ability to describe the collaborative process, but replication of this research with multiple assessments and multiple reporters might help provide suggestions for intervention when clients do not agree with treatment goals.

Provision of therapist empathy, or the ability to understand and relate to the client's struggles, may also correlate with improved clinical outcomes. In a meta-analysis evaluating the role of empathy in adult psychotherapy, empathy accounted for nearly 10% of the variance in treatment outcomes

($r = .32$; Greenberg, Elliott, Watson, & Bohart, 2001). Empathy and outcome relations were strongest for client report ($r = .25$) and observer report ($r = .23$), but therapist-reported empathy also significantly correlated with clinical improvement ($r = .18$). Although they represent small to moderate effect sizes (accounting for 3%–10% of treatment outcome variance), these correlations support a consistent relationship between outcomes and therapist-offered conditions found in the literature. As stated earlier, this literature suggests possible useful techniques but provides less guidance for how therapists should identify problems in session and be responsive to negative client process over therapy.

ALLIANCE RUPTURES: NECESSARY STRUGGLES?

Assessing alliance at multiple points in therapy or observing changes in alliance over time is certain to capture the dynamic nature of the alliance better. Research exploring the phenomenon of alliance ruptures might provide insight into the process of alliance building and maintenance. *Alliance ruptures* have been conceptualized within Bordin's (1979) framework as disagreements about the goals or tasks of treatment or strains in the affective bond (Safran, Muran, Samstag, Wallner, & Stevens, 2002). These ruptures are thought of as a series of negotiations that occur throughout therapy. For example, goal disagreement might occur when a client presents for treatment of social phobia, but the therapist believes that the client's substance abuse symptoms should be addressed before treating the anxiety. Task disagreement might occur if a client is unwilling to complete assigned out-of-session homework tasks. A strain in the affective bond may occur when the client feels misunderstood or disrespected by the therapist.

In each example, the needs or agendas of the client and therapist conflict, and this rupture may require either explicit or implicit negotiation to mend (Safran et al., 2002). Implicit negotiation may occur, for example, when a client decides to attempt out-of-session tasks, despite feelings of hesitation or anxiety. If a therapist explicitly discusses the therapeutic rationale for prioritizing substance abuse over social anxiety and works toward mutual agreement, this negotiation is more observable and overt. In dynamically based therapies, such alliance ruptures are often considered expected and even necessary for the client to grow in therapy. In cognitive–behavioral therapies, such ruptures may be attributed to client resistance or limited therapist skill. In either case, resolution of alliance ruptures is essential once they have been identified.

In therapy with adolescents, mood irregularities and the need for autonomy associated with this developmental period may increase the likelihood that therapeutic ruptures will occur. Initial resistance to therapy tasks and activities should not automatically be labeled as defiance or rejection (Holmbeck et al., 2000). There is some evidence to suggest that adolescents who show the highest degree of satisfaction with treatment and the most in-session collaboration had therapists who used specific techniques that are respectful of this stage (Church, 1994). Therapists who earnestly collaborated with clients, emphasized the sincerity of confidentiality, encouraged clients to actively work toward solutions, and provided structure for sessions had adolescent clients with more open views of the therapeutic relationship and solicited more therapist advice (Church, 1994). This study did not link specific alliance behavior with outcome, but it suggests possible factors that contribute to effective relationships in therapy.

RESOLVING ALLIANCE RUPTURES

Ruptures in any collaborative working relationship threaten the potential for success. Resolving ruptures and strengthening alliance have been associated with increased retention in therapy (Tryon & Kane, 1990, 1993, 1995) and positive clinical outcomes (Horvath & Symonds, 1991; Martin et al., 2000; Shirk & Karver, 2003), but resolving ruptures is no easy task for a therapist. First, clients may be uncomfortable bringing ruptures to the attention of a therapist out of fear that they will further damage the relationship (Rennie, 1994). A common pattern appears to be that clients leave dissatisfaction unsaid and terminate treatment soon after an unresolved rupture (Hill, Nutt-Williams, Heaton, Thompson, & Rhodes, 1996; Rhodes, Hill, Thompson, & Elliott, 1994).

It may be even more difficult for some adolescents to initiate a conversation about an alliance rupture given the added potential for perceived power differences between therapist and client. In addition, adolescents, particularly those experiencing an internalizing form of pathology, are still developing the basic social maturity needed for interpersonal confrontations and assertiveness. Likewise, even seasoned therapists have difficulty recognizing therapeutic ruptures when clients do not draw attention to them (Hill, Thompson, Cogar, & Denman, 1993). Naturally, if the therapist fails to acknowledge a rupture, and the client is unable or unwilling to bring attention to it, the rupture is likely to go unresolved and subsequently increase the likelihood of attrition (Tryon & Kane, 1990, 1993, 1995) and poorer clinical outcomes (Horvath & Symonds, 1991; Martin et al., 2000; Shirk & Karver, 2003). When working with adolescents, the therapist will want to be sensitive to client resistance (e.g., minimal disclosure or responses, distractibility, lateness to the session) or disagreement with therapy tasks or goals (e.g., refusal to participate, poor homework compliance, dismissing therapist suggestions). This resistance may be expressed either overtly or covertly, so it is incumbent on the therapist to monitor closely.

Once a rupture has been identified, how the therapist responds will likely have a strong impact on how the rupture is resolved. The therapist should be prepared to initiate discussion about potential alliance ruptures, focusing on both real problems and disagreements while modeling socially appropriate forms of confrontation and compromise. The extent to which therapists directly address such problems may predict desirable therapy process later in therapy. For example, in poor outcome cases of CBT for depressed adults, one pattern observed was that therapists responded to alliance ruptures with overly rigid adherence to particular cognitive–behavioral techniques (Castonguay, Goldfried, Wiser, Raue, & Hayes, 1996). For instance, some therapists in this study interpreted perceived ruptures in the alliance as related to dysfunctional client thinking. Not surprisingly, these clients felt misunderstood and ultimately had poorer outcomes. Therapists who directly addressed perceived ruptures and their own potential role in the discord tended to repair the alliance better.

It is important to note that a steady, linear growth in alliance should not always be expected and such a pattern may not be necessary for positive treatment outcomes. Growth curve analysis of alliance suggests that curvilinear patterns in alliance (e.g., a high early level of alliance that decreases over time but returns by the end of treatment) may be common in some forms of treatment (Golden & Robbins, 1990; Hentschel & Bjileveld, 1995; Horvath & Marx, 1990), and hierarchical linear modeling found that a quadratic, but not a linear, pattern of alliance development was positively related to client outcome (Patton, Kivlighan, & Multon, 1997). In contrast, Kivlighan and Shaughnessy (1995) found that a linear change in therapist alliance ratings was significantly related to treatment outcome. In a subsequent study using cluster analysis, however, Kivlighan and Shaughnessy (2000) found three distinct patterns of client-reported alliance development (stable alliance, linear growth, and quadratic growth), and the quadratic pattern was associated with greater improvement on measures of interpersonal problems. Thus, several alliance patterns may be natural in therapy, and it is not clear which is most associated with clinical outcomes. Acute alliance ruptures that occur in response to specific disagreements between therapist and client may then be superimposed onto these larger patterns. The therapist will want to be careful to distinguish specific ruptures from longer term fluctuations in the alliance because they may signal different processes that call for separate responses.

DEVELOPMENTAL CONSIDERATIONS
AND CLINICAL RECOMMENDATIONS

Our review has highlighted several client and therapist factors associated with engagement in diverse therapies across age groups. Few of the studies focused exclusively on adolescence, even as the rapid social development and interpersonal challenges of this period signify special consideration (see also Holmbeck & Kendall, 2002). To make recommendations on how to accommodate the unique needs of adolescents, we integrate findings from the engagement and developmental literatures.

First, the clinical lore that adolescents are impossible to engage in therapy or present an insurmountable challenge to the therapist is likely an overstatement. Some adolescents may be averse to beginning therapy, but hesitation, resistance, and disengagement can be challenges in any age group. The belief that adolescents are particularly difficult to engage in therapy stems, in part, from the belief that adolescents are moody and disagreeable. Although occasionally true, a review of the research suggests that adolescents are not inherently moody and that mood changes may be associated more with changes in activity than with the hormonal fluctuations (Larson & Lampman-Petraitis, 1989) that characterize this developmental period. Moreover, the idea that adolescents are disagreeable is likely related to rapid changes in cognitive development during this period, which gives them increased ability to form independent ideas and to question the ideas of those around them. Development from childhood to adolescence is significant and may be more stressful at times for those around the adolescent than for the teen. Thus, this developmental period may not necessarily be one of emotional turbulence, contrary to early notions of adolescence (Steinberg & Morris, 2001). Nonetheless, this period still contains the most developmental changes since infancy (Holmbeck et al., 2000), and such vast biological, social, and psychological changes are likely to cause at least some distress, even for well-adjusted teens. For the therapist, appreciating this possibility will undoubtedly facilitate the therapeutic process.

In addressing the mental health needs of adolescents, Cicchetti and Rogosh (2002) highlighted the need for contexts to be structured to facilitate germane developmental tasks. Psychological maladjustment may result when the adolescent's developmental needs are mismatched with the larger context in which the teen functions. When applied to the therapeutic context, therapists should be aware of the salient developmental tasks of adolescence and structure the therapy environment to match the teen's needs. For instance, overly didactic or doctrinaire methods of intervention are likely to bore or irritate adolescents who are vying for increased independence, for example, a rigid session agenda that does not incorporate client input or using manualized treatment procedures that are developmentally young (e.g., using a workbook that has cartoons appropriate for younger children). Specific developmental issues for the therapist to consider include biological, cognitive, social, and emotional changes during adolescence (for additional review, see Oetzel & Sherer, 2003; Weisz & Hawley, 2002).

Biological Development

Some of the major changes during adolescence take place in the biological domain. Puberty signals multiple important changes including the development of secondary sex characteristics, changes in height, proportion of body mass, and the start of menarche for girls. Puberty may affect a teen's psychosocial development in any number of ways and may depend on the timing of puberty, gender, and the context in which puberty occurs. It appears that early-maturing girls may be at risk for self-image difficulties and emotional distress, whereas late-maturing boys are at increased risk for self-esteem difficulties (e.g., Ge, Conger, & Elder, 1996; Graber, Lewinsohn, Seeley, & Brooks-Gunn, 1997; Hayward, Killen, Wilson, & Hammer, 1997). More important, however, both early-maturing girls and boys are at risk for early sexual activity, drug and alcohol use, and other age-inappropriate activities. Recent reviews have suggested that the effect of puberty on psychosocial functioning is dependent on the context in which puberty occurs (see Steinberg, 2002). For example, early-maturing girls may be affected most negatively in coeducational schools (Caspi, Lynam, Moffitt, & Silva, 1993). Thus, the interaction between biological transitions and the teen's social context will be an important indication of the teen's adjustment.

In the therapeutic context, it is important for the therapist to consider the age at which the adolescent began puberty relative to his or her peers. Therapists might expect early-maturing girls and late-maturing boys to undergo a more difficult time, particularly in coeducational environments. Early-maturing adolescents may experience an increased self-consciousness that moderates their emotional distress. Assessing biological changes accurately and addressing the issues frankly may help adolescents feel understood in therapy. Even for adolescents experiencing biological development at a similar rate to same-age peers, the bodily changes may be emotionally upsetting, leading to a heightened self-consciousness. Any adolescent beginning puberty may appear reticent or defensive, particularly in the therapeutic environment where he or she may feel scrutinized. Providing education about normal biological development, and allowing the adolescent to discuss his or her experiences, may help allay the distress the teen is experiencing.

Discretion should be used when deciding whether developmental issues are relevant to the treatment focus and when they should be discussed. There is some evidence to suggest that the alliance can be negatively affected if therapists push youth to talk too soon (Creed & Kendall, 2005), although it is not yet known how this might affect eventual treatment outcomes. Ultimately, the therapist is encouraged to be responsive to the adolescent's own views about his or her development to determine whether the rapid changes during this time are affecting the teen's emotional distress or participation in therapy. Furthermore, given the multitude of biological transitions during puberty, the adolescent's views, attitudes, and feelings about the maturation process are likely to fluctuate over time. The therapist should expect that the youth's willingness to discuss these matters, as well as his or her opinions, may change throughout therapy.

Cognitive Development

As with biological developments, numerous cognitive changes occur during adolescence. Adolescents are able to think more abstractly and hypothetically and to reason at a more complex level (Piaget, 1972). Likewise, they are able to engage in deductive reasoning (Klaczynski & Narasimham, 1998) and metacognition. Adolescents show advances in information processing, including development in storage and efficiency abilities. Although these developments are natural and necessary, they result in some confusing (to both adults and teens) experiences. For instance, it is common for adolescents to experience an imaginary audience—a belief that they are the focus of those around them. Adolescents may also experience the personal fable, in which they believe that their experiences are unique. Although normative, such phenomena may be magnified in adolescents with additional psychological difficulties, contributing to further maladjustment.

The range of cognitive development is likely to vary widely from teenage client to teenage client. Tailoring the structure, content, and process of therapy to match the cognitive abilities of the teen is likely necessary for therapeutic success. A therapist who uses childlike terms to communicate may insult or alienate the teen. Adolescents may in fact welcome the therapist's use of more technical terms and in-depth explanations that show greater respect for the teen. For example, clinical experience in the provision of CBT for anxiety suggests that teens appreciate when therapists introduce technical terms like *exposure tasks* and *habituation* and provide the rationale for their use. Teens often feel more mature and may be more likely to take ownership of their problems and treatment. Helping instill a sense of ownership may facilitate the teen's engagement in and compliance with treatment.

The cognitive changes of adolescence also allow the therapist to maximize the use of cognitive components in therapy (e.g., problem solving, self-monitoring one's thoughts, identifying maladaptive cognition). Adolescents' increased ability to think abstractly and develop metarules may allow them to absorb and individualize cognitive skills more than younger clients. However, this increased ability to reason and think abstractly also allows adolescents to question things around them. Instead of following adult rules and believing as they are told, adolescents often require additional explanation. Therapists should not instantly equate a teen's questioning to insolence. Taking such questioning as a sign of active engagement instead of opposition may help prevent potential power struggles. The sensitive therapist can respond nondefensively, offer additional explanation about the problem and treatment, and invite additional questions and thoughts.

Soliciting a teen's thoughts and feelings about therapy may be particularly important for an adolescent who feels that he or she was coerced into therapy. For such adolescents, normalizing the youth's skepticism and his or her inclination to question will demonstrate good faith. As suggested in the literature, positive attitudes toward therapy are important for maintaining attendance and engagement (e.g., Garcia & Weisz, 2002); attending to the client's concerns and opinions is essential to ensure a collaborative working alliance.

Finally, adolescents' increased social–cognitive abilities may also give them a greater sense of when therapists are being disingenuous. Genuineness and candor will go far in facilitating the therapeutic relationship even when an adult disagrees with the teen's behavior or beliefs (Oetzel & Sherer, 2003; Rubenstein, 1996). Adolescents value a therapist who is empathic, knowledgeable, and understanding but tend to lose respect for therapists who appear to pander to their need for approval or participation.

Social Development

During adolescence, teens experience four primary status changes: interpersonal, economic, political, and legal (Steinberg, 2002). During early adolescence, teens can obtain employment, and during late adolescence, they can vote. Under some circumstances, adolescents can be tried as adults in the legal system. Social role expectations for adolescents vary widely as a function of culture, socioeconomic status, and gender and are not always clearly delineated. Adolescence is a time frequently filled with new and varied role changes and increased responsibility. For adolescents who are experiencing clinical levels of emotional distress, negotiating new social roles may be particularly challenging.

The role that parents play in therapy is sure to arise when treating an adolescent. During adolescence, teens spend much less time with family and increased time with peers (Larson & Verma, 1999). Parent–child conflict tends to increase and is experienced as especially stressful to parents (Silverberg &

Steinberg, 1990). There is also a developmental normative expectation for increased autonomy in the teen years. Collectively, such factors may contribute to parent–teen conflict regarding parental involvement in the treatment process. Because parents often bring the youth to treatment, they may expect to play an active role. However, the therapist must balance the teen's desire and willingness for parental involvement with the need to have the parent play an active role. Limiting parental involvement is consistent with the developmental goal of facilitating teen autonomy—a goal that may be particularly salient for anxious adolescents. When therapeutic gains are made in the context of little parental involvement in therapy sessions, teens may be more likely to attribute success to themselves than to their parents.

However, when treating defiance, acting-out behavior, or rule breaking, the need for family participation (e.g., contingency management, setting house rules) may outweigh the teen's interests in limiting parent involvement. The therapist may also choose to include an intrusive parent to teach parent anxiety management skills. Even in cases in which the therapist believes it would be beneficial to include parents, the level of involvement can be restricted to times where it is necessary to include parents. In this way, there is still ample opportunity for teens to gain a sense of increased autonomy and self-efficacy in managing their anxiety. The need to involve parents may also change over the course of therapy depending on the particular phase of treatment. During assessment or psychoeducational phases, individual work with the teen may be sufficient and may help the therapist know the adolescent independently. As the therapy initiates homework, exposure tasks, behavioral activation, or contingency management, the need for parent participation (increased or decreased) may change. It is best when the therapist is clear about his or her intentions and plans throughout therapy to avoid surprises for either the teen or the parent. Such attempts to respect family members and keep each member involved at different stages of therapy may help each person feel supported and involved, which may be a necessary element for successful family-based therapy (Diamond, Diamond, and Liddle, 2000).

Overall, evidence for how best to include parents in therapy is still accumulating and difficult to experimentally test. For example, in the case of anxiety treatments, large reviews and meta-analyses have failed to find consistent benefit from incorporating parents into treatments (Barmish & Kendall, 2005; Ishikawa, Okajima, Matsuoka, & Sakano, 2007). Direct experimental comparisons (in the form of randomized clinical trials) do show an advantage for treatments that either explicitly incorporate parents in child sessions or provide separate parent training (Barrett, 1998; Barrett, Dadds, & Rapee, 1996; Spence, Donovan, & Brechman-Touissant, 2000), but positive effects are seen mostly in child, not adolescent, populations. Few studies have assessed within-session parent participation directly in treatment studies, so we have little information about the impact of parent involvement in specific therapy activities. Fjermestad, Haugland, Heiervang, and Ost (2009) identified three studies in which parent involvement was rated by either therapist report or by independent coders reviewing audiotaped sessions. The study directly observing sessions (Choudhury, 2004) did find an association between parent involvement and clinician-rated child functioning. Again, this was primarily a child, not an adolescent, sample. Further research is needed, particularly in the definition and assessment methods of parent involvement. It would be important to consider both positive and interfering parental involvement as well as within-session and extrasession involvement. One could make the argument that a parent's help in facilitating homework and incorporating lessons at home is as important if not more so than "simple" involvement in session.

Autonomy and Identity Formation

Autonomy and identity formation is a critical developmental task for all adolescents (Erikson, 1968). Adolescents are expected to demonstrate more autonomous emotional and behavioral functioning (e.g., increasing self-reliance and expecting less emotional comfort from parents). Accordingly, teens seek comfort from peers and begin making their own decisions about their actions and life choices. In therapy, this need for autonomy may affect the process in several ways. Teens who do not come to therapy of their own volition may feel their autonomy and choice have been disregarded. Therapists can appeal to the teen's sense of autonomy by collaboratively assessing the teen's willingness and motivation for treatment.

Prochaska, Norcross, and DiClemente (1995) suggested using the stages of change model to match therapist strategies with the client's readiness for change. For example, teens who enter treatment in the precontemplative stage of change may not be aware of the impact their behavior or emotional functioning has on themselves and others. They may also not appreciate the level of control they have over their actions. Helping these teens understand the link between stressors and their reactions, as well as their control over outcomes, can help prepare them for change. Therapists are encouraged to reassess teens' readiness for change throughout therapy because their awareness and readiness may wax and wane over time.

As teens increasingly define themselves in terms of values, beliefs, and goals (i.e., identity development; Erikson, 1968), the therapist may notice increased role exploration in therapy. Attending to an adolescent's stage of identity development (e.g., identity moratorium, foreclosure, diffusion, or achievement) may guide the therapist in how to interpret the teen's behavior. For example, therapists might expect a senior in high school to frequently discuss whether to attend college and for which career he or she might best be suited. Similarly, an adolescent might argue with parents about attending religious services that have been a part of the family's routine for several years. These examples highlight typical exploration as a teen develops a sense of identity and do not necessarily indicate rejection or rebellious behavior. Understanding and validating the teen's need to explore will facilitate the therapy relationship. Therapists might also encourage the teen to view his or her work in therapy as an extension of his or her continued identity development. The therapist may also need to provide education to the parents who are concerned about the teen's apparent rapid change.

INTEGRATION

Managing engagement with an adolescent client requires an alert and flexible therapist, even when implementing empirically supported and manual-based treatments (Kendall & Beidas, 2007; Kendall, Chu, Gifford, Hayes, & Nauta, 1998). The literature review points to several useful client processes that the therapist can monitor to detect withdrawal, disinterest, or resistance. Positive initial attitudes toward therapy, hopefulness for positive outcomes, and early commitment to treatment appear to predict who might remain in therapy. Behavioral participation, including verbal disclosures and task involvement, and playing an active role in the working alliance are also important to treatment retention and positive outcomes. Research examining the fluctuating process of involvement suggests that changes in client engagement during therapy (e.g., negative involvement shifts, alliance ruptures) may be even more important to monitor than baseline involvement. For example, anxious youth who demonstrated a large drop in engagement over the first half of therapy had half the success rate in clinical outcomes as youth who simply maintained initial levels of involvement (Chu & Kendall, 2004). Adult clients who experienced a rupture or change in the alliance tended to exhibit high dissatisfaction with treatment and drop out (Hill et al., 1996; Rhodes et al., 1994).

Once a therapist has identified a disengaged client, how should he or she respond? The search continues for reliable, effective engagement strategies, but the literature has suggested that efforts to establish a strong collaborative stance (Creed & Kendall, 2005) and efforts to actively engage a child by incorporating personalized activities and matching lessons to child interests may be key (Chu & Kendall, 2009). Directly discussing ruptures when they occur rather than disregarding them also seems to be helpful in handling confrontations in therapy.

When the client is an adolescent, additional developmental processes may complicate therapeutic engagement. Motivation can be suspect because few adolescents refer themselves to treatment, and teens tend to be self-focused and less aware of how their actions and emotions affect others. Adolescents' desire for increased autonomy and individualization may also affect their receptivity to therapeutic goals identified by others. Adolescence is a period of rapid change, and the therapist will need to adjust for the possible variations in cognitive, emotional, and interpersonal functioning that will occur even within members of the same age group.

To ensure that a treatment is developmentally sensitive, the therapist is encouraged to be attentive to the biological, social, and cognitive developments that may affect the teen's presentation in therapy. Treatment approaches should then match the teen's developmental needs. If a teen expresses a need for greater autonomy, the therapy might benefit from giving the youth more control in session activities. Conversely, if the teen appears more self-conscious, the therapist should not assume this reticence is resistance. It could be natural self-consciousness in reaction to rapid developmental changes. Greater patience and space might be recommended here.

As one example, Kendall, Choudhury, Hudson, and Webb (2002a, 2002b) made changes in the therapeutic approach, structure, and content to adapt their child-oriented (ages 7–13) cognitive–behavioral treatment (i.e., Coping Cat program; Kendall & Hedtke, 2006a, 2006b) to accommodate teen clients. This adolescent program, which adopted the more mature moniker of "C.A.T. Project" (Kendall, Choudhury, Hudson, & Webb, 2002a, 2002b), encourages the adolescent to take charge of therapy throughout treatment. Teens are asked at the start to choose a name for the treatment using the letters C, A, and T (e.g., "Coping with Anxiety for Teens," "Changing Anxious Thinking") to encourage ownership over the program. The therapy materials are engaging and contain age-appropriate graphics, and the teen leads many of the tasks by individualizing exercises and helping to design the exposure tasks. Therapists routinely describe themselves as coaches rather than therapists to minimize their image as an authority figure (therapist is not an agent of society). In addition, many of the tasks from the Coping Cat that were specialized for younger children were adapted. For example, relaxation training in the teen version includes greater psychoeducation about the fight-or-flight phenomenon and anxious physiology to appeal to a teen's interest in detail and adult language. Challenging anxious self-talk includes a lesson on formal cognitive errors, or "thinking traps" (e.g., catastrophic thinking, discounting the positive), which appeals to the teen's greater sophistication in thinking about cognitions and interest in technical skills. This developmentally adapted protocol has recently been tested as part of a large multisite trial including both children and adolescents, and results have shown similar clinical benefits as previous trials with children (Walkup et al., 2008). Such findings continue to support conventional and clinical wisdom that attending to developmental needs, just as with any form of therapeutic flexibility, is beneficial to the therapy process and subsequent treatment outcomes.

REFERENCES

Adelman, H. S., Kaser-Boyd, N., & Taylor, L. (1984). Children's participation in consent for psychotherapy and their subsequent response to treatment. *Journal of Clinical Child Psychology, 13,* 170–178.

Allart-van Dam, E., Hosman, M. H., & Keijsers, G. P. J. (2004). A new instrument to assess participant motivation for involvement in preventive interventions. *Journal of Clinical Psychology, 60,* 555–565. doi:10.1002/jclp.10236

Barmish, A. J., & Kendall, P. C. (2005). Should parents be co-clients in treating anxious youth? *Journal of Clinical Child and Adolescent Psychology, 34,* 569–581. doi:10.1207/s15374424jccp3403_12

Barrett, P. M. (1998). Evaluation of cognitive–behavioral group treatments for childhood anxiety disorders. *Journal of Clinical Child Psychology, 27,* 459–468. doi:10.1207/s15374424jccp2704_10

Barrett, P. M., Dadds, M. R., & Rapee, R. M. (1996). Family treatment of childhood anxiety: A controlled trial. *Journal of Consulting and Clinical Psychology, 64,* 333–342. doi:10.1037/0022-006X.64.2.333

Bordin, E. S. (1979). The generalizability of the psychoanalytic concept of the working alliance. *Psychotherapy: Theory, Research, and Practice, 16,* 252–260.

Braswell, L., Kendall, P. C., Braith, J., Carey, M. P., & Vye, C. S. (1985). "Involvement" in cognitive-behavioral therapy with children: Process and its relationship to outcome. *Cognitive Therapy and Research, 9,* 611–630. doi:10.1007/BF01173021

Caspi, A., Lynam, D., Moffitt, T. E., & Silva, P. A. (1993). Unraveling girls' delinquency: Biological, dispositional, and contextual contributions to adolescent misbehavior. *Developmental Psychology, 29,* 19–30. doi:10.1037/0012-1649.29.1.19

Castonguay, L. G., Goldfried, M. R., Wiser, S., Raue, P. J., & Hayes, A. M. (1996). Predicting the effect of cognitive therapy for depression: A study of unique and common factors. *Journal of Consulting and Clinical Psychology, 64,* 497–504. doi:10.1037/0022-006X.64.3.497

Chambless, D. L., & Ollendick, T. H. (2001). Empirically supported psychological interventions: Controversies and evidence. *Annual Review of Psychology, 52,* 685–716. doi:10.1146/annurev.psych.52.1.685

Chiu, A. W., McLeod, B. D., Har, K., & Wood, J. J. (2009). Child-therapist alliance and clinical outcomes in cognitive behavioral therapy for child anxiety disorders. *Journal of Child Psychology and Psychiatry and Allied Disciplines, 50,* 751–758. doi:10.1111/j.1469-7610.2008.01996.x

Choudhury, M. S. (2004). *The role of parent-training in the treatment of anxiety disorders in children and adolescents* (Doctoral dissertation, Temple University, United States—Pennsylvania). Available from Dissertations & Theses: A&I database. (Publication No. AAT 3150990)

Chu, B. C., & Kendall, P. C. (2004). Positive association of child involvement and treatment outcome within a manual-based cognitive–behavioral treatment for children with anxiety. *Journal of Consulting and Clinical Psychology, 72,* 821–829. doi:10.1037/0022-006X.72.5.821

Chu, B. C., & Kendall, P. C. (2009). Therapist responsiveness to child engagement: Flexibility within manual-based CBT for anxious youth. *Journal of Clinical Psychology, 65,* 736–754. doi:10.1002/jclp.20582

Church, E. (1994). The role of autonomy in adolescent psychotherapy. *Psychotherapy: Theory, Research, Practice, Training, 31*, 101–108.

Cicchetti, D., & Rogosh, F. A. (2002). A developmental psychopathology perspective on adolescence. *Journal of Consulting and Clinical Psychology, 70*, 6–20. doi:10.1037/0022-006X.70.1.6

Creed, T. A., & Kendall, P. C. (2005). Empirically supported therapist relationship-building behavior within a cognitive–behavioral treatment for anxiety in youth. *Journal of Consulting and Clinical Psychology, 73*, 498–505. doi:10.1037/0022-006X.73.3.498

Crits-Christoph, P., Connolly Gibbons, M., Barber, J. P., Gallop, R., Beck, A. T., Mercer, D., . . . Frank, A. (2003). Mediators of outcome of psychosocial treatments for cocaine dependence. *Journal of Consulting and Clinical Psychology, 71*, 918–925. doi:10.1037/0022-006X.71.5.918

Dakof, G. A., Tejeda, M., & Liddle, H. A. (2001). Predictors of engagement in adolescent drug abuse treatment. *Journal of the American Academy of Child & Adolescent Psychiatry, 40*, 274–281. doi:10.1097/00004583-200103000-00006

Diamond, G. M., Diamond, G. S., & Liddle, H. A. (2000). The therapist-parent alliance in family-based therapy for adolescents. *Journal of Clinical Psychology, 56*, 1037–1050. doi:10.1002/1097-4679(200008)56:8<1037::AID-JCLP4>3.0.CO;2-4

DiGiuseppe, R., Linscott, J., & Jilton, R. (1996). Developing the therapeutic alliance in child-adolescent psychotherapy. *Applied and Preventive Psychology, 5*, 85–100. doi:10.1016/S0962-1849(96)80002-3

Erikson, E. H. (1968). *Identity: Youth and crisis.* New York, NY: Norton.

Estrada, A., & Russell, R. (1999). The development of Child Psychotherapy Process Scales (CPPS). *Psychotherapy Research, 9*, 154–166. doi:10.1093/ptr/9.2.154

Eugster, S. L., & Wampold, B. E. (1996). Systematic effects of participant role on evaluation of the psychotherapy session. *Journal of Consulting and Clinical Psychology, 64*, 1020–1028. doi:10.1037/0022-006X.64.5.1020

Fjermestad, K. W., Haugland, B. S. M., Heiervang, E., & Ost, L. (2009). Relationship factors and outcome in child anxiety treatment studies. *Clinical Child Psychology and Psychiatry, 14*, 195–214. doi:10.1177/1359104508100885

Garcia, J. A., & Weisz, J. R. (2002). When youth mental health care stops: Therapeutic relationship problems and other reasons for ending youth outpatient treatment. *Journal of Consulting and Clinical Psychology, 70*, 439–443. doi:10.1037/ 0022-006X.70.2.439

Ge, X., Conger, R. D., & Elder, G. H. (1996). Coming of age too early: Pubertal influences on girls' vulnerability to psychological distress. *Child Development, 67*, 3386–3400. doi:10.2307/1131784

Golden, B. R., & Robbins, S. B. (1990). The working alliance within time-limited therapy. *Professional Psychology: Research and Practice, 21*, 476–481. doi:10.1037/0735-7028.21.6.476

Gomes-Schwartz, B. (1978). Effective ingredients in psychotherapy: Prediction of outcome from process variables. *Journal of Consulting and Clinical Psychology, 46*, 1023–1035. doi:10.1037/0022-006X.46.5.1023

Graber, J. A., Lewinsohn, P. M., Seeley, J. R., & Brooks-Gunn, J. (1997). Is psychopathology associated with the timing of pubertal development? *Journal of the American Academy of Child & Adolescent Psychiatry, 36*, 1768–1776. doi:10.1097/00004583-199712000-00026

Greenberg, L. S., Elliot, R., Watson, J. C., & Bohart, A. C. (2001). Empathy. *Psychotherapy: Theory, Research, Practice, Training, 38*, 380–384.

Hayward, C., Killen, J. D., Wilson, D. M., & Hammer, L. D. (1997). Psychiatric risk associated with early puberty in adolescent girls. *Journal of the American Academy of Child & Adolescent Psychiatry, 36*, 255–262.

Henggeler, S. W., Schoenwald, S. K., Borduin, C. M., Rowland, M. D., & Cunningham, P. B. (1998). *Multisystemic treatment of antisocial behavior in children and adolescents*. New York, NY: Guilford Press.

Hentschel, U., & Bjileveld, C. C. J. H. (1995). It takes two to do therapy: On differential aspects in the formation of therapeutic alliance. *Psychotherapy Research, 5*, 22–32.

Hill, C. E., Nutt-Williams, E., Heaton, K. J., Thompson, B. J., & Rhodes, R. H. (1996). Therapist retrospective recall impasses in long-term psychotherapy: A qualitative analysis. *Journal of Counseling Psychology, 43*, 207–217. doi:10.1037/ 0022-0167.43.2.207

Hill, C. E., Thompson, B. J., Cogar, M. C., & Denman, D. W. (1993). Beneath the surface of long-term therapy: Therapist and client report of their own and each other's covert processes. *Journal of Counseling Psychology, 40*, 278–287. doi:10.1037/0022-0167. 40.3.278

Holmbeck, G. N., Colder, C., Shapera, W., Westhoven, V., Kenealy, L., & Updegrove, A. (2000). Working with adolescents: Guides from developmental psychology. In P.C. Kendall (Ed.), *Child & adolescent therapy: Cognitive-behavioral procedures* (2nd ed., pp. 334–385). New York, NY: Guilford Press.

Holmbeck, G. N., & Kendall, P. C. (2002). Clinical adolescent psychology: Developmental psychopathology and treatment. *Journal of Consulting and Clinical Psychology, 70*, 3–5. doi:10.1037/0022-006X.70.1.3

Holtzworth-Munroe, A., Jacobson, N. S., DeKlyen, M., & Whisman, M. A. (1989). Relationship between behavioral marital therapy outcome and process variables. *Journal of Consulting and Clinical Psychology, 57*, 658–662. doi:10.1037/ 0022-006X.57.5.658

Horvath, A. O., & Marx, R. W. (1990). The development and decay of the working alliance during time-limited counselling. *Canadian Journal of Counselling, 24*, 240–260.

Horvath, A. O., & Symonds, B. D. (1991). Relation between working alliance and outcome in psychotherapy: A meta-analysis. *Journal of Counseling Psychology, 38*, 139–149. doi:10.1037/ 0022-0167.38.2.139

Ishikawa, S., Okajima, I., Matsuoka, H., & Sakano, Y. (2007). Cognitive behavioural therapy for anxiety disorders in children and adolescents: A meta-analysis. *Child and Adolescent Mental Health, 12*, 164–172. doi:10.1111/j.1475-3588. 2006.00433.x

Karver, M. S., Handelsman, J. B., Fields, S., & Bickman, L. (2006). Meta-analysis of therapeutic relationship variables in youth and family therapy: The evidence for different relationship variables in the child and adolescent treatment outcome literature. *Clinical Psychology Review, 26*, 50–65. doi:10.1016/j.cpr.2005.09.001

Kazdin, A. E. (1996). Dropping out of child psychotherapy: Issues for research and implications for practice. *Clinical Child Psychology and Psychiatry, 1*, 133–156. doi:10.1177/ 1359104596011012

Kazdin, A. E. (2004). Psychotherapy for children and adolescents. In A. Bergin & S. Garfield (Eds.), *Handbook of psychotherapy and behavior change* (5th ed., pp. 543–589). New York, NY: Wiley.

Kazdin, A. E., Holland, L., & Crowley, M. (1997). Family experience of barriers to treatment and premature termination from child therapy. *Journal of Consulting and Clinical Psychology, 65*, 453–463. doi:10.1037/0022-006X.65.3.453

Kazdin, A. E., & Wassell, G. (1999). Barriers to treatment participation and therapeutic change among children referred for conduct disorder. *Journal of Consulting and Clinical Psychology, 28*, 160–172.

Kendall, P. C., & Beidas, R. S. (2007). Smoothing the trail for dissemination of evidence-based practices for youth: Flexibility within fidelity. *Professional Psychology: Research and Practice, 38*, 13–20. doi:10.1037/0735-7028.38.1.13

Kendall, P. C., Choudhury, M., Hudson, J., & Webb, A. (2002a). *The C.A.T. project therapist manual.* Ardmore, PA: Workbook.

Kendall, P. C., Choudhury, M., Hudson, J., & Webb, A. (2002b). *The C.A.T. project workbook for the cognitive–behavioral treatment of anxious adolescents.* Ardmore, PA: Workbook.

Kendall, P. C., Chu, B. C., Gifford, A., Hayes, C., & Nauta, M. (1998). Breathing life into a manual: Flexibility and creativity with manual-based treatments. *Cognitive and Behavioral Practice, 5,* 177–198. doi:10.1016/S1077-7229(98)80004-7

Kendall, P. C., Comer, J., Marker, C., Creed, T., Puliafico, A., Hughes, A., . . . Hudson, J. (2009). In-session exposure tasks and therapeutic alliance across the treatment of childhood anxiety disorders. *Journal of Consulting and Clinical Psychology, 77,* 517–525. doi:10.1037/a0013686

Kendall, P. C., & Hedtke, K. (2006a). *Coping cat workbook* (2nd ed.). Ardmore, PA: Workbook. (Available at http://www.WorkbookPublishing.com)

Kendall, P. C., & Hedtke, K. (2006b). *Cognitive-behavioral therapy for anxious children: Therapist manual* (3rd ed.). Ardmore, PA: Workbook. (Available at http://www.WorkbookPublishing.com)

Kendall, P. C., & Sugarman, A. (1997). Attrition in the treatment of childhood anxiety disorders. *Journal of Consulting and Clinical Psychology, 65,* 883–888. doi:10.1037/0022-006X.65.5.883

Kivlighan, D. M., & Shaughnessy, P. (1995). Analysis of the development of the working alliance using hierarchical linear modeling. *Journal of Counseling Psychology, 42,* 338–349. doi:10.1037/0022-0167.42.3.338

Kivlighan, D. M., & Shaughnessy, P. (2000). Patterns of working alliance development: A typology of client's working alliance ratings. *Journal of Counseling Psychology, 47,* 362–371. doi:10.1037/0022-0167.47.3.362

Klaczynski, P. A., & Narasimham, G. (1998). Representations as mediators of adolescent deductive reasoning. *Developmental Psychology, 34,* 865–881. doi:10.1037/0012-1649.34.5.865

Larson, R., & Lampman-Petraitis, C. (1989). Daily emotional states as reported by children and adolescents. *Child Development, 60,* 1250–1260. doi:10.2307/1130798

Larson, R. W., & Verma, S. (1999). How children and adolescents spend time across the world: Work, play, and developmental opportunities. *Psychological Bulletin, 125,* 701–736. doi:10.1037/0033-2909.125.6.701

Luborsky, L. (1994). Therapeutic alliances as predictors of psychotherapy outcomes: Factors explaining the predictive success. In A.O. Horvath & L.S. Greenberg (Eds.), *The working alliance: Theory, research, and practice* (pp. 38–50). New York, NY: Wiley.

Martin, D. J., Garske, J. P., & Davis, M. K. (2000). Relationship of the therapeutic alliance with outcome and other variables: A meta-analytic review. *Journal of Consulting and Clinical Psychology, 68,* 438–450. doi:10.1037/0022-006X.68.3.438

Oetzel, K. B., & Sherer, D. G. (2003). Therapeutic engagement with adolescents in psychotherapy. *Psychotherapy: Theory, Research, and Practice, Training, 40,* 215–225.

Ollendick, T. H., & King, N. J. (2000). Empirically supported treatments for children and adolescents. In P.C. Kendall (Ed.), *Child & adolescent therapy: Cognitive–behavioral procedures* (2nd ed., pp. 386–425). New York, NY: Guilford Press.

O'Malley, S. S., Suh, C. S., & Strupp, H. H. (1983). The Vanderbilt Psychotherapy Process Scale: A report on the scale development and a process-outcome study. *Journal of Counseling Psychology, 51,* 581–586. doi:10.1037/0022-006X. 51.4.581

Patton, M. J., Kivlighan, D. M., & Multon, K. D. (1997). The Missouri Psychoanalytic Counseling Research Project: Relation of changes in counseling process to client outcomes. *Journal of Counseling Psychology, 44,* 189–208. doi:10.1037/ 0022-0167.44.2.189

Piaget, J. (1972). Intellectual evolution from adolescence to adulthood. *Human Development, 15*, 1–12.

Prochaska, J. O., Norcross, J. C., & DiClemente, C. C. (1995). *Changing for good*. New York, NY: Avon.

Reandeau, S. G., & Wampold, B. E. (1991). Relationship of power and involvement to working alliance: A multiple-case sequential analysis of brief therapy. *Journal of Counseling Psychology, 38*, 107–114. doi:10.1037/0022-0167.38.2.107

Rennie, D. L. (1994). Clients' deference in psychotherapy. *Journal of Counseling Psychology, 41*, 427–437. doi:10.1037/0022-0167.41.4.427

Rhodes, R. H., Hill, C. E., Thompson, B. J., & Elliott, R. (1994). Client retrospective recall of resolved and unresolved misunderstanding events. *Journal of Counseling Psychology, 41*, 473–483. doi:10.1037/0022-0167.41.4.473

Rubenstein, A. K. (1996). Interventions for a scattered generation: Treating adolescents in the nineties. *Psychotherapy: Theory, Research, Practice, Training, 33*, 353–360.

Safran, J. D., Muran, J. C., Samstag, L., Wallner, L. K., & Stevens, C. L. (2002). Repairing alliance ruptures. In J. C. Norcross (Ed.), *Psychotherapy relationships that work: Therapist contributions and responsiveness to patients* (pp. 235–254). London: Oxford University Press.

Safran, J. D., & Wallner, L. K. (1991). The relative predictive validity of two therapeutic alliance measures in cognitive therapy. *Psychological Assessment, 3*, 188–195. doi:10.1037/1040-3590.3.2.188

Shirk, S. R., & Karver, M. (2003). Prediction of treatment outcome from relationship variables in child and adolescent therapy: A meta-analytic review. *Journal of Consulting and Clinical Psychology, 71*, 452–464. doi:10.1037/0022-006X. 71.3.452

Shirk, S. R., & Saiz, C. (1992). Clinical, empirical, and developmental perspectives on the therapeutic relationship in child psychotherapy. *Development and Psychopathology, 4*, 713–728. doi:10.1017/S0954579400004946

Silverberg, S., & Steinberg, L. (1990). Psychological well-being of parents at midlife: The impact of early adolescent children. *Developmental Psychology, 26*, 658–666. doi:10.1037/0012-1649.26.4.658

Sommers-Flanagan, J., & Sommers-Flanagan, R. (1995). Psychotherapeutic techniques with treatment-resistant adolescents. *Psychotherapy, 32*, 131–140. doi:10.1037/0033-3204.32.1.131

Spence, S. H., Donovan, C., & Brechman-Touissant, M. (2000). The treatment of childhood social phobia: The effectiveness of a social skills training-based, cognitive-behavioral intervention, with and without parental involvement. *Journal of Child Psychology and Psychiatry and Allied Disciplines, 41*, 713–726. doi:10.1111/1469-7610.00659

Steinberg, L. D. (2002). *Adolescence* (6th ed.). New York, NY: McGraw-Hill.

Steinberg, L., & Morris, A. S. (2001). Adolescent development. *Annual Review of Psychology, 52*, 83–110. doi:10.1146/annurev.psych.52.1.83

Tryon, G. S., & Kane, A. S. (1990). The helping alliance and premature termination. *Counselling Psychology Quarterly, 3*, 233–238. doi:10.1080/09515079008254254

Tryon, G. S., & Kane, A. S. (1993). Relationship of working alliance to mutual and unilateral termination. *Journal of Counseling Psychology, 40*, 33–36. doi:10.1037/0022-0167.40.1.33

Tryon, G. S., & Kane, A. S. (1995). Client involvement, working alliance, and type of therapy termination. *Psychotherapy Research, 5*, 189–198.

Tryon, G. S., & Winograd, G. (2002). Goal consensus and collaboration. In J. C. Norcross (Ed.), *Psychotherapy relationships that work* (pp. 109–125). New York, NY: Oxford University Press.

Walkup, J. T., Albano, A. M., Piacentini, J., Birmaher, B., Compton, S., Sherrill, J., . . . Kendall, P. C. (2008). Cognitive behavioral therapy, sertraline, or a combination in childhood anxiety. *New England Journal of Medicine, 359,* 2753–2766. doi:10.1056/NEJMoa0804633

Weisz, J. R., & Hawley, K. M. (2002). Developmental factors in the treatment of adolescents. *Journal of Consulting and Clinical Psychology, 70,* 21–43. doi:10.1037/0022-006X.70.1.21

Windholz, M. J., & Silberschatz, G. (1988). Vanderbilt Psychotherapy Process Scale: A replication with adult outpatients. *Journal of Consulting and Clinical Psychology, 56,* 56–60. doi:10.1037/0022-006X.56.1.56

4

TEEN: TECHNIQUES FOR ENHANCING ENGAGEMENT THROUGH NEGOTIATION

DAVID CASTRO-BLANCO

The majority of adolescents referred for treatment of mental disorders do not want to be there (Evans & Seligman, 2005). Many may acknowledge the presence of problems, although they may still resent the idea of being coerced to attend treatment sessions and resist engaging in psychotherapy.

There is overwhelming evidence to support the idea that a limited window of opportunity exists in which to engage and successfully treat significant psychological disorders with adolescents (Jamieson & Romer, 2005; Kazdin & Wassell, 2000). The groundbreaking report by the Surgeon General (U.S. Public Health Service, 1999) and recent reports by others (Evans et al., 2005; Roberts, Roberts, & Chan, 2009) have suggested that nearly 20% of adolescents meet the diagnostic criteria for at least one mental disorder. However, the evidence has suggested that these at-risk adolescents are not receiving mental health services. The Surgeon General's 1999 report on mental health stated that the majority of adolescents referred for psychological treatment failed to receive adequate intervention. Kazdin, Holland, and Crowley (1997) have reported that as many as 40% to 60% of teens referred for treatment fail to attend more than a handful of sessions, and Spirito,

Boergers, Donaldson, Bishop, and Lewander (2002) reported that the majority of significantly mentally ill adolescents fail to attend more than two psychotherapy sessions.

Although alarming, these findings are anything but new. Spirito, Brown, Overholser, and Fritz (1989) reported that 75% of a sample of adolescents treated at a hospital emergency room after a suicide attempt failed to attend a single psychotherapy session within 12 months of their attempt. Trautman, Stewart, and Morishima (1993) reported similar results following a cohort of adolescents seen in an emergency room for suicidal ideation or attempts. Rotheram-Borus, Piacentini, Miller, et al. (1994; Rotheram-Borus, Piacentini, Miller, et al., 1996a) reported that more than 80% of a sample of 250 adolescents treated for suicide attempts failed to attend more than four psychotherapy sessions in the year after their emergency room discharge.

Given the risk for recurrence of risk taking, or the development of longer-term problem behaviors stemming from early dangerous behaviors (Loeber, Green, & Lahey, 1990; Loeber, Wung, & Keenan, 1993), interventions offering the promise of actively engaging potential treatment dropouts while aiming to reduce high-risk adolescent behaviors are critical. More to the point, interventions that encourage engagement and participation by adolescents who are, by and large, reluctant to take part in treatment are needed and warranted.

In this chapter, I describe and provide guidelines on a family engagement approach built on the idea that encouraging intrafamilial negotiation and cooperation is likely to produce treatment participants who are more willing to work together in therapy to problem solve to reach commonly agreed-on treatment goals. This approach makes sense given that prior research has shown a relationship between high family conflict and treatment dropout (Armbruster & Fallon, 1994). It may be that if a clinician does not immediately address high levels of family conflict, a condition that is commonly associated with adolescent psychopathology (e.g., Grant et al., 2006), then family members may immediately disengage from any participation in treatment. Interestingly, Brookman-Frazee, Haine, Gabayan, and Garland (2008) found that higher parent–youth treatment goal agreement, but not clinician–youth treatment goal agreement, was a significant predictor of more frequent therapy sessions attended. In fact, they suggested that it may be critical for clinicians to address parent–youth goal agreement very early in treatment to prevent treatment dropout. Given the aforementioned findings, the emphasis in the approach described in this chapter is not directly on therapist–client negotiation but on a therapeutic relationship built by the role the therapist plays in getting an adolescent and family members to successfully negotiate with one another fairly early on in treatment. This approach builds on the work of Rotheram-Borus, Piacentini, Graae, et al. (1994), which emphasizes teaching suicidal adolescents and their families how to communicate with one another so that they can be better at problem solving together. At the heart of good family problem solving is the ability for all members to effectively negotiate with one another (Robin, 1981).

NEGOTIATION

> Never let us negotiate out of fear, but never let us fear to negotiate.
> —John F. Kennedy

Negotiation requires a number of basic skills, all of which can be easily taught if the basic goal of improved problem solving is made clear at the outset. Some people may react to negotiation with ambivalence, believing that to achieve a negotiated solution, they may have to surrender something of value for the process to advance.

Learning to negotiate effectively requires an individual to learn many of the basic skills associated with adaptive problem solving. Among these are clarity in defining desires, wants, and needs; identifying and establishing goals; and focusing attention on issues rather than on the individuals involved.

Why Negotiate?

> In business, you don't get what you deserve, you get what you negotiate.
> —Chester L. Karrass

The same can be said of life. Learning the skills of negotiation increases the ability of the adolescent and his or her family to be effective communicators, with each other and outside the home. The essential goal of negotiation is equitable gain. For everyone to benefit in a negotiation, every party to the negotiation has to abandon the notion of zero-sum gain. Many familial conflicts center around the goal of winning rather than attaining a specific goal. In a zero-sum situation, for one party to win, the other needs to lose.

Effective negotiation is predicated on the principle that any solution in which one side wins and another loses results in loss for everyone. Rather than concentrate on defeating an opponent, adaptive negotiation focuses on the win–win scenario, in which each party makes some gain (Rotheram-Borus, Piacentini, van Rossem, et al., 1996).

For many families, a solution in which every participant can win is a novelty. Beginning with the expectation that an argument must have a winner motivates many to avoid losing rather than to achieve a desired goal through cooperation. Unlike many familial and other group arguments, in a well-conducted negotiation winning does not necessarily have to come at the expense of the other negotiator.

By fostering cooperation rather than an adversarial, winner-take-all stance, the basic premise of negotiation is that part of something is better than all of nothing.

Concerns About Negotiation

> Insanity is doing the same thing over and over, and expecting different results.
>
> —Albert Einstein

Teaching adolescents and their parents to effectively negotiate requires them to do something with which they have difficulty: Communicate. If this was simply and easily accomplished, there would be no need to teach these skills to troubled teens and their families.

Among the concerns expressed by many parents when first introduced to the concept of negotiating with their troubled adolescent is threat to the hierarchical structure of the family. Many parents express reluctance to negotiate with the adolescent, citing the concern that doing so will normalize arguments in the family, legitimize adolescent rebellion, and undermine parental authority within the family (McLeod, Wood, & Weisz, 2007).

The fundamental problem in many family arguments and fights is the dedication to winning at all costs. The result of this style of argument is ever-increasing stakes. By using the threat of risk taking, many adolescents are able to maneuver their parents toward ceding what is demanded. The counter-stroke to this approach is to assert a strong, restrictive parental authority, effectively barring the adolescent from any opportunity to engage in potentially risky behavior. Ultimately, this stalemate is maintained (or reiterated) until one party capitulates. Unfortunately, this sets the stage for a perpetual war of attrition within the family.

Undermining parental authority and fomenting revolution are clearly not the primary goals of effective treatment. The integrity of the family and maintaining its credibility and viability are essential to effective therapy. Rather than subvert the authority of parents, the goal of teaching effective negotiation can actually reinforce the hierarchical structure of the family.

Parents who can negotiate effectively demonstrate their flexibility and reason. They reinforce the premise that rules and strictures have a rationale and are not capricious or arbitrary. Indeed, by demonstrating a willingness to negotiate some aspects of family life, parents make a more valid and reasonable case for differentiating between negotiable and non-negotiable behaviors and issues.

Guidelines of Effective Negotiation

> If you treat people as they are, you will be instrumental in keeping them as they are. If you treat people as they could be, you will be instrumental in making them what they ought to be.
>
> —Goethe

Effective negotiation is based on a set of principles that can be taught to both adolescents and their family members. The following list briefly describes these guidelines:

1. *State each want (goal) in a single sentence.* More than one sentence means more than one goal.
2. *State only what you want to see or hear.* Goals need to be framed as tangible, proactive, measurable behaviors.
3. *State what you do want to happen, not what you do not.* State goals positively, indicating what you want to see increased rather than eliminated.
4. *State what you think others with whom you are negotiating want as well.* One of the most difficult tasks of negotiation is trying to figure out what the other person wants.
5. *Explain without blame.* Keeping the focus on issues rather than individuals helps ensure that arguments are about competing goals rather than competing people.
6. *Listen, without interruption.* Perhaps the most difficult task in negotiation is listening to opposing views without leaping to defend one's own position. Respectful listening sometimes says far more than any argument could and is far more persuasive.
7. *Value disagreement.* If two people agree about everything, it's a good bet that at least one of them is not doing much thinking. Problems are not caused by people disagreeing. They arise out of the ways in which people disagree.
8. *Remember that you are negotiating to get something.* In any negotiation, the goal is to obtain something desired, not to defeat an opponent. Remember, part of something is better than all of nothing.
9. *Remember that you have to give to get.* Negotiation only works when all the parties are prepared to give ground to gain ground. The most effective solution is the one in which all participants give equally to gain equally.
10. *If everyone is equally unhappy, it's probably a good solution.* If you dispense with the idea of winning and losing, then each person ought to give and receive in a roughly equivalent manner. This

means no one should be in the position of getting the better end of the deal. In a successful negotiation, there ought to be no truly better deal.

Negotiation and Treatment Engagement

The main thing is to keep the main thing the main thing.
—Steven Covey

There is ample evidence that adolescents receiving treatment for psychological disorders benefit (Jamieson & Romer, 2005). Unfortunately, there is also considerable evidence that many teens who could benefit from psychotherapy do not receive an adequate level of intervention for their problems (Evans & Seligman, 2005). Enhancing engagement in the initial stages of treatment can increase the adolescent's potential to remain in treatment and garner the benefits from intervention.

How can learning the skills of effective negotiation accomplish this goal? By incorporating the teen and family members as parties to a negotiation rather than as adversaries, the focus of treatment can remain on the goals and issues in contention rather than on recrimination and blame avoidance. The adolescent is enlisted as a collaborative partner in the treatment team, participating in the formulation of treatment goals, identification of desired outcomes, and steps toward compromise.

Psychotherapists routinely use and model the skills of effective negotiation in their work. By teaching these skills to adolescents and their family members, potential adversaries can effectively become members of the same treatment team.

TECHNIQUES FOR ENHANCING ENGAGEMENT THROUGH NEGOTIATION

Things do not change, we change.
—Henry David Thoreau

Techniques for Enhancing Engagement through Negotiation (TEEN) was developed to increase the engagement of adolescents and their family members in treatment by teaching them the skills of negotiation. The main premise underlying the development of TEEN is the need for the adolescent to participate in treatment to benefit from treatment.

TEEN has its roots in adolescent suicide prevention research. As part of a National Institute of Mental Health–supported study examining a specialized emergency room intervention, Rotheram-Borus, Piacentini, Graae, et al. (1994) developed a six-session intervention model designed to increase the effective communication skills of suicide-attempting adolescents and their families. SNAP (Successful Negotiation/Acting Positively) combines psychoeducation and exercises to help suicidal teens and their family members work together to actively generate problem-solving options. Initial results using this intervention appeared to support the utility of negotiation training and cooperative problem solving as a major treatment component with high-risk adolescents (Piacentini, Rotheram-Borus, & Gillis, 1995; Rotheram-Borus, Piacentini, Cantwell, Belin, & Song, 2000; Rotheram-Borus, Piacentini, Graae, et al., 1994; Rotheram-Borus, Piacentini, Miller, et al., 1996; Rotheram-Borus, Piacentini, van Rossem, et al., 1996).

The experience of developing and implementing the SNAP protocol highlighted two very important points related to engaging adolescents and their families in treatment. First, much of the alliance literature had focused on the establishment and maintenance of the patient–therapist bond. The success of SNAP appeared to rely more on the remaining two legs of Bordin's (1979) stool: collaborative agreement about the goals and tasks of treatment. The second point is intimately connected to the first. Negotiation facilitates talking and discussion among parties who might otherwise not communicate. Learning negotiation skills permitted treatment participants to identify and agree to the goals of therapy and the procedures to attain those goals.

SNAP was designed as an intervention specific to the needs of Latina adolescent suicide attempters and their families. Nonetheless, the experience of working with the SNAP protocol demonstrated the great potential for developing negotiation-based strategies for broader application.

Engagement and, by extension, the alliance, predicated on developing agreeable goals, offers great promise to therapists working with adolescents. Being incorporated in the goal-setting and decision-making aspects of treatment provides manifest benefits to the teen. Negotiation training permits a definable and skill-based set of procedures to be learned by the adolescent and family members in treatment.

SNAP offered a preliminary view of the utility of teaching negotiation skills to adolescents at risk for treatment dropout. It is from this experience that the seeds of TEEN found fertile ground.

Overview of TEEN

We don't see things as they are, we see them as we are.

—Anaïs Nin

TEEN was developed to promote treatment engagement in potentially resistant adolescents through the development of negotiating skills.

The overarching goal of the intervention is to increase the ability of adolescents to communicate, identify problems, generate options, and accept compromise.

TEEN has its foundation in cognitive–behavioral theory. Like standard cognitive–behavioral therapy, TEEN uses a mix of psychoeducation, cognitive restructuring, and behavioral experimentation designed to identify, isolate, challenge, and re-form distorted and dysfunctional patterns of belief, feeling, and action. Like more traditional cognitive–behavioral therapy models, TEEN is an active treatment, requiring considerable practice and homework between sessions. Early in the process of treatment, the adolescent and family are advised that the bulk of treatment will actually take place outside of the therapy office. The goal of TEEN is to aid the adolescent and family to become their own primary therapists, training them to solve problems and, more important, avoid them.

Although arguments in families seem inevitable, the goal of TEEN is to teach the adolescent and his or her family how to argue differently, so that rather than reiterating the same argument, a new, more productive argument can be substituted.

TEEN is not intended to replace psychotherapy and all other engagement strategies used with the adolescent and family. Rather, the protocol is an adjunct to existing treatment and existing engagement strategies (e.g., following the client's lead [Creed & Kendall, 2005], validation [Linehan, 1993]). This is important because DiGiuseppe, Linscott, and Jilton (1996) found that bond-focused engagement strategies alone were more likely to be rejected by oppositional adolescents. On the contrary, oppositional adolescents may need to be approached in a more active manner to be engaged in treatment. The primary purpose of TEEN is to make existing treatment more available and accessible to the adolescent and increase the likelihood that the benefits of attending treatment can be had.

TEEN was developed to be administered in a series of modules. Although the suggested number of sessions using the model is eight, the techniques and exercises can be modified and presented in more or fewer sessions, depending on time availability.

Each TEEN module is focused on the achievement of a component of effective problem-solving. The six modules, shown in Exhibit 4.1 (http://pubs.apa.org/books/supp/elusive/), reflect the progression of achievement through the protocol and are designed to be used in an integrative fashion.

TEEN's structure provides a framework that is simple for a therapist to use and easily adapted to the needs of the adolescent and family. By instituting a highly structured framework from the outset of therapy while attending to the therapeutic alliance, the therapist ensures that all participants are able to understand and predict the organization and course of a session. Each participant's role in the therapy is clearly outlined from the first session: The therapist proceeds with a focus on intervention fidelity and adherence to the model, the therapist records all activities during the sessions, both the adolescent and the therapist maintain a homework record (they can compare notes), and the adolescent is fully and respectfully used as a partner in treatment planning and implementation.

USING POSITIVES TO BREAK THROUGH TREATMENT RESISTANCE

> There is nothing in a caterpillar that tells you it's going to be a butterfly.
> —Buckminster Fuller

Part of being viewed as a respectful partner in therapy is related to how the therapist views the adolescent client and his or her family. If the therapist views the adolescent as an individual with only a collection of problems to be focused on, the adolescent is more likely to feel stigmatized and less likely to feel respected, less likely to be hopeful, and thus less likely to be receptive to and energized by treatment (Smith, 2006; Weisz, Hawley, & Doss, 2004). Often adolescents are referred to treatment against their will, and thus it is not a surprise that they are resistant to treatment (DiGiuseppe et al., 1996). However, a focus on strengths, especially when youth and family members are used to being criticized, can be quite validating. Neither the adolescent nor the family is likely to enter therapy expecting to identify, discuss, and use their individual and collective strengths. This unexpected and more respectful focus may enhance the sense of the adolescent and family members alike that the therapist is worth the effort of working with. These identified strengths then become the very mechanisms that will enable the participants in therapy to learn to negotiate, treat each other respectfully, and, ultimately, resolve their problems in more effective and less painful ways.

The following sections outline a set of approaches designed to maximize the focus on the positive attributes of the entire family.

Setting Positive Rather Than Negative Expectations

The therapist models positivity. Through the use of social reinforcement, reframing of behaviors as positive and strong, the importance of positive, prosocial behavior is emphasized. Treatment participants are encouraged to adopt a positive rather than a negative set of expectations regarding treatment and its outcome.

Establishing Competence Rather Than Failure

Through the use of social reinforcement by both the therapist and the family, all the participants in treatment are encouraged to look for, identify, and reward success. Experiencing competence, positive consequences, and encouragement serve as the impetus for greater and continuing change.

Problems Are Soluble and Transient Events in People's Lives

Many of the events precipitating family conflict are actually transient and capable of resolution. A child who bobs in the ocean's waves will occasionally have a wave wash over his or her head. The wave will pass, and the child will remain unharmed if she or he realizes being overwhelmed is temporary and will quickly change. If she or he is able to remain calm and focus on the next wave, then the child can resurface and recover without further incident.

Often assumptions and habitual methods for dealing with problems aid in their perpetuation. A view of problems as soluble decreases hopelessness. Regarding problems with the expectation that they will be resolved aids the family members in focusing on the search for options for how, rather than whether, the problem will be solved.

Success Breeds Success: Positive Choices Remove Negative Expectations

It is beneficial for the therapist to have clients initially target easier goals. Once the participants successfully problem solve, they will have greater motivation to try dealing with other problems. Successful resolution of one problem increases the expectation that subsequent problems may also be dealt with successfully.

When the family realizes that problem solving involves choice, the range of options available to them will increase. The willingness of the participants to explore this expanded range of options can also be seen to grow as the positive benefits of doing so are realized.

Proactive Behavior Changes in the Future as a Goal of Treatment Now

Although acting to resolve current problems, a major goal of treatment is to improve the skills of the participants to problem solve in the future. By improving the skills of all participants as communicators and problem solvers, methods and options for preventing recurrences of problems with teachers, peers, and each other in the future can be developed.

Negotiation Makes the Adolescent a Partner in the Treatment Team

A considerable risk factor for treatment dropout is the perception of being ignored in the process of clinical decision making. Negotiation involves the adolescent as a fully contributing member of the treatment team. This increases both the responsibility of the adolescent to contribute to the process of treatment and the likelihood that the teen's motivation to continue in treatment will grow. As Bordin's (1979) working alliance model suggests, joint agreement between patient and therapist as to the goals and tasks of treatment ensures greater potential for success. There is every reason to believe that this is even more the case when the alliance between family members is strengthened.

Communication With, Rather Than Dictation to, the Adolescent

Involving the adolescent as a partner within the treatment team aids in increasing the motivation for treatment. By involving the adolescent in an agreement as to the tasks and goals of therapy, the teen's contribution to the process of treatment is reinforced. This, in turn, makes the adolescent's contribution to the therapy more meaningful and potentially long lasting. The establishment of mutually agreed-on goals aids in the maintenance of an effective, goal-directed working alliance.

Engaging the Adolescent in the Treatment Contract Helps Maintain Family Involvement in Therapy

Often, the family will lower their expectations of treatment outcome if they perceive the adolescent as uninvolved and resistant to the therapy process. Any strategy that offers the promise of increasing the adolescent's motivation to continue and participate actively is important. This is especially so when intervention discourages efforts to shift the focus of treatment to blaming of the family members or the teen for current problems rather than to cooperation of all to solve them. This should increase the motivation for all participants to actively engage in therapy.

TECHNIQUES USED IN TEEN

We are what we repeatedly do. Excellence then, is not an act, it is a habit.
—Aristotle

TEEN makes use of a number of techniques and adjunctive aids. Many of these are easily incorporated into standard psychotherapy practice and can be developed with little difficulty.

To encourage positive focus in sessions, the therapist uses frequent social reinforcement. This can be aided by the use of social tokens. Poker chips, colored cards, or other small tokens can be provided to all participants and exchanged in recognition of positive, therapeutic behaviors during the session. The therapist must model the use of these tokens, as well as the liberal application of verbal praise, for other participants to follow suit.

The feeling thermometer features prominently in the TEEN protocol. Adapted from Wolpe's (1973) Subjective Units of Discomfort scale, the thermometer requires participants to quantify the degree of severity or intensity of a given feeling. Many adolescents (and adults) experience difficulty in the accurate and precise identification and discussion of feelings. Although their emotional vocabulary may be limited, the thermometer provides a quick, easy, and very internally reliable measure of how much an individual is feeling, even if she or he has difficulty articulating precisely what is being felt. Changes in intensity are a fast and useful way of demonstrating both the transience of problems and the positive consequences of their resolution.

Many conflicts within the family are fostered by the adherence to older ways of transacting discipline and resistance. Rather than having frequent fights, many families engage in reiterations of the same fight. Learning to identify expectations and attributions about other family members can open the door to option generation. Learning that each individual is not as gifted a mind reader as she or he might believe can be a sobering experience and a powerful impetus to change. To facilitate this awareness, the therapist can use a set of assumption cards, with statements such as "If I work hard enough, I can get anything I want" or "Bad behavior is just a way of trying to get attention." The family members assess their agreement with these statements and open the discussion of the assumptions underlying such attributions.

Within many families, each member assumes a number of roles. For the most part, the roles, and the rules that accompany them, are implicit, although violations are frequently met with severe consequences. Articulating those roles, and their accompanying rules, and determining how fixed they truly are is another component of learned negotiation. The therapist can use a set of Rules and Roles cards, including such descriptors as "'The Trouble Maker': She or he makes sure there is always confusion and difficulty so everyone can focus their concerns" or "'The Fixer': She or he 'takes care of things' and 'works things out.'"

Exploring the roles performed by each family member in a safe setting can allow the exploration of assumptions held by the teen and others regarding not only his or her own behavior but that of the other members of the family. Exploring these roles and rules through the use of cards and in the context of problem solving can permit the family members to learn new ways to disagree in a more productive manner.

Given the risk of premature treatment dropout, as well as potentially injurious behaviors on the part of the adolescent, the development of an emergency action plan is a key goal of the first session. The emergency action plan can be constructed on an index card and instructs the adolescent, as well as the other participants, in what to do if a crisis occurs. The progression of crisis remedy, from telling a trusted family member to transport to a local emergency room, is spelled out in sequence. The rationale for the plan is having "done all the thinking" ahead of time. While preparing for how to deal with a crisis, the participants are subtly trained to prepare for the eventuality of a crisis during treatment. By modeling the belief that such events are common and can be weathered without great distress, the family can get down to the business of change, without a crisis intervening each week to derail treatment.

TEEN uses frequent role-play activities. The adolescent and family members are encouraged to exchange places and argue realistically and vigorously on each other's behalf. This permits each participant to experience the goals of the others and allows the rational rather than emotional discussion of negotiating. In addition, role plays can prepare the family members for interactions with a more hostile environment than the therapist's office. Every participant should be encouraged to use the negotiating skills taught in treatment broadly and generally in the real world.

Finally, TEEN emphasizes a collective approach to problem solving. Just as problems are seen to be systemic, rather than idiopathic, so too are their resolutions.

The TEEN protocol uses a metaphoric approach to identifying problems, approaches to their solution, and how faulty expectations and assumptions can defeat these efforts. The story about "The Immigrant and 'the Magic Phrase'" (see Exhibit 4.2, http://pubs.apa.org/books/supp/elusive/), which humorously highlights the process of problem solving, is a useful one.

Many adolescents and families seeking assistance, particularly in response to dangerous, risk-taking behaviors, are prone to ask for advice and seek a magic phrase. Unfortunately, when participants learn tactics, rather than strategies, the use of new techniques and phrases may become overly general, and the family may well become overly dependent on them as a panacea.

The more widely a technique is applied, the more general the assumption that it should be. This can get in the way of genuine success and prompt premature termination of treatment. Brainstorming possible solutions for the sad immigrant in the story about the magic phrase can result in a number of productive avenues in which each participant can play the part of the distressed immigrant (see Exhibit 4.3, http://pubs.apa.org/books/supp/elusive/).

The most effective problem-solving interventions are those that aid participants in learning to solve their own problems rather than relying on an expert to do so. Problem solving is a process, not a technique. Like any process, it has a series of steps and tasks that have to be learned and mastered. Effective problem solving relies on an approach to treating problems as temporary, resolvable issues rather than as threats to the integrity of the self and family. Learning to recognize, access, and use all the options available rather than relying on a "quick fix" of solutions and techniques that work on paper, but not in reality, will not only lead participants to becoming better problem solvers but to becoming better problem avoiders.

Negotiation provides a framework for family members to remember something that is often assumed but not frequently recalled on entering treatment: They are all part of the problem and solution. Approaching treatment of the adolescent with the idea and promise that "we are all in this together" can have powerful, and one hopes, long-lasting impact on the teen and his or her family.

SUMMARY

Treating interpersonal and behavioral difficulties of adolescents in isolation appears to increase the risk for premature treatment termination and inadequate treatment of potentially severe problems. In large part because of unique developmental factors, adolescents experiencing psychopathology and behavioral problems are particularly vulnerable to long-standing problems and risks. Treating problems as systemic and working with the adolescent and family as a team offers opportunities for systemic, sustainable change, not only in target behaviors, but in reshaping the environments in which these behaviors occur (McLeod & Weisz, 2005).

Negotiation is a proven problem-resolution strategy. TEEN is an intervention designed to train adolescents and their family members in the skills of effective negotiation. Improving communication, increasing the specificity of goals and stated desires, and working toward compromise are all potential benefits of negotiated settlements. TEEN teaches the adolescent and family members to work toward defining and achieving common goals, even when initial stances appear to be quite disparate.

Although TEEN derives from a cognitive–behavioral tradition, it is most effectively conceived as a treatment-enhancing adjunct to any treatment modality that attempts to change problem and risk behaviors in adolescents. By providing real, attainable benefits, TEEN is designed to increase the engagement of the adolescent and his or her family in treatment. The costs of failing to do so are, indeed, too great to risk.

REFERENCES

Armbruster, P., & Fallon, T. (1994). Clinical, sociodemographic, and systems risk factors for attrition in a children's mental health clinic. *American Journal of Orthopsychiatry, 64*, 577–585. doi:10.1037/h0079571

Bordin, E. S. (1979). The generalizability of the psychoanalytic concept of the working alliance. *Psychotherapy: Theory, Research, & Practice, 16*, 252–260.

Brookman-Frazee, L., Haine, R. A., Gabayan, E. N., & Garland, A. F. (2008). Predicting frequency of treatment visits in community-based youth psychotherapy. *Psychological Services, 5*, 126–138. doi:10.1037/1541-1559.5.2.126

Creed, T. A., & Kendall, P. C. (2005). Therapist alliance-building behavior within a cognitive–behavioral treatment for anxiety in youth. *Journal of Consulting and Clinical Psychology, 73*, 498–505. doi:10.1037/0022-006X.73.3.498

DiGiuseppe, R., Linscott, J., & Jilton, R. (1996). Developing the therapeutic alliance in child–adolescent psychotherapy. *Applied & Preventive Psychology, 5*, 85–100. doi:10.1016/S0962-1849(96)80002-3

Evans, D. L., Beardslee, W., Biederman, J., Brent, D., Charney, D., Coyle, J., . . . Weller, E. (2005). Defining depression and bipolar disorders. In D. L. Evans, E. B. Foa, R. E. Gur, H. Hendin, C. P. O'Brien, M. E. P. Seligman, & B. T. Walsh, (Eds.), *Treating and preventing adolescent mental health disorders: What we know and what we don't know, a research agenda for improving the mental health of our youth* (pp. 3–76). New York, NY: Oxford University Press.

Evans, D., & Seligman, M. E. P. (2005). Introduction. In D. L. Evans, E. B. Foa, R. L. Gur, H. Hendin, C. P. O'Brien, E. P. Seligman, & B. T. Walsh (Eds.), *Treating and preventing adolescent mental health disorders: What we know and what we don't know* (pp. xxv–xl). New York, NY: Oxford University Press. doi:10.1093/9780195173642.003.0001

Grant, K. E., Compas, B. E., Thurm, A. E., McMahon, S. D., Gipson, P. Y., Campbell, A. J., . . . Westerholm, R. I. (2006). Stressors and child and adolescent psychopathology: Evidence of moderating and mediating effects. *Clinical Psychology Review, 26*, 257–283. doi:10.1016/j.cpr.2005.06.011

Jamieson, K. H., & Romer, D. (2005). A call to action on adolescent mental health. In D. L. Evans, E. B. Foa, R. L. Gur, H. Hendin, C. P. O'Brien, M. E. P. Seligman, & B. T. Walsh (Eds.), *Treating and preventing adolescent mental health disorders: What we know and what we don't know* (pp. 617–623). New York, NY: Oxford University Press. doi:10.1093/9780195173642.003.0033

Kazdin, A. E., Holland, L., & Crowley, M. (1997). Barriers to Treatment Participation scale: Evaluation and validation in the context of child outpatient treatment. *Journal of Clinical Child Psychology and Psychiatry, 38*, 1051–1062. doi:10.1111/j.1469-7610.1997.tb01621.x

Kazdin, A. E., & Wassell, G. (2000). Therapeutic changes in children, parents and families resulting from treatment of children with conduct problems. *Journal of the American Academy of Child & Adolescent Psychiatry, 39*, 414–420.

Linehan, M. M. (1993). *Cognitive–behavioral treatment of borderline personality disorder*. New York, NY: Guilford Press.

Loeber, R., Green, S. M., & Lahey, B. B. (1990). Mental health professionals' perception of the utility of children, mothers and teachers as informants on childhood psychopathology. *Journal of Clinical Child Psychology, 19*, 136–143. doi:10.1207/s15374424jccp1902_5

Loeber, R., Wung, P., & Keenan, K. (1993). Developmental pathways in disruptive child behavior. *Development and Psychopathology, 5*, 103–133. doi:10.1017/S0954579400004296

McLeod, B. D., & Weisz, J. R. (2005). The Therapy Process Observational Coding System-Alliance Scale: Measurement characteristics and prediction of outcome in usual clinical practice. *Journal of Consulting and Clinical Psychology, 73*, 323–333. doi:10.1037/0022-006X. 73.2.323

McLeod, B. D., Wood, J. J., & Weisz, J. R. (2007). Examining the association between parenting and child anxiety: A meta-analysis. *Clinical Psychology Review, 27*, 155–172. doi:10.1016/j.cpr.2006.09.002

Piacentini, J., Rotheram-Borus, M. J., & Gillis, J. R. (1995). Demographic predictors of treatment attendance among adolescent suicide attempters. *Journal of Consulting and Clinical Psychology, 63*, 469–473. doi:10.1037/0022-006X.63.3.469

Roberts, R. E., Roberts, C. R., & Chan, W. (2009). One-year incidence of psychiatric disorders and associated risk factors among adolescents in the community. *Journal of Child Psychology and Psychiatry and Allied Disciplines, 50*, 405–415. doi:10.1111/j.1469-7610.2008.01969.x

Robin, A. L. (1981). A controlled evaluation of problem-solving communication training with parent-adolescent conflict. *Behavior Therapy, 12*, 593–609. doi:10.1016/S0005-7894(81)80132-3

Rotheram-Borus, M. J., Piacentini, J., Cantwell, C., Belin, T. R., & Song, J. (2000). The 18-month impact of an emergency-room intervention for adolescent female suicide attempters. *Journal of Consulting and Clinical Psychology, 68*, 1081–1093.

Rotheram-Borus, M. J., Piacentini, J., Graae, F., Castro-Blanco, D., & Miller, S. (1994). Family intervention to increase treatment adherence of Latina adolescent suicide attempters. *Journal of the American Academy of Child & Adolescent Psychiatry, 33*, 508-517.

Rotheram-Borus, M. J., Piacentini, J., Miller, S., Graae, F., & Castro-Blanco, D. (1994). *Successful negotiation/acting positively: Family-based cognitive-behavioral intervention for female adolescent suicide attempters.* New York, NY: Columbia University College of Physicians and Surgeons.

Rotheram-Borus, M. J., Piacentini, J., Miller, S., Graae, F., Dunne, E. & Cantwell, C. (1996). Toward improving treatment adherence among adolescent suicide attempters. *Clinical Child Psychology and Psychiatry, 1*, 99–108

Rotheram-Borus, M. J., Piacentini, J., van Rossem, R., Graae, F., Cantwell, C., Castro-Blanco, D., & Feldman, J. (1996). Enhancing treatment adherence with a specialized emergency room intervention for adolescent suicide attempters. *Journal of the American Academy of Child & Adolescent Psychiatry, 35*, 654–663.

Smith, E. J. (2006). The strength-based counseling model. *Counseling Psychologist, 34*, 13–79.

Spirito, A., Boergers, J., Donaldson, D., Bishop, D., & Lewander, W. (2002). An intervention trial to improve adherence to community treatment by adolescents after a suicide attempt. *Journal of the American Academy of Child & Adolescent Psychiatry, 41*, 435–442.

Spirito, A., Brown, L., Overholser, J., & Fritz, G. (1989). Attempted suicide in adolescence: A review and critique of the literature. *Clinical Psychology Review, 9*, 335–363.

Trautman, P., Stewart, N., & Morishima, A. (1993). Are adolescent suicide attempters non-compliant with outpatient care? *Journal of the American Academy of Child & Adolescent Psychiatry, 32*, 89–94.

U.S. Public Health Service. (1999). *The Surgeon General's call to action to prevent suicide.* Washington, DC: Author.

Weisz, J. R., Hawley, K. M., & Doss, A. J. (2004). Empirically tested psychotherapies for youth internalizing and externalizing problems and disorders. *Child and Adolescent Psychiatric Clinics of North America, 13*, 729–815.

Wolpe, J. (1973). *The practice of behavior therapy.* New York, NY: Pergamon Press.

5

ENGAGING ADOLESCENTS WITH DISRUPTIVE BEHAVIOR DISORDERS IN THERAPEUTIC CHANGE

RICHARD GALLAGHER, STEVEN KURTZ,
AND SASHA COLLINS BLACKWELL

For youth enrolled in therapy for disruptive behavior disorders (DBDs), cooperation and effective participation are never easy to obtain, but doing so is especially difficult when the primary targets for change include substance use and abuse, delinquent acts, limited participation in school, or full school refusal. Youth with attention-deficit/hyperactivity disorder (ADHD), oppositional defiant disorder, or conduct disorder rarely experience psychological distress that might motivate them to change. In fact, they are usually requested or mandated to enroll in therapy because they are causing distress to others rather than to themselves.

The problem of engaging adolescents with DBDs is substantial from the outset of treatment. In general, a large percentage (15%–30%) of adolescents do not attend the first appointment (Morrissey-Kane & Prinz, 1999), but the rate of absence is nearly twice as high for adolescents with externalizing disorders (36%) as for internalizing disorders (19%; Pelkonen, Marttunen, Laippala, & Lonnqvist, 2000). Rates of dropout after initiating treatment are also very high for all adolescents, but they are especially high (up to 60%) for those with DBDs.

The actions that result in a diagnosis of a DBD and referral for treatment often provide overt or implicit rewards for the adolescent. Behaviors such as substance use or theft often result in powerful immediate gratification. Other actions result in social advantages. Those teens who use aggression to gain an advantage as opposed to simply in reaction to frustration (instrumental aggression) are rewarded when others give in to their threats and wishes.

Many disruptive behaviors are maintained by powerful positive reinforcement from peers through laughter, attention, and subsequent praise and social conversation (Gifford-Smith, Dodge, Dishion, & McCord, 2005). Moreover, many behaviors such as classroom disruption, temper outbursts when requests are made, physical aggression, and threats to those in authority are negatively reinforced by aiding the adolescent's escape from or avoidance of unpleasant or dull tasks.

As a result of these factors, adolescents can perceive treatment as a process in which they are supposed to forgo many benefits to engage in "appropriate behaviors" in settings in which they have often been highly unsuccessful and not rewarded. The full and willing participation of adolescents with DBDs requires careful thought, concentration, and actions from therapists and therapeutic agents.

The potential harm and the financial, social, and public health costs represented by adolescent treatment dropout are particularly acute when dealing with teens diagnosed with DBDs. Adolescents presenting with ADHD, oppositional defiant disorder, and conduct disorder are far more likely to engage in many problematic actions, including dangerous behaviors that are risky to themselves, physical fights, unprotected and high-risk sexual behaviors, and substance use as well as being at heightened risk of arrest and incarceration. They are also more likely to have poor adult outcomes if left untreated or inadequately treated (Frick & Loney, 1999).

Adolescents with DBDs may be presented with special barriers to treatment because of their condition. Their actions often lead to negative encounters with school officials, the police, juvenile justice authorities, and other agencies that are likely to take constraining actions. One such action often involves mandated treatment, putting treatment in the context of a punishment rather than offering it as a beneficial aid to problem solving. In this context, a teen may develop psychological barriers to even consideration of treatment because it is perceived as an instrument of control rather than as a help. Low motivation to engage in treatment, on the teen's part because the adolescent does not demonstrate distress and on the part of the parents because families often label the behavior as the result of poor moral character as opposed to a mental health issue, is also present. Other systemic barriers include limits in service availability for adolescents in general and, in particular, limits for those with DBDs because service providers are reluctant to take on such challenging cases with the oft ill-founded impression that nothing can be done to significantly alter the trajectory of DBDs after puberty.

THE ELUSIVE ALLIANCE EXPANDED

A full discussion of engagement of adolescents with DBDs must incorporate more than the adolescent because the adolescent, the family, and, at times, other people involved in the adolescent's life need to be targets of therapeutic efforts. The most successful methods for treating DBDs involve the adolescent and the family at least, so engaging the teen and his or her parents is necessary (Boxer & Frick, 2008). Extensive improvements in effectiveness are also obtained when the school, work settings, and the juvenile justice system and other components of the community are engaged in the process (Henggeler et al., 2006). This discussion focuses on means to engage the adolescent and family and other components of the adolescent's system. The means for obtaining support in the teen's school; the adolescent's present or potential work setting; legal authorities, including parole officers, police, and the courts; and the wider community that provides financial support for youth services need to be considered. High levels of success with serious conduct problems have been obtained in programs that have creatively combined the financial and personnel resources of the juvenile justice system, health care system, substance abuse treatment system, and mental health system to form a pool of resources that can adequately and flexibly address the needs of individual teens and their families. Important systemic and political interactions are required to support these efforts to create a comprehensive treatment program that most effectively engages troubled adolescents and their families in therapy (Henggeler et al. 2006).

Defining Engagement

For the purposes of this discussion, we describe full engagement as including consistent attendance, having a positive perception of the relationship with the therapeutic agent or agents, and agreement with the methods and tasks in therapy. We wish to focus on therapeutic agents as opposed to a single therapist because engagement by adolescents and their families is influenced by the relationship with the therapist and the therapeutic setting, including support staff. One important fact about the existing research is that studies have focused on one or two aspects of engagement with the result that our understanding of what variables affect adolescent treatment participation is fragmented and piecemeal. Rather than an overly broad and vague body of knowledge about adolescent treatment engagement, we strive for a more detailed and comprehensive view of the process of engagement. A second important point to consider is that much of the treatment literature has focused on dropout and early termination as opposed to active engagement in the process, so in many ways it is easier to understand what factors drive teens from treatment without a better grasp of what factors can successfully attract teens to treatment and maintain their participation through the process of therapeutic change.

Our discussion of engagement includes variables known to influence the broad range of therapeutic activities, from simple attendance to full and enthusiastic engagement. These variables can be grouped into categories including characteristics of the therapists or the therapeutic settings in which care is provided, actions by the therapist or therapeutic agents before and during therapy that influence participation and cooperation, and characteristics of the adolescents themselves and their families who are presented with the option to pursue treatment.

For adolescents with externalizing disorders, engagement seems to be more critical for therapeutic success. Shirk and Karver (2003) reported that the influence of the therapeutic relationship on treatment outcome was higher in cases with DBDs than in those with other conditions. Their meta-analysis suggested that the combined variables of treatment attendance, positive interactions in therapy, and mutually agreed-on goals and tasks for treatment were most central and crucial in the treatment outcome of children and adolescents with DBDs. Overall, then, results appear to support the idea that engagement with the adolescents with DBDs is truly more difficult but more critical for success than with any other adolescent group.

Once it is clear that engaging adolescents with DBDs is more challenging but also more critical for successful treatment outcome, the active and goal engagement of parents is crucial. It is important to review the variables that enhance the therapeutic alliance for both the adolescent and his or her parents and which are most likely to enhance engagement. The next sections divide these variables into two groups: (a) characteristics of the therapist and therapeutic setting and (b) therapeutic activities and therapeutic structure.

Therapist and Therapeutic Setting Characteristics

In general, psychotherapy effectiveness is fostered by extratherapeutic factors (e.g., spontaneous recovery, the impact of social support), expectancy factors (e.g., whether the patient expects treatment to work), therapeutic techniques, and factors in the patient–therapist relationship, including the level of warmth experienced, the amount of empathy demonstrated, and the alliance formed in treatment to collaboratively use specific therapeutic goals and tasks (Lambert & Barley, 2001). If therapists are perceived as warmer, if they demonstrate more empathic understanding of the patient, and if therapists and patients perceive that there are shared goals with agreed-on tasks to reach those goals, outcomes are more positive (Lambert & Barley, 2001).

It is assumed that success is related to engagement, so it is likewise assumed that engagement with adolescents in general, and those with DBDs in particular, is influenced by the same variables of warmth, understanding, and the collaborative establishment of goals. Unfortunately, very little research has investigated these factors in therapy with teens with DBDs.

Results have clearly indicated that the therapist's characteristics in the relationship contribute to outcome, but research has not provided clear indications about what specific actions, in which order, and in what amount result in the best outcomes for adolescents in general or for those with DBDs in particular. A number of alliance-building strategies have been proposed (DiGiuseppe, Linscott, & Jillian, 1996), and the therapies that use such strategies have been effective (Cunningham & Henggeler, 1999). The exact dosing, timing, and interactive effects of strategies to increase warmth, move toward agreed-on goals, and designate therapeutic tasks remain unclear.

Some support for the importance of therapist characteristics can be found in studies on the therapeutic alliance. Garcia and Weisz (2002) found that therapy relationship problems and money issues were the only two factors reliably predicting treatment dropout. A factor termed *therapy relationship problems*, composed of items reflecting a poor alliance as reported by the child participants, was highly related to early termination. Those who terminated endorsed many concerns about staff competence, including "the therapist did not seem to be doing the right thing," "the therapist did not seem to understand," and "the therapist did not talk about the right problems." Parents of teens who dropped out also endorsed more alliance problems, including the statement "My child's problems were not clearly explained to me." Additionally, parents are more likely to stop treatment if they do not believe that the therapist spent enough time alone with the child or if the therapist did not seem to be helping. Thus, parents who drop out may not fully grasp the rationale for heavy involvement of the family group and do not see the connections between therapist actions and advances in their child's adjustment.

In contrast, alliances are effectively built when the therapist elicits and attends to the adolescent's experience, when the therapist provides validation of the adolescent's perspective by listening to it and clarifying any misunderstandings rather than challenging its accuracy, and when the therapist takes the time to explore the adolescent's subjective experience (Diamond, Liddle, Hogue, & Dakof, 1999; Robbins, Alexander, & Turner, 2000). However, when therapists fail to acknowledge an adolescent's expression of emotion, criticize or express anger with an adolescent's actions, and misunderstand or misconstrue an adolescent's statements, diminished alliance and collaboration often result (Karver et al., 2008; Robbins et al., 2000). Given that adolescents are not always facile with explaining themselves, misunderstandings can occur easily, so therapists need to be patient while requesting repetition of statements and clarification of statements.

A therapist who is able to attend to the story of the adolescent, even when disturbing or antisocial actions are described, is likely to fare better than a therapist who is perceived as judgmental. To maintain the engagement of the parents, the therapist also needs to communicate that the problems bringing a teen into treatment are acknowledged and will be addressed. After providing indications that the teen will be heard, an empathically listening therapist may gain more traction in the treatment of the teen with DBDs. For teens who need to discuss problematic actions, disclosures about delinquent acts and dishonest behaviors, although boastful in nature, are more likely to occur when the adolescent's statements are attended to, when reflection of statements is used, and when the teen is given an opportunity to tell his or her personal history (Fong & Cox, 1983).

Setting characteristics that reduce barriers to treatment facilitate engagement at a significant level. This is demonstrated by one of the most effective innovations in the treatment of serious adolescent conduct disorder: multisystemic therapy (Borduin et al., 1995; Henggeler, Pickrel, Brondino, & Crouch, 1996; Santos, Henggeler, Burns, Arana, & Meisler, 1995). Therapy and supportive assistance to families and teens are provided in ways that eliminate barriers. Services are administered to teens and their families in the home at times that are convenient to the family. Consultation and support are available 24 hours a day, 7 days a week. The combination of these delivery characteristics and therapeutic modalities such as behavior therapy, family communication, and problem-solving training along with collaborative assistance helping families connect with needed educational and health care resources has led to completion rates far in excess of those found in typical community care. The activity of the therapist certainly plays a role in these exemplary results, but it is clear that meeting families in their setting and on their schedule facilitates engagement and alliance.

It is useful to consider the success of multisystemic therapy and its approach. Working with several samples of adolescents presenting with a variety of conduct problems including violation of laws, drug use, truancy, and major family conflicts, Henggeler et al. (2006) established a program in which teens and their families are assigned an intensive case manager who visits with them in their homes and is available on a 24-hour basis to provide consultation and behaviorally based and family systems–based therapeutic services for periods ranging from 6 to 10 weeks (Henggeler et al., 2006).

An essential component of multisystemic therapy is the adoption of a treatment orientation. Training and supervision for therapists stresses collaboration with the family members. Family members are expected to discuss and recognize problems present in the home to engage in problem-oriented discussions and solution-focused actions. Youth and families are not criticized for having the problems revealed in these discussions. The success of this effort suggests that engagement will be facilitated when those in therapy are expected to play a role in change but are not made to experience shame for their dilemmas.

Therapeutic Activity and Structure

The interactions within families play an important role in the development and treatment of DBDs. When conduct disorder or externalizing disorders have been successfully addressed, family treatments are almost always a component of successful efforts. Many factors that seem likely candidates to influence the establishment of an alliance with teens and other family members have yet to be explored. For example, the causal attributions about referral problems brought to treatment by both the teen and his or her parents may have a powerful influence in predicting readiness for change, treatment motivation, help seeking, and participation (Reimers, Wacker, Derby, & Cooper, 1995; Snarr, Slep, & Grande, 2009). However, this raises the question of whether it is preferable to support and not blame the teen and family because disruptive behaviors result from problematic and hard-to-control biological factors, environmental factors, or both, or whether it is more effective to hold the youth, parent, or both responsible for their circumstances by confronting youth or parental thoughts, actions, and emotions that are believed to have led to the problems. The approach taken may affect whether families and teens will engage in treatment with more or less energy.

Engagement in therapeutic interchanges is also affected by therapists' actions. Robbins et al. (2000) studied the responses to varied therapist statements in the initial family session for delinquent adolescents. Therapists encountered fewer defensive statements—including blaming, sarcasm, and disagreements—from family members when their reactions to responses by families included reframing as opposed to statements reflecting content and seeking to clarify or structure the input. Initial sessions using alternative explanations for behaviors in which the adolescent has engaged facilitate a positive impression of treatment for adolescents. This suggests that helping families consider an alternative perspective, as is done in reframing, facilitates productive communication and enhances the adolescent's interest in therapy. This step has a negative effect on fathers, who generally look to therapists to join in criticism of the teen, but if reframing is conducted in balance with clear-cut agendas spelling out the goals of therapy, parents and teens are more likely to willingly participate.

Ford, Millstein, Halpern-Felsher, and Irwin (1997) reported that teens were much more likely to discuss sensitive topics and return to future health care when complete or conditional confidentiality was discussed and explained as compared with when no aspect of confidentiality received consideration. Teens appeared to feel more comfortable when provided with information about how interactions and information would be managed. Contrary to the impression that adolescents would be comfortable only when complete confidentiality was assured, even when conditional confidentiality was described, more adolescents indicated they would seek future health care and disclose sensitive information in comparison to situations in which confidentiality was not discussed at all. This implies that adolescents are more likely to engage when the parameters of treatment are disclosed, even when those parameters include informing parents and involving them in the process, providing teens with an open understanding of the procedures to be used. This appears to suggest that in general, adolescents will engage more effectively if they know how the professionals will operate rather than having a set of vague or unclear expectations.

A number of practical implications can be drawn from this research. The data on confidentiality suggest that clear descriptions of the actions and a collaborative relationship in which the adolescent is informed of what steps might be taken enhance a teen's interest in continuing in and cooperating with treatment. For parents, actions conveying competence and clear plans addressing their complaints about a teen's behavior result in better outcomes. Finally, making certain that all treatment contacts, from receptionists to therapists, behave respectfully, demonstrate competence, enhance convenience, and collaborate in setting goals and therapeutic tasks leads to therapy with more success and greater likelihood of completion. This process is especially important in work with teens with DBDs because comorbid language disorders and learning problems are so frequent that adolescents with disabilities may need time and repeated effort to make themselves understood and to understand others in verbal interactions (Brownlie et al., 2004).

Adolescent and Family Characteristics

Pelkonen et al. (2000) reported about additional factors that impede early engagement. In addition to minority status and low socioeconomic status (SES), their research revealed that older age, male gender, higher numbers of problems, more severe levels of psychopathology, and externalizing disorders were all associated with low levels of early engagement. In fact, externalizing disorders played a major role in failure to attend the initial session. Of adolescents accepted for outpatient treatment, nearly twice as many diagnosed with externalizing disorders failed to report for their first session when compared with those diagnosed with internalizing problems.

Although much has been written about economic, social, and institutional barriers to health care availability, particularly for those in lower SES strata, the precise reasons why families with lower SES status, especially those with minority group membership and lower levels of education, drop out remain unclear. Understanding how these factors contribute to their problems with engagement is important for adolescents with DBDs because these low-SES families make more requests for treatment to address externalizing behaviors than to address internalizing disorders (Halfon & Newacheck, 1999). Data on the acceptability of treatment for conduct disorders may provide some insight. Generally, parents report that they find treatment more acceptable and experience fewer barriers to participation when they perceive therapy to be more relevant and less demanding of time and energy and when they have a positive relationship with the therapist (Kazdin, 2000). In many circumstances, parents with less education may not grasp the relevance of treatment unless it is explained explicitly, so they may not see treatment as relevant unless special efforts are made to enhance their understanding of the therapeutic process. Establishing a positive relationship with the therapist may also be harder for families from minority or poverty-level backgrounds because there may be mismatches between a family's background and that of the therapist (Whaley & Davis, 2007). Finally, families from lower SES backgrounds may have less time and energy to devote to treatment because of the demands of their day-to-day survival. A number of barriers to obtaining services are present for families with low financial resources because of limited insurance coverage; problems in transportation, especially in nonurban areas; and difficulties obtaining child care while engaging in therapy work with the adolescent (Owens et al., 2002; Pumariega, Glover, Holzer, & Nguyen, 1998).

Successful engagement is likely to require special attention to family background, the level of psychopathology present, the family's comprehension of the proposed treatment, and the level of demands placed on the family in relation to their circumstances and daily responsibilities (Kazdin, 2000). Respect for diversity, understanding a family's culture and orientation to therapy and psychopathology, clear behavioral contracts, and enhanced explanations of how therapy will influence the referral problems will likely go a long way to improve impressions of acceptability, which, in turn, will likely foster engagement (Dakof, Tejeda, & Liddle, 2001; Diamond, Diamond & Liddle, 2000).

The family's and adolescent's motivational set and perception of the referral problem also influence engagement. Dakof et al. (2001) reported that only the age of the adolescent discriminated between engaged and not-engaged teens in a drug treatment, whereas conduct disorder therapy, and economic, ethnic, and educational factors had no influence. Older adolescents were more likely to participate in at least four sessions. If parents perceived that their teens had serious externalizing problems, it was more likely for the parents and teens to participate. Highly engaged teens had parents who typically had higher educational aspirations than did the parents of nonengaged teens. Parents who perceived more problems while holding out hope for the future of their teens were more likely to participate and to have their children participate.

Parent attributions as to the causes of referral problems are important to consider. Parents who attribute their teens' problems to stable, internal characteristics that are out of the parents' control are much less likely to seek treatment or become engaged in the treatment process when their children are enrolled (Morrissey-Kane & Prinz, 1999). The type of treatment interacts predictably with parental attributions. Parents who believe the teen's characteristics are the source of the problem are not likely to accept behavioral interventions requiring their own participation (Reimers et al., 1995), but they may be willing to accept medication interventions or individual psychotherapy that they believe will have an impact on their child's characteristics.

SPECIAL CONSIDERATIONS FOR ADHD

A full consideration of adolescent ADHD is far beyond the scope of this chapter. However, several important points require discussion. First, when considering engagement of adolescents diagnosed with ADHD, the nature of the disorders should be kept in mind. The core symptoms of ADHD often interfere with engagement in the therapeutic process from beginning to end. Inattentiveness, a component of at least two subtypes making up the majority of cases, often results in adolescents being unaware of the negative consequences generated by their condition (Robin, 1998). Teens with ADHD may not be motivated to use treatment to change because they are inattentive to negative feedback about the impact of a lack of attention on learning in school performance and the impact of distractibility, impulsivity, and restlessness on social relations.

Engagement in treatment often requires teens to use a slow, deliberate, and careful review of the details of interactions and one's own actions followed by careful consideration of numerous alternative means to overcome problems. However, such slow consideration is not an easy task for a motorically restless, quick-to-respond youth with ADHD (Bitsakou, Psychogiou, Thompson, & Sonuga-Barke, 2009; Marco et al., 2009). Third, despite all the appearances to the contrary, those with ADHD have distinct difficulties controlling their actions, especially their attention to detail, their level of arousal and activity, and the appropriateness of their responses so that they may not be capable of gaining a handle on the means to alter the responses that led to their treatment referral.

Engagement for effective treatments is especially important for teens with ADHD. The role of therapy in changing the core conditions of the disorder—impulsivity, hyperactivity, and inattention—has very little support no matter what type, although it is continually tried and recommended in clinical practice (see Harris & Rice, 1997). Neither comprehensive review of treatments completed in the past 2 decades has found either an efficacious or a probably efficacious treatment effect for any form of individual therapy or behavioral therapy that incorporates parent or school interventions for teens (Pelham & Fabiano, 2008; Pelham, Wheeler, & Chronis, 1998). Caution is strongly advised against overapplication of techniques with empirical support for other DBD conditions to the treatment of ADHD. Many of these efforts, including anger management, social problem solving, and impulse control training, have not worked well with ADHD (see Barkley, Edwards, Laneri, Fletcher, & Metevia, 2001).

Given the likely neurobiological underpinning of ADHD, engagement in several therapeutic efforts is suggested, including consideration of medication treatment. The adolescent's status in contrast to younger children needs to be considered for this effort. A teen who is being presented with an option for medication treatment for the first time needs to be included in discussions about benefits and side effects more extensively than do children to obtain compliance and consistent self- or other administration. Adolescents are much more likely to want to control themselves and be in charge of their lives rather than rely on medication as a means of control. Considering themselves as people not fully in charge of their lives runs counter to adolescents' emerging self-direction and independence. Therefore, more extensive and collaborative discussions to motivate continued use of medication will likely be required.

Despite the cautions described, therapeutic engagement for three goals can be strongly encouraged. Requesting that an adolescent participate in medication treatment makes good sense. Addressing comorbid conditions is also reasonable. Many teens with ADHD will have other disorders, including other DBDs, learning disorders, and, often, anxiety disorders. Continued engagement can be enhanced by collaboratively developing and altering the goals to address the comorbid conditions or impairments while validating the teen's difficulties. Finally, an adolescent can be requested to participate in a time-limited effort to cope effectively with ADHD, with a particular focus on increasing cooperative interactions to reduce conflict in the family and attain better school success (Robin, 1998). Some promise has been shown with interventions improving academic performance with young adolescents through the collaborative efforts of therapists, parents, and teachers (Langberg, Epstein, Urbanowitz, Simon, & Graham, 2008), suggesting that engagement strategies that incorporate not only interdisciplinary collaboration but active collaboration with the familial members of the treatment team are warranted.

PRACTICAL GUIDELINES FOR THERAPEUTIC ENGAGEMENT

On the basis of this review of research, a number of practical steps can be suggested. If considered from the initial contact, some of these recommended actions will appear obvious. This may, however, be somewhat deceptive because often what might seem an obvious clinical step may also be one that is overlooked. In this section, we address both seemingly obvious and more nuanced intervention steps to foster engagement of the teen and the family. For many of these actions, the sequence in which they are applied may be as important as their overall application.

Steps Following Initial Contact

It would be useful to help the adolescent and family better understand and develop realistic expectations about therapy because many do not know what to expect in therapy (DiGiuseppe et al., 1996). Overcoming negative expectations and impressions about therapy from pop culture and substituting these with more positive and optimistic goals and beliefs about treatment and about the nature of the problems being addressed is critical for early session attendance and receptivity to therapists and treatment. Frequently, this change in expectations must begin from the outset, even before the first session, because the window for engaging the adolescent and family may be not only small but narrowing. Over the years, pretherapy preparation, such as brief brochures sent to family members, has been found to be useful in successfully encouraging the participation of people who have formerly underused therapy services, including low-income adults, minority individuals, and candidates for group therapy (Yalom, 1995). With technological advances, depending on the clients, a link to a website with a video or audio description of therapy might be appealing to teens who are used to wired communications.

Invitations for All Relevant Parties and the Effective Structure of First Meetings

Efforts to develop and take steps to involve all members of the family in treatment should be designed. Research has indicated that engagement of teens in therapy requires steps to engage not only the teen but other family members as well. Although the adolescent may be the identified patient, it is especially the case when the referral stems from DBDs that the entire family and, in fact, the broader macro system are clients. The structure of the initial contact should take into account that members of the family may have different motivations for change and that the family as a whole may be experiencing a high degree of conflict. Assuming that many families with teens diagnosed with DBDs perceive themselves to be in intractable and mutually painful and coercive relationships (Robbins et al., 2000), structuring initial interactions to minimize repetitions of these patterns in the therapy space is highly important. Scheduling separate times to meet with and gather data from the teen and the family (teen first) after a brief initial meeting is recommended (Sarles, 1998; Sperling, 1997).

Adolescents, and in particular those with DBDs, are not likely to consider themselves or their behaviors problematic. Rather, they are likely to be tuned into the conflicts they experience. Gaining an empathic understanding of their circumstances and beliefs about why problems are present, with attention paid to the amount and nature of conflict and irritation experienced, can provide information that motivates the teen to participate. An adolescent who is uncomfortable will likely respond positively to a treatment rationale designed to lessen the conflicts producing discomfort. Similarly, parents worried about their teen's future will likely engage more swiftly if the problems being addressed are cast as consequences of conflicts rather than innate shortcomings on the part of the adolescent.

Given the strength of negative responses provoked by many disruptive behaviors, it is important to explore how the adolescent views such behaviors. If the teen believes that the behaviors are beyond his or her responsibility, treatment that offers the promise of decreasing external stressors can facilitate swift and effective engagement. Parents who believe that the adolescent's behaviors are the product of internal, dispositional characteristics will also be less likely to engage in family-based treatment. Empathic listening and validating concerns while respectfully dispelling faulty attributions is a key to effective treatment engagement of adolescents and parents.

Developing Treatment Plans for Differing Change Readiness

Parents and teens often enter treatment with apparent differences in their readiness for clinical change. Prochaska and DiClemente (1983, 1984) proposed the transtheoretical model of change to explain how patients develop a readiness for clinical intervention. Although a complete treatment of this theory is beyond the scope of this chapter, it is important that the initial contract for treatment match the level of readiness for change of each party (Treasure et al., 1999) and that any disparity between parental readiness for change and that of the adolescent is addressed.

Often, what seems to be a gulf in the relative readiness for clinical change and a lack of agreement about the need for change may actually be rooted in differing understanding of what constitutes a problem, what needs to change, and who is expected to be involved in change actions. To suggest that adolescents with DBDs lack motivation for significant change is not only erroneous in many cases, but risks doing a great disservice to the teen and family by ignoring the adolescent's desire for problems to be solved and for things to be different. In fact, the therapist can formulate a treatment sequence that is aimed at reducing interpersonal tension desired by the adolescent (perhaps by asking parents to alter their responses to the teen) in trade for the teen's reducing the disruptive behaviors, which is desired by parents.

A combination of motivational interviewing techniques and appropriate pressure from external sources can be used to move parties along the path of change. From the very beginning of treatment, fostering agreement about the negative consequences of the conflicts experienced by all members of the family provides a common basis for engaging in goal-directed pursuits that avoid the traps of blame assignment and mutual recriminations. Agreeing that everyone desires change, even if those changes seem mutually in conflict, permits the therapist to focus on methods for how desired changes can be achieved rather than what they should be.

Parents may balk at the suggestion that they and the adolescent might need to change. In such cases, reviewing the benefits and costs of maintaining the status quo rather than mutual change can prove useful and facilitate engagement. The treatment plan should also be well delineated, detailing the expectations for all members because participation may be limited in direct relation to their sense that treatment is generally vague, too indirect in guiding the adolescent to address behaviors that the parents see as highly threatening to their child's life course, and too nonspecific in spelling out what actions parents can take to facilitate change. Alliances and level of engagement seem to be best when participants know and agree with the proposed goals of therapy, the therapeutic tasks that are planned, and the actions that will be required to complete the therapeutic tasks (DiGiuseppe, Leaf, & Linscott, 1993).

The scope and nature of early therapeutic tasks require careful consideration. It should be remembered that many teens with DBDs experience difficulty with academic demands and may perceive tasks that are similar to schoolwork such as requiring them to write down problems and potential solutions as aversive. Thus, tasks and homework assignments need to be negotiated. When they are not fulfilled, exploring the barriers to completion is preferred over scolding the adolescent. After a bond and a collaborative relationship are established, exploring barriers to completion of therapeutic tasks can lead to joint work to avoid or overcome those barriers.

Establishing and Maintaining Alliances
With the Adolescent and Parents

Once treatment has been initiated, empathic listening, negotiating agreed-on goals, collaborating on the completion of therapeutic tasks, and remaining open to exploring disruptions in the working relationship are all essential to establishing and maintaining treatment engagement. The therapist should avoid efforts to "act like an adolescent." Adolescents are adept at recognizing disingenuous efforts at connection and engagement. Teens with DBDs, many of whom have extensive experience with social rejection, are especially ready to reject insincere or superficial efforts to induce them to participate.

Making an effort to understand the adolescent's interests and ways of relating through reflective listening and questioning can often lead him or her into an effective relationship. Therapists also need to avoid becoming distressed with the details of the actions and behaviors enacted by the adolescent. Adolescents in treatment should be rewarded for the positive steps they take, not corrected for all missteps along the way. This is an important behavior to model for the family, and it is hoped that the teen will eventually reciprocate.

It is essential for the therapist to keep in mind that true engagement is based on activity and not merely attendance. The fact that a teen continues to attend sessions does not in itself mean therapeutic intervention is taking place. Teens who find the therapist to be supportive, pleasant, and nonjudgmental may wish to attend sessions but not engage in the behavior-changing goals of treatment. Adolescents with DBDs benefit not only from support but also from clear and consistent encouragement to modify their behaviors and achieve personal goals. Graduated assignments that require minimal effort at first with gradual increases in time and effort demands should be used. In effect, it is helpful to consider cooperative effort as a "feared" response that requires the use of systematic desensitization to increase the teen's tolerance for providing effort and time.

Maintaining Alliances During Termination

Although this may seem controversial, for the true goals of engagement to be met, adolescents should have a say in when active treatment ends. A negotiated hold to treatment may make the teen more comfortable and amenable to seeking services in the future even if and when the therapist believes termination is premature. Although lack of engagement and early dropout are associated with significantly worse outcomes, there are no significant differences in adolescents and other patients who complete most of a treatment sequence compared with those who complete a full sequence (Luk, Staiger, & Mathai, 2001). Treatment termination of an engaged adolescent offers the promise of returning to treatment and framing problems as solvable, whereas there is ample evidence to suggest that termination of the adolescent without engagement is simply another term for dropout without consideration of return.

PRAGMATIC RECOMMENDATIONS FOR ASSESSING THE WORKING ALLIANCE AND ENGAGEMENT

Assessing the therapeutic alliance as treatment progresses is both necessary and valuable. Formal assessment of the alliance can be planned at intervals in treatment to help the therapist and family understand where there are problems requiring attention. Such assessment allows the treatment participants to gauge not only the quality of interpersonal relationships between the various family members and the therapist and how well the therapist understands them, but also the perception of collaboration in formulating and enacting the goals and tasks of treatment. A measure demonstrating great promise is the adolescent adaptation of the Working Alliance Inventory (Florsheim, Shotorbani, Guest-Warnick, Barratt, & Hwang, 2000). This measure is relatively short, has been used in repeated assessments with adolescents with DBDs, and provides information tied to treatment outcome, in that higher scores predict better treatment results (Florsheim et al., 2000).

SUMMARY

Efforts to gain insights from recent research on adolescent psychotherapy have led to some broad conclusions about helping adolescents with DBDs engage in therapeutic change. Factors influencing engagement include personal characteristics of the adolescent and family, characteristics of the therapist and therapeutic setting, and specific therapist actions.

Of particular import when working with adolescents diagnosed with DBDs is the therapist's willingness to convey warmth in the face of antagonistic and sometimes antisocial behaviors. The ability to validate the teen and family members without validating the problematic behaviors and conflicts that precipitated treatment is an essential element to affective engagement with DBD diagnosed adolescents.

Therapists using empathic listening, negotiation of treatment roles, and an openness to discussing the quality of the therapist–family relationship have adolescent patients who are more engaged and make more progress. Guidelines generated from the research review and sound clinical literature suggest that efforts to enhance engagement and increase the power of the alliance between therapy agents and their clients should be incorporated in all stages of therapy from initial contact through termination and follow-up. Those guidelines emphasize a number of steps. Therapists are encouraged to make the process of treatment clear to all participants; to review each family member's understanding of the problems, their origins, and the willingness to collaborate in negotiating treatment goals and tasks; and to respect all participants while challenging the impact of disruptive actions and counterproductive responses.

Special consideration for the impact of ADHD on therapeutic efforts is suggested in recognition that neurobiological factors make consistent behavior change difficult to attain and maintain. Assessment of the working alliance throughout the course of treatment is highly recommended.

Finally, a considerable amount of empirical work remains to be done before we can truly understand and improve the effectiveness of therapeutic interventions in the treatment of DBDs. We are at an early stage in our understanding of the change process and in particular of what will interest and motivate youth with attentional and behavioral limitations. We have yet to discover what exact actions in which sequence and in what dose will prove optimal in increasing the participation of reluctant teen patients.

For adolescents with DBDs, the most prevalent of youth disorders, such research efforts are critical if we are to diminish the costs of these disorders to the adolescent, the family, and society at large.

REFERENCES

Barkley, R. A., Edwards, G., Laneri, M., Fletcher, K., & Metevia, L. (2001). The efficacy of problem-solving communication training alone, behavior management training alone, and their combination for parent–adolescent conflict in teenagers with ADHD and ODD. *Journal of Consulting and Clinical Psychology, 69*, 926–941. doi:10.1037/0022-006X.69.6.926

Bitsakou, P., Psychogiou, L., Thompson, M., & Sonuga-Barke, E. J. S. (2009). Delay aversion in attention deficit/hyperactivity disorder: An empirical investigation of the broader phenotype. *Neuropsychologia, 47*, 446–456. doi:10.1016/j.neuropsychologia.2008.09.015

Borduin, C. M., Mann, B. J., Cone, L. T., Henggeler, S. W., Fucci, B. R., Blaske, D. M., & Williams, R. A. (1995). Multisystemic treatment of serious juvenile offenders: Long-term prevention of criminality and violence. *Journal of Consulting and Clinical Psychology, 63*, 569–578. doi:10.1037/0022-006X.63.4.569

Boxer, P., & Frick, P. J. (2008). Treating conduct problems, aggression, and antisocial behavior in children and adolescents: An integrated view. In R. C. Steele, T. D. Elkin, & M. C. Roberts (Eds.), *Handbook of evidence-based therapies for children and adolescents* (pp. 241–259). New York, NY: Springer. doi:10.1007/978-0-387-73691-4_14

Brownlie, E. B., Beitchman, J. H., Escobar, M., Young, A., Atkinson, L., Johnson, C., . . . Douglas, L. (2004). Early language impairment and young adult delinquent and aggressive behavior. *Journal of Abnormal Child Psychology, 32*, 453–467. doi:10.1023/B:JACP. 0000030297.91759.74

Cunningham, P. B., & Henggeler, S. W. (1999). Engaging multiproblem families in treatment: Lessons learned throughout the development of multisystemic therapy. *Family Process, 38*, 265–281. doi:10.1111/j.1545-5300.1999.00265.x

Dakof, G. A., Tejeda, M., & Liddle, H. A. (2001). Predictors of engagement in adolescent drug abuse treatment. *Journal of the American Academy of Child & Adolescent Psychiatry, 40*, 274–281. doi:10.1097/00004583-200103000-00006

Diamond, G. M., Diamond, G. S., & Liddle, H. A. (2000). The therapist-patient alliance in family-based therapy for adolescents. *Journal of Clinical Psychology, 56,* 1037–1050.

Diamond, G. M., Liddle, H. A., Hogue, A., & Dakof, G. A. (1999). Alliance-building interventions with adolescents in family therapy: A process study *Psychotherapy: Theory, Research, Practice, Training, 36,* 355–368.

DiGiuseppe, R., Leaf, R., & Linscott, J. (1993). The therapeutic relationship in rational-emotive therapy: Some preliminary data. *Journal of Rational-Emotive & Cognitive-Behavior Therapy, 11,* 223–233. doi:10.1007/BF01089777

DiGiuseppe, R., Linscott, J., & Jilton, R. (1996). Developing the therapeutic alliance in child-adolescent psychotherapy. *Applied & Preventive Psychology, 5,* 85–100. doi:10.1016/S0962-1849(96)80002-3

Florsheim, P., Shotorbani, S., Guest-Warnick, G., Barratt, T., & Hwang, W. C. (2000). Role of the working alliance in the treatment of delinquent boys in community-based programs. *Journal of Clinical Child Psychology, 29,* 94–107. doi:10.1207/S15374424jccp2901_10

Fong, M., & Cox, B. G. (1983). Trust as an underlying dynamic in the counseling process: How clients test trust. *Personnel and Guidance Journal, 62,* 163–166.

Ford, C. A., Millstein, S. G., Halpern-Felsher, B. L., & Irwin, C. E., Jr. (1997). Influence of physician confidentiality assurances on adolescents' willingness to disclose information and seek future health care: A randomized controlled trial. *JAMA, 278,* 1029–1034. doi:10.1001/jama.278.12.1029

Frick, P. J., & Loney, B. (1999). Outcomes of children with oppositional defiant disorder and conduct disorder. In H. C. Quay & A. E. Hogan (Eds.), *Handbook of disruptive behavior disorders* (pp. 507–524). New York, NY: Plenum Press.

Garcia, J. A., & Weisz, J. R. (2002). When youth mental health care stops: Therapeutic relationship problems and other reasons for ending youth outpatient treatment. *Journal of Consulting and Clinical Psychology, 70,* 439–443. doi:10.1037/0022-006X.70.2.439

Gifford-Smith, M., Dodge, K. A., Dishion, T. J., & McCord, J. (2005). Peer influence in children and adolescents: Crossing the bridge from developmental to intervention science. *Journal of Abnormal Child Psychology, 33,* 255–265. doi:10.1007/s10802-005-3563-7

Halfon, N., & Newacheck, P. W. (1999). Prevalence and impact of parent-reported disabling mental health conditions among U.S. children. *Journal of the American Academy of Child & Adolescent Psychiatry, 38,* 600–609. doi:10.1097/00004583-199905000-00023

Harris, G. T., & Rice, M. E. (1997). Mentally disordered offenders: What research says about effective service. In C. D. Webster & M. A. Johnson (Eds.), *Impulsivity: Theory, assessment, and treatment* (pp. 361–393). New York, NY: Guilford Press.

Henggeler, S. W., Halliday-Boykins, C. A., Cunningham, P. B., Randall, J., Shapiro, S. B., & Chapman, J. E. (2006). Juvenile drug court: Enhancing outcomes by integrating evidence-based treatments. *Journal of Consulting and Clinical Psychology, 74,* 42–54. doi:10.1037/0022-006X.74.1.42

Henggeler, S. W., Pickrel, S. G., Brondino, M. J., & Crouch, J. L. (1996). Eliminating (almost) treatment dropout of substance abusing or dependent delinquents through home-based multisystemic therapy. *American Journal of Psychiatry, 153,* 427–428.

Karver, M., Shirk, S., Handelsman, J. B., Fields, S., Crisp, H., Gudmundsen, G., & McMakin, D. (2008). Relationship process in youth psychology: Measuring alliance, alliance-building behaviors, and client involvement. *Journal of Emotional and Behavioral Disorders, 16,* 15–28. doi:10.1177/1063426607312536

Kazdin, A. E. (2000). Perceived barriers to treatment participation and treatment acceptability among antisocial children and their families. *Journal of Child and Family Studies, 9,* 157–174. doi:10.1023/A:1009414904228

Lambert, M. J., & Barley, D. E. (2001). Research summary on the therapeutic relationship and psychotherapy outcome. *Psychotherapy: Theory, Research, Practice, Training, 38*, 357–361.

Langberg, J. M., Epstein, J. N., Urbanowicz, C. M., Simon, J. O., & Graham, A. J. (2008). Efficacy of an organization skills intervention to improve the academic functioning of students with attention-deficit/hyperactivity disorder. *School Psychology Quarterly, 23*, 407–417. doi:10.1037/1045-3830.23.3.407

Luk, E. S., Staiger, P., & Mathai, J. (2001). Evaluation of outcome in child and adolescent mental healthcare services: Children with persistent conduct problems. *Clinical Child Psychology and Psychiatry, 6*, 109–124. doi:10.1177/1359104501006001009

Marco, R., Miranda, A., Schlotz, W., Melia, A., Mulligan, A., Muller, U., . . . Edmund, J. S. (2009). Delay and reward choice in ADHD: An experimental test of the role of delay aversion. *Neuropsychology, 23*, 367–380. doi:10.1037/a0014914

Morrissey-Kane, E., & Prinz, R. J. (1999). Engagement in child and adolescent treatment: The role of parental cognitions and attributions. *Clinical Child and Family Psychology Review, 2*, 183–198. doi:10.1023/A:1021807106455

Owens, P. L., Hoagwood, K., Horowitz, S. M., Leaf, P. J., Poduska, J. M., Kellam, S. G., & Ialongo, N. S. (2002). Barriers to children's mental health services. *Journal of the American Academy of Child & Adolescent Psychiatry, 41*, 731–738. doi:10.1097/00004583-200206000-00013

Pelham, W. E., & Fabiano, G. A. (2008). Evidence-based psychosocial treatments for attention deficit/hyperactivity disorder. *Journal of Clinical Child and Adolescent Psychology, 37*, 184–214. doi:10.1080/15374410701818681

Pelham, W. E., Wheeler, T., & Chronis, A. (1998). Empirically supported psychosocial treatments for attention deficit hyperactivity disorder. *Journal of Clinical Child Psychology, 27*, 190–205. doi:10.1207/s15374424jccp2702_6

Pelkonen, M., Marttunen, M., Laippala, P., & Lonnqvist, J. (2000). Factors associated with early dropout from adolescent psychiatric outpatient treatment. *Journal of the American Academy of Child & Adolescent Psychiatry, 39*, 329–336. doi:10.1097/00004583-200003000-00015

Prochaska, J. O., & DiClemente, C. C. (1983). Stages and processes of self-change of smoking: Toward an integrative model of change. *Journal of Consulting and Clinical Psychology, 51*, 390–395. doi:10.1037/0022-006X.51.3.390

Prochaska, J. O., & DiClemente, C. C. (1984). *The transtheoretical approach: Crossing the boundaries of traditional therapy.* Homewood, IL: Dow Jones-Irvin.

Pumariega, A. J., Glover, S., Holzer, C. E., & Nguyen, H. (1998). Utilization of mental health services in a tri-ethnic sample of adolescents. *Community Mental Health Journal, 34*, 145–156. doi:10.1023/A:1018788901831

Reimers, T. M., Wacker, D. P., Derby, K. M., & Cooper, L. J. (1995). Relation between parental attributions and the acceptability of behavioral treatments for their child's behavior problems. *Behavioral Disorders, 20*, 171–178.

Robin, A. L. (1998). *ADHD in adolescents: Diagnosis and treatment.* New York, NY: Guilford Press.

Robbins, M. S., Alexander, J. F., & Turner, C. W. (2000). Disrupting defensive family interactions in family therapy with delinquent adolescents. *Journal of Family Psychology, 14*, 688–701. doi:10.1037/0893-3200.14.4.688

Santos, A. B., Henggeler, S. W., Burns, B. J., Arana, G. W., & Meisler, N. (1995). Research on field-based services: Models for reform in the delivery of mental health care to populations with complex clinical problems. *American Journal of Psychiatry, 152*, 1111–1123.

Sarles, R. M. (1998). Individual psychotherapy with adolescents. In H. S. Ghuman & R. M. Sarles (Eds.), *Handbook of child and adolescent outpatient treatment* (pp. 259–263). Philadelphia, PA: Brunner/Mazel.

Shirk, S. R., & Karver, M. (2003). Prediction of treatment outcome from relationship variables in child and adolescent therapy: A meta-analytic review. *Journal of Consulting and Clinical Psychology, 71*, 452–464. doi:10.1037/0022-006X.71.3.452

Snarr, J. D., Slep, A. M. S., & Grande, V. P. (2009). Validation of a new self-report measure of parental attributions. *Psychological Assessment, 21*, 390–401. doi:10.1037/a0016331

Sperling, E. (1997). The collateral treatment of parents with children and adolescents in psychotherapy. *Child and Adolescent Psychiatric Clinics of North America, 6*, 81–95.

Treasure, J. L., Katzman, M., Schmidt, U., Troop, N., Todd, G., & de Silva, P. (1999). Engagement and outcome in the treatment of bulimia nervosa: First phase of a sequential design comparing motivation enhancement therapy and cognitive behavioural therapy. *Behaviour Research and Therapy, 37*, 405–418. doi:10.1016/S0005-7967(98)00149-1

Whaley, A. L., & Davis, K. E. (2007). Cultural competence and evidence-based practice in mental health services: A complementary perspective. *American Psychologist, 62*, 563–574. doi:10.1037/0003-066X.62.6.563

Yalom, I. D. (1995). *The theory and practice of group psychotherapy*. New York, NY: Basic Books.

6

ENGAGEMENT OF ADOLESCENTS IN COGNITIVE–BEHAVIORAL THERAPY FOR OBSESSIVE–COMPULSIVE DISORDER

ANNALISE CARON AND JOANNA ROBIN

The quality of the therapeutic alliance has been shown to be an important predictor of adolescent treatment outcome (e.g., Shirk & Karver, 2003). For adolescents with obsessive–compulsive disorder (OCD), commitment to cognitive–behavioral therapy (CBT) can often be tenuous, given the anxiety-provoking nature of some of the treatment components (e.g., exposure). Moreover, children with OCD often have a history of being misunderstood or reprimanded by parents, teachers, and other adults, which makes them wary of therapists' intentions. Thus, in this population, the need for explicit attention to engagement of the adolescents and their families is particularly important to maintain regular attendance and prevent premature treatment dropout. In this chapter, we briefly review cognitive–behavioral techniques used in treating OCD and then outline six important clinical engagement strategies for working with adolescents and their families. Although many of the engagement strategies discussed have already been incorporated into empirically supported cognitive–behavioral treatments, the purpose of this chapter is to elaborate on them in more detail and discuss their application in clinical practice.

OCD is a chronic and debilitating condition that often initially presents during childhood or adolescence. Although OCD was once thought to be rare during childhood, recent epidemiological studies have suggested that prevalence rates increase with age and range from 1% to 4% in children and adolescents (Douglass, Moffitt, Dar, McGee, & Silva, 1995; Heyman et al., 2003; Maina, Albert, Bogetto, & Ravizza, 1999). Approximately one third to one half of adults with OCD experienced its onset during childhood or adolescence (Geller, 2006). Increased awareness of the prevalence of the disorder before adulthood has led to a wide expansion of research and clinical attention to the development and refinement of empirically supported treatments for OCD in youth.

Both CBT using exposure plus response prevention (E–RP) and medication treatment with either selective serotonin reuptake inhibitors or the tricyclic antidepressant clomipramine have proven effective, to differing degrees, in the treatment of pediatric OCD (for a review of CBT, see Turner, 2006; for a review of medication trials, see Geller et al., 2003). In open and randomized controlled trials, CBT has been associated with clinically significant reductions in OCD symptoms for children and adolescents, with mean symptom reductions in the range of 40% to 66% (Benazon, Ager, & Rosenberg, 2002; Bolton & Perrin, 2008; de Haan, Hoogduin, Buitelaar, & Keijsers, 1998; Piacentini, Bergman, Jacobs, McCracken, & Kretchman, 1994; Pediatric OCD Treatment Study [POTS] Team, 2004; Waters, Barrett, & March, 2001). On the basis of these findings, as well as trials of medication alone (e.g., March, Biederman, & Wolkow, 1998) and CBT with adjunctive medication as needed (e.g., Barrett, Healy-Farrell, & March, 2004), treatment guidelines have been developed to help practitioners choose appropriate interventions for children on the basis of age and severity of OCD symptoms (e.g., American Academy of Child and Adolescent Psychiatry, 1998).

Of particular importance in solidifying these treatment guidelines for youth was the groundbreaking POTS (POTS Team, 2004). This multisite randomized controlled trial was notable for both its design (CBT vs. sertraline vs. CBT plus sertraline vs. placebo) and for its large sample size of 112 children and adolescents. Most prior studies had been open trials that did not directly examine the efficacy of CBT versus medication (e.g., Piacentini et al., 2002) or randomized controlled trials with smaller sample sizes (Barrett et al., 2004; de Haan et al., 1998). Findings indicated that youth treated with CBT alone or CBT in combination with medication fared better than youth treated with medication alone or placebo. Remission rates were numerically higher for youth in the CBT plus medication group (53.6%) than for those in the CBT-alone group (39.3%), but these remission rates were not statistically different from each other. However, both groups that received CBT treatment had remission rates that were significantly better than those for treatment with medication alone (21.4%) or placebo (3.6%). This confirmed previous expert consensus guidelines suggesting that CBT (with or without medication) should be the first-line treatment for children and adolescents with OCD. For more information regarding treatment algorithms for clinical decision making and managing treatment of mental health comorbidities, see *Practice Parameters for the Assessment and Treatment of Children and Adolescents With Obsessive-Compulsive Disorder* (American Academy of Child and Adolescent Psychiatry, 1998) and the briefly summarized recommendations in March and Benton (2007).

Even with the positive aforementioned treatment outcome data and clear treatment guidelines for children and adolescents to start with CBT, engagement and maintenance of youth in CBT for OCD is a difficult undertaking. Not only must the clinician be well trained in E–RP techniques, but he or she must also be sensitive to the many issues that make engaging with and adhering to treatment difficult. In this chapter, we focus specifically on engaging adolescents in treatment for OCD because their particular developmental stage and emerging needs for autonomy may affect the therapeutic alliance and their willingness to engage in what can be anxiety-provoking and arduous treatment (DiGiuseppe, Linscott, & Jilton, 1996). Before discussing six important strategies for enhancing adolescent engagement in treatment, we briefly review general information about OCD in youth and components of cognitive–behavioral treatment for pediatric OCD.

COGNITIVE–BEHAVIORAL TECHNIQUES FOR OCD IN YOUTH

OCD in youth presents with a gradual (and frequently misdiagnosed) onset and chronic course. OCD symptoms include recurrent obsessions (i.e., intrusive thoughts, images, or impulses) and compulsions (i.e., ritualized behavioral responses) that are distressing to the child or adolescent. These symptoms are associated with negative affect, typically anxiety. Some of the more likely obsessions during childhood include fears of contamination or harm and hyperfocus on numbers, symmetry, or exactness (e.g., Franklin et al., 1998). Although OCD symptom profiles appear to be relatively congruent across the life span, with symptom dimensions in childhood similar to those described in adult populations (Stewart et al., 2007), there is some evidence of developmental differences that may emerge around adolescence (e.g., religious and sexual obsessions becoming more prominent; Geller et al., 2001).

Although the presence of both obsessions and compulsions is not required to meet diagnostic criteria for OCD, typically compulsions serve to reduce the anxiety or distress associated with obsessions (American Psychiatric Association, 2000). However, compulsions themselves can be highly distressing as well because of their tendency to interfere with daily life activities and cause functional impairment with schoolwork, peer relationships, and family life (e.g., Renshaw, Steketee, & Chambless, 2005). Unlike with adults, youth need not find their symptoms to be "excessive and unreasonable" to receive a diagnosis of OCD (American Psychiatric Association, 2000), although they often do have this insight. Obsessions and compulsions tend to wax and wane over time, which can be confusing to parents and children who may think the condition has improved, only to have it reemerge or intensify later.

COMPONENTS OF CBT FOR YOUTH OCD

Although how and when the techniques are presented vary by manual (e.g., March & Mulle, 1998; Piacentini, Langley, & Roblek, 2007), cognitive–behavioral approaches for youth with OCD tend to have five general components. These are some form of (a) psychoeducation; (b) creation of an OCD stimulus hierarchy; (c) cognitive techniques, anxiety management techniques, or both; (d) E–RP; and (e) family or parental involvement. Clinicians implement these treatment components only after a thorough assessment and evaluation of the adolescent's symptoms to confirm the OCD diagnosis, as well as an assessment of the family's response to these symptoms. Throughout all of these stages of treatment, the clinician's attention to engaging the family is important, part and parcel of good treatment. From our perspective, without developing an alliance with the adolescent, these treatment components have little hope of being implemented because they require hard work and maintained endurance of discomfort on the part of the patient.

Depending on the clinician's approach, psychoeducation can vary from a uniquely cognitive explanation of OCD and its treatment (Williams, Salkovskis, Forrester, & Allsopp, 2002) to conceptualizing OCD as a neuropsychiatric illness (e.g., "brain hiccup"; March & Mulle, 1998) to very brief psychoeducation solely about treatment content itself (Bolton & Perrin, 2008). Cognitive and anxiety management techniques include strategies to externalize and detach from the OCD (i.e., "OCD is not me"), cognitive restructuring to confront and manage OCD thoughts, coping self-statements, and sometimes other more traditional anxiety management strategies (e.g., relaxation, diaphragmatic breathing). Family involvement in treatment also varies but typically includes psychoeducation, clarifying parents' role in the adolescent's symptoms and treatment, family problem solving, and reward strategies. See March and Mulle (1998; March & Benton, 2007) or Piacentini et al. (2007) for a more detailed description of treatment components.

The main mechanism of treatment action is assumed to be E–RP, that is, the combination of exposure to the triggers for obsessions while preventing acting on compulsive urges (e.g., rituals) to reduce anxiety or distress.

Over time, the adolescent learns that exposure does not produce the feared consequence, for example, touching the bathroom doorknob did not result in the adolescent's becoming sick or counting food items in even numbers while eating is not required to reduce distress (i.e., distress reduces over time anyway). This process is thought be facilitated by the process of habituation. Treatments emphasize the need for the adolescent to work at his or her own pace and do so in a hierarchical fashion starting with the least anxiety-provoking stimuli and working up to more difficult exposures.

When implementing E–RP and other CBT techniques with teenagers, clinicians benefit from being mindful of the developmental needs of adolescence. One of the most important developmental tasks of adolescence is developing autonomy of thoughts and ideas while decreasing reliance on parents for decision making (Steinberg, 1990). Often, a shift occurs during this time, particularly in early adolescence, from relying on parents to relying on peers. Awareness of these normative developmental changes is important for facilitating the treatment process. For example, emphasizing the adolescent's ownership of the treatment and that he or she is in charge (i.e., not his or her parents) can be helpful. Being sensitive to how the adolescent came to initiate treatment can be important. Was the adolescent pressured to come to treatment by the parent? Discussion of these issues can be helpful to alliance between the adolescent and the therapist. Moreover, peer issues can sometimes prove particularly relevant to adolescent patients. In particular, concerns regarding possible peer rejection in response to OCD-related behaviors and difficulties engaging in activities with peers because of OCD symptoms can be additionally impairing. Helping to identify these issues and prioritizing them in treatment is useful and may help increase the adolescent's willingness to follow through on treatment goals.

SIX THERAPY ENGAGEMENT STRATEGIES WITH ADOLESCENTS

This section details six engagement strategies for working with adolescents experiencing OCD. Although some of the engagement strategies are incorporated in the CBT protocols, the purpose of this section is to elaborate on them in more detail, providing examples of how to implement them in clinical practice.

Assessment as Engagement

The initial appointment with a clinician for possible OCD treatment involves a thorough assessment, including a full clinical interview with a thorough evaluation of current and past OCD symptoms, as well as an assessment of symptom severity, associated functional impairment, comorbid psychopathology, and information regarding medical, psychosocial, and familial factors related to the presenting illness. Moreover, the clinician provides psychoeducation on OCD and its treatment (described in the next section). This meeting can be time consuming (approximately 90 minutes) and arduous for both the parent and the adolescent and can be particularly anxiety provoking for family members who may be hearing the diagnosis for the first time. Furthermore, many parents and adolescents come with healthy skepticism as a result of previous treatments that have not worked to alleviate impairing OCD symptoms. Thus, the initial meeting is a pivotal time for gaining the adolescent's (and parent's) buy-in and preliminary commitment to treatment.

A thorough review of all the components of an OCD evaluation is beyond the scope of this chapter on engagement strategies. Thus, the reader is referred to March and Mulle (1998) and Merlo, Storch, Murphy, Goodman, and Geffken (2005) for a more complete discussion of the assessment process, topics covered, and specific measures of OCD symptoms and comorbid psychopathology domains used in the initial meeting.

When conducting the initial assessment, it is important for clinicians to be sensitive to the fact that adolescents and parents may have different levels of comfort answering questions and discussing mental health concerns. One simple way to ease this concern is to normalize it and let the adolescent and parents know that you are aware that answering questions can feel awkward or uncomfortable. Furthermore, providing the parent and adolescent with multiple ways to report their symptoms can help with uneasiness and result in a more thorough evaluation. Typically, a clinical interview is completed individually with the adolescent and then with the parent. We think it is useful to let the adolescent meet with the clinician first (after initial joint introductions and confidentiality review) so that he or she feels validated and autonomous in his or her treatment. Second, both the adolescent and the parent can fill out self-report rating scales of OCD symptoms (e.g., Leyton Obsessional Inventory—Child Version; Berg, Whitaker, Davies, Flament, & Rapoport, 1988) and comorbid psychopathology domains (e.g., Children's Depression Inventory; Kovacs 1996). The anonymity of writing on paper can sometimes provide information that adolescents and parents may be embarrassed or unwilling to admit verbally to a new person. It is generally believed that adolescents are better reporters on their internal symptoms (e.g., in the case of OCD, obsessions) and parents are better reporters of outward behaviors (in the case of OCD, compulsions; Herjanic & Reich, 1982).

If the clinical interview or self-report measures suggest possible OCD, clinicians should follow up by administering the Children's Yale-Brown Obsessive Compulsive Scale (Goodman, Price, Rasmussen, Riddle, & Rapoport,

1991). This clinician-rated instrument is particularly useful because it combines information gathered from observation and from adolescent and parent report. Because this scale provides a rather comprehensive list of obsessions and compulsions, adolescents and parents affected by OCD often seem relieved when completing a Children's Yale-Brown Obsessive Compulsive Scale interview for two reasons. The interview provides evidence that the clinician has knowledge of the types of impairing symptoms the family faces, and it offers the family some perspective about the symptoms because they can see that they likely have not endorsed all possible OCD symptom areas. This instrument is useful for the clinician because it provides much more detailed information about the severity of the adolescent's symptoms and can be used in developing a treatment hierarchy later.

Most adolescents presenting to treatment for the first time may not be coming with an awareness that they have OCD; instead, they may be coming because of a parent's perception that the adolescent is overly anxious, is difficult, or has a behavior problem. Thus, if the initial evaluation is conducted without a prior referral for assessment of OCD, it is important for the mental health practitioners to ask fairly detailed and specific questions about obsessions and compulsions anyway. Because of embarrassment, fear, or familial stress associated with OCD symptoms, individuals tend to be secretive about their obsessions and compulsions. Thus, it is important for clinicians to have a matter-of-fact style when discussing OCD symptoms and provide multiple examples of obsessions and compulsions. Below is an excerpt of an initial interview with an adolescent and therapist. Notice the therapist's straightforward style and normalizing tone, even when the adolescent becomes uncomfortable with the discussion:

Therapist:	Besides the worries you have mentioned about your schoolwork, I'm wondering if you have any other worries, thoughts, ideas, or images that bother you.
Adolescent:	Besides my schoolwork and the public speaking worries? No, I don't have any problems besides the school stuff.
Therapist:	Oh, OK. The types of thoughts I was wondering about are ideas or pictures that seem to pop into your mind out of the blue, as though you cannot control them. They can be silly, weird, or unusual, and can be distressing—the kinds of things you might not feel comfortable sharing with your buddies.
Adolescent:	I don't have any funky thoughts like that. I mean, maybe some weird thoughts, everyone has weird thoughts.
Therapist:	Let me give you an example of some "funky thoughts" that other adolescents I know have had. Some teens have funky

thoughts about germs—that something bad will happen if they don't wash their hands a lot, for example. Other teens have funky thoughts about violence or sexual things—they have images flash through their minds of hurting people, or they fear doing something embarrassing. Another teen I know has a fear of losing things that she just couldn't shake. The thought that she was going to lose her keys kept popping into her mind over and over, so much so that she would need to check for them a lot. These are just some examples, but these types of thoughts tend to come even though you may not want them to, and it feels hard to control them.

Adolescent: [*pause*] I don't have thoughts like that, really. I do have one weird thing, that's kind of like the checking you mentioned, but there's no worry about it. It's just that I have to get out of my bed the same way every day, and if I don't, I feel pretty uncomfortable. My brother makes fun of me for it, and that makes me mad.

Therapist: Tell me more.

In this example, the adolescent initially denies experiencing obsessions, and if the therapist had stopped probing, she or he would have missed important information. After the therapist provides further examples, the adolescent likens the example of the person with a checking ritual to his own morning ritual, which opens the door to further discussion.

Although providing examples such as contamination, symmetry, and hoarding obsessions and washing, repeating, and checking compulsions is a solid start, providing examples of rarer obsessions and compulsions is also important during general clinical interviews. For example, Annalise Caron conducted an intake evaluation and diagnosed an adolescent with anxiety, not otherwise specified; transient tic disorder; and sensory concerns, after initially thinking she had ruled out OCD by providing the aforementioned categories of obsessions and compulsions as examples. The following week, it became apparent that the child had less typical obsessions about which he felt great shame because of their, as he put it, "weird content." He was fearful to admit these thoughts during the initial evaluation. He had beliefs that if he looked at certain people (i.e., including Caron), he would turn into those people or take on the gender of those people. His compulsions included blinking and other ticlike behaviors to alleviate the anxiety associated with these intrusive thoughts. His admission of these beliefs and compulsions led Caron to follow up with the Children's Yale-Brown Obsessive Compulsive Scale, confirming a diagnosis of OCD that she would otherwise have missed. Sometimes, inquiring simply if the adolescent has any repetitive thoughts or behaviors about which he or she feels embarrassment or shame can lead to admission of OCD symptoms.

Finally, it is important that the initial assessment and diagnosis of OCD and comorbidities lead directly into a treatment plan that the adolescent and parent agree on. Treatment targets should be kept clear and distinct. For example, if an adolescent is diagnosed with mild to moderate OCD, major depressive disorder, and attention deficit/hyperactivity disorder, then the proposed treatment strategies should be clearly defined for the adolescent and parent relating to each concern. Thus, the treatment plan might include E–RP for OCD, CBT for depression, and the combination of behavior therapy strategies and a medical referral for treatment of attention-deficit/hyperactivity disorder (ADHD). If the clinician is a psychologist, he or she might refer the adolescent to a child psychiatrist for a medical evaluation for the concentration difficulties associated with ADHD but would also clarify to initially hold off on any medication for the OCD. Moreover, the family and clinician would decide together whether to target the OCD first or the depression first or to address them in concert, depending on what was most impairing and the treatment goals. Thus, if behavioral activation as part of CBT for depression was the first treatment approach, the parent and adolescent should be informed that the OCD was not immediately being targeted (i.e., not to expect symptoms changes in that psychopathology domain until later in the treatment plan when E–RP is initiated).

Psychoeducation as Engagement

Once a thorough evaluation is completed and the diagnosis of OCD is confirmed, one of the first treatment goals should be the provision of psychoeducation to both the adolescent and the parents. *Psychoeducation* refers to providing information about the causes, symptoms, risks, clinical course, and treatment options for a particular disorder. Presumably, increasing adolescents' and parents' knowledge about OCD and its treatment will help with both (a) reducing misconceptions or shame about the illness and (b) engaging in the treatment process. Psychoeducation for OCD typically focuses on two main areas: (a) providing information and a conceptual framework for the diagnosis of OCD itself and (b) providing a description of the planned treatment approach.

First, the clinician provides general information about the disorder, including its prevalence. Letting adolescents and parents know that a conservative estimate suggests that two or three adolescents per 100 have OCD (Douglass et al., 1995; Heyman et al., 2003; Maina et al., 1999) is often comforting, as is pointing out that this number means there may be two to

10 other students in the adolescent's very own high school class struggling with the disorder, depending on full class size. Such information can be helpful in reducing stigma and anxiety.

A conceptual framework serves to aid the adolescent's and parent's understanding of the illness. Typically, OCD is conceptualized as either a neurobehavioral–neuropsychiatric illness (March & Mulle, 1998; Piacentini et al., 2007) or simply an anxiety disorder resulting from misattributed normal anxious thoughts (Williams et al., 2002). These authors follow the March, Biederman, and Wolkow (1998; March & Benton, 2007; March & Mulle, 1998) approach of framing OCD as a neuropsychiatric disorder (i.e., medical illness). Discussing OCD as a medical illness that can be likened to diabetes or asthma helps reduce blame and guilt for the OCD-related behaviors, both the adolescent's self-blame and parental blame. Clinically, this seems to help adolescents feel better about themselves and their illness, as well as helping parents understand their therapeutic role later (e.g., not to punish the adolescent for OCD-related behavior). Decreasing parental criticism for OCD-related behaviors is likely helpful in validating the adolescents and maintaining them in treatment, but it also may be helpful in increasing treatment response, as has been suggested in studies of perceived criticism by relatives of adult patients in treatment for OCD (Renshaw, Chambless, & Steketee, 2003). Unlike with children, to whom OCD may be explained as a simple "brain hiccup" (March & Mulle, 1998), adolescents often resonate with a more direct discussion of the neurochemical basis of their OCD being an imbalance or dysfunction in serotonin that can be likened, for example, to having a dysfunction in insulin that occurs with Type II diabetes. In the example that follows, the therapist provides developmentally appropriate psychoeducation that leads to increased engagement. Notice how the therapist validates the teenager's experience of OCD while also suggesting that she or he can change.

Therapist: So, does the idea that OCD is not your fault and instead is due to chemicals in your brain resonate with you? Your brain is sending you the fear messages that are giving you the obsessive thoughts because of low levels of a brain chemical called serotonin.

Adolescent: So, it's not my fault? Mom, are you listening to what she just said?

Therapist: You're absolutely right, Joe. OCD, and the thoughts and behaviors associated with OCD, are not your fault and are not under your control, at least not yet. So, you should not be punished for them. That said, though it is not your "fault," it is your responsibility to work on it.

Adolescent:	Mom, did you hear that? You can't get mad at me when I take too long in the bathroom! It's my brain's fault, and it's not under my control.
Therapist:	You're right, Joe. However, you and I are going to work together, possibly even with your mom's help, to make it so that OCD has less control over you and you take more control over it. Over time, you will gain more control over your OCD-related behavior and won't have to stay in the bathroom so long.
Adolescent:	That sounds hard, but maybe I can try.
Therapist:	Good. We will do it together. OCD is a medical problem much like diabetes or asthma. In diabetes, for example, there are problems with the body's regulation of a hormone called insulin. So, just like OCD, this illness is treated with a two-pronged approach: behavioral homework from the doctor, such as diet and exercise, and prescribed medicine options, such as taking insulin. With OCD, the problem is not with regulation of insulin but with regulation of the brain chemical serotonin. So, the treatment involves a two-pronged approach of therapy sessions with me, including behavioral homework, as well as the possibility of medication with a selective serotonin reuptake inhibitor if we do not see enough improvement from the behavioral therapy alone. Make sense?

The second step of psychoeducation with the family is setting realistic expectations for treatment. This helps with engagement by letting the family know what to expect, so that they are not surprised at the effort required on the part of both adolescent and parent, and to prevent any misconceptions about the process or length of treatment. First, treatment is framed as a collaborative enterprise involving the adolescent, the therapist, and the parent, where the adolescent takes the lead in setting the pace. Notably, therapists' use of collaborative strategies (e.g., encouraging youth feedback on treatment, use of words like *we* and *us*, active goal setting with youth input) predicts therapeutic alliance in treatment of other anxiety disorders (Creed & Kendall, 2005), and such therapeutic alliance predicts engagement with therapy tasks (Chu et al., 2004).

Next, treatment components are clearly described and possible projected progress and an individualized treatment plan are discussed up front, with family members being encouraged to ask questions and engage in any adjustments to the treatment plan. The treatment plan for mild to moderate OCD will typically include an initial trial of CBT alone for 12 weeks. If no symptom reduction is evident at the end of that period, then the family may be referred for an evaluation by a psychiatrist to assess the appropriateness of adding medication to the treatment plan. With severe cases of OCD, a therapist will likely suggest starting with a combination of CBT and medication. If the family has concerns about initiating treatment with medication, the therapist may provide information regarding the treatment outcome research with combined treatment and may also encourage setting up a consultation appointment with a psychiatrist to get further information to consider in making the decision. Often, collaboration may come into the treatment planning itself. If a parent is hesitant about considering medication for a child with moderate to severe OCD, the therapist might suggest a middle path of starting with CBT alone for an agreed-on specified time period, with a plan to add medication intervention if clinically significant symptom reduction is not evident after a certain time period to which all family members agree. Again, this process engages the family with solid information and a collaborative and active role in the treatment process.

Focus on the Whole Adolescent as an Engagement Strategy

One of the most impairing aspects of OCD is adolescents' sense that OCD equates to who they are. They receive feedback from siblings, parents, and teachers that their compulsive behaviors are bad or disruptive but often interpret those responses to mean they, themselves, are bad. These behaviors can lead to further familial distress (Renshaw et al., 2005) or peer rejection (Storch et al., 2006). Adolescents with OCD often feel responsible for their behaviors and for letting other people down, even though they have neither volitionally engaged in the OCD-related behavior nor learned the skills necessary to be able to exert control over them (yet).

A pivotal aspect of OCD treatment to clarify during initial sessions is that the OCD-related behaviors are not intentional. For example, if an adolescent is always late for school because he spends too long in the bathroom washing his hands after breakfast or takes an hour to get out of his bedroom in the morning because of his need to engage in walking and touching rituals, this behavior is not simple disobedience. The behaviors, however, can appear that way to the rest of the family. Siblings may be late for school or a parent may become angry because of how this behavior affects her or his ability to get to work in a timely fashion. Tensions often run high, with siblings resenting the extra attention the adolescent receives and parents becoming exasperated with power struggles and the ineffectiveness of consequences, punishment, or both in decreasing their son's apparent disobedience.

A useful technique to clarify that the OCD-related behaviors are not purposeful is to externalize the OCD. That is, the adolescent and parent are taught to distinguish between what is behavior resulting from OCD and what is not (e.g., "That's my OCD talking"). This externalizing of OCD has already begun with the provision of OCD as a neurobehavioral disorder during the psychoeducation aspect of treatment. As a further method of externalizing OCD, March and Mulle (1998) suggested the technique of giving the OCD a silly nickname to further separate the OCD behaviors from the adolescent. Sometimes adolescents prefer simply to refer to the term *OCD* instead of finding a nickname, which may be more appealing to younger children. That said, one teen with whom Annalise Caron worked chose "Stinker" as the name for his OCD. The adolescent, parent, and clinician all used Stinker when discussing his OCD, which not only served to disengage the adolescent from his OCD but also brought humor and levity into sessions and family life. The therapist can model disengagement strategies for family members and give examples of how to externalize OCD in a supportive and calm manner. For example, a parent might be coached to say, "You're worried that if you touch the color orange, something bad will happen? Hmm . . . this sounds to me like it might be your OCD [Stinker] talking."

Another important part of this process of clarifying that the adolescent is not a bad teenager is fostering the combination of externalizing the OCD behaviors with internalizing the adolescent's strengths. Early sessions should include an assessment of the adolescent's interests and hobbies. Gathering this information can serve to enhance treatment engagement in two ways. First, doing so lets the adolescent know that OCD is not all that the therapist sees in him or her. Through the treatment process, fostering development in these other interests and hobbies can help to deemphasize the importance of OCD while these interests gain greater importance to the adolescent's sense of self. Second, Franklin, Rynn, Foa, and March (2003) pointed out that learning about the adolescent's other interests can enhance engagement in treatment if the therapist incorporates these interests in the treatment vocabulary. For example, a boy's keen interest in baseball could be used as a metaphor for OCD treatment. OCD could be conceptualized as the team ahead in the first inning (i.e., beginning of treatment), with the boy being conceptualized as the pitcher on the opposing team (i.e., the one to make the other team players [OCD] strike out).

Clarifying Roles of the Adolescent and Parent as an Engagement Strategy

Current research has suggested that family involvement in treatment for childhood OCD is associated with decreased OCD symptoms (Piacentini, 1999). As previously discussed, treatment protocols focus on providing parents with psychoeducation about OCD and E–RP, helping prepare the family for treatment (Barrett et al., 2004) and gradually reducing the family's accommodations to the child's rituals (e.g., March & Mulle, 1998; Piacentini, Gitow,

Jaffer, Graae, & Whitaker, 1994). In addition, treatment protocols suggest that therapists conduct sessions that are devoted to teaching parents different strategies (e.g., parental anxiety management, differential reinforcement of behavior, problem-solving skills training) to help their child overcome OCD (e.g., Barrett et al., 2004; Waters et al., 2001). Typically, the degree of family involvement in treatment protocols is left to the clinical judgment, and there is little research on whether children and adolescents require different levels of parent involvement to remain engaged in treatment. Given the increased need for autonomy during adolescence, maintaining an adolescent's engagement in treatment while involving parents can be challenging. In this section, we discuss several factors that need to be assessed before determining the level of parental involvement needed to maintain engagement in treatment, including (a) the developmental stage of the adolescent, (b) the role that OCD plays in the family system, and (c) the occurrence of helpful versus harmful family patterns.

Developmental Level

For young children, parent involvement is customary: The parents, child, and therapist all join together to "boss back" OCD (March & Mulle, 1998). Ideally, the parent acts a cheerleader for the child by supporting the child when he or she is able to boss back OCD. When appropriate, parents may also play the role of the cotherapist. The parents coach the child through resisting compulsive behavior during exposures and help the child with therapy homework. Without this level of parent involvement, the younger child may not be able to complete the goals of treatment.

In contrast, the adolescent (depending on developmental level) may require less parental involvement to complete goals and maintain engagement in the treatment. Given that many adolescents may not feel comfortable attending therapy sessions with parents, individual sessions with the teenager and separate parent sessions may be more appropriate. Alternatively, some adolescents may prefer to have their parents attend the first part of the session and then leave so the adolescent can speak with the therapist privately. In addition to conducting separate sessions with parents, the therapist can direct parents to empirically informed popular audience reading on OCD (March & Benton, 2007) as a way to give parents useful information while not interfering with the adolescent's individual session time. Although the adolescent may prefer to have individual sessions with the therapist, there are times when parental participation is necessary. If an adolescent is not able to complete tasks, such as monitoring of symptoms, reporting on progress, or completing exposures at home, the therapist may have to increase parental participation in treatment.

Determining the appropriate level of parent involvement when working with adolescents coping with autonomy issues can be difficult. We discuss an example of an adolescent (Molly, age 16) to illustrate how the therapist can best balance the therapeutic goals with an adolescent's desire for autonomy.

Molly had always been a very independent child who liked to accomplish goals that she set for herself. She enjoyed it when her parents were proud of her accomplishments and independence. When Molly was diagnosed with OCD, she felt embarrassed and frustrated because she felt that she had let herself and her parents down. The therapist worked with her on these issues by providing psychoeducation about OCD, helping her identify and challenge cognitive errors, and helping her talk to her parents about her fears. Her parents were surprised to hear about the pressure that Molly placed on herself and were open to working on how they could change their behavior to help her. In this situation, the therapist was able to help Molly advocate for herself with her parents, which was empowering for her. Whether the therapist helps the client advocate for him- or herself to the parents or works in conjunction with the adolescent to advocate on his or her behalf, both methods serve to enhance adolescent buy-in and engagement with therapy.

As treatment progressed, Molly was able to discuss her symptoms with her parents, moved up on her exposure hierarchy, and was motivated in individual therapy sessions. However, Molly continued to struggle with one particular ritual that she completed at night. Before she fell asleep, she had specific images of her parents when she swallowed. If she did not have the "correct" image of her parents, she needed to repeat her image, causing her frustration and lack of sleep. Molly's parents were somewhat aware of her nighttime rituals but were confused because they seemed to keep changing. When Molly was unable to sleep, she would go to her parents' bedroom. When her parents asked her if OCD was telling her to do things, she denied it. Molly's parents became frustrated with her because she could not tell them why she could not sleep. Molly was embarrassed and annoyed with herself but could not ask for help.

In session, Molly revealed that she did not want to tell her parents about her nightly ritual because she wanted to be able to cope with OCD by herself. She became annoyed when her parents asked her if her OCD was bothering her. To help Molly engage with the treatment, it was important for the therapist to acknowledge her wish for independence while discussing how her parents could support her if and when exposures became too difficult. Although Molly wanted to be able to cope with her OCD by herself, she needed her parents' help when she became overwhelmed. After a few sessions that involved (a) helping Molly accept her struggle with OCD, (b) cognitive restructuring around her ability to work on OCD, and (c) imaginal exposures about asking for help, Molly was able to recognize that she may need support from her parents and agreed to have her parents come to a family session to discuss how they could help her when she felt overwhelmed by OCD.

Role of OCD in the Family

When an adolescent has OCD, it is likely that the family system will be affected in some way. Research on family involvement in children's OCD shows that 70% of parents with a child with OCD reported involvement with their child's symptoms. Almost 75% of the parents accommodated the child's rituals, and the rest reacted with hostility (Allsopp & Verduyn, 1990). When parents are involved in obsessions or rituals, an increase in parent involvement in treatment may be indicated. Although this may help to decrease symptoms of OCD, it may also be difficult for the adolescent to work on these exposures with his or her parents. For example, one adolescent with whom we worked (Joseph, age 15) reported that he was having intrusive sexual thoughts about his mother, Kathy. Joseph felt very guilty about having these thoughts, so he would tell his mother that he "had a bad thought" whenever he experienced an intrusive thought about her. Kathy was unsure how to respond and tried to reassure him by telling him that it was OK to have bad thoughts. Yet Joseph would continue to ask for reassurance several more times until he felt that his mom forgave him. Although Kathy was trying to help Joseph feel less anxious, her reassurance was maintaining his compulsion to tell on himself. Because of the nature of Joseph's obsessions and Kathy's role in providing reassurance, it was clear that Kathy needed to be involved in the treatment. Before having Joseph and Kathy talk about his obsessions and work on exposures together, the therapist worked with Joseph on understanding that his obsessions were unwanted intrusive thoughts and not hidden desires. They worked on developing cognitive strategies to effectively cope with the intrusive thoughts when they occurred, and he was told about other children who had experienced similar symptoms to help him understand he was not the only child experiencing these types of obsessive thoughts. Joseph worked with the therapist on developing this hierarchy:

1. Talk to mom about nonsexual intrusive thoughts.
2. Accept mom's not providing reassurance about nonsexual intrusive thoughts.
3. Experience a nonsexual intrusive thought and do not tell mom.
4. Talk to mom about sexual intrusive thoughts and accept mom's not providing reassurance.
5. Do not tell mom about sexual intrusive thoughts to tell on myself.

Using these graded exposures gave Joseph a sense of control during the exposure sessions and helped him to feel proud of his ability to cope with his OCD.

Although it was difficult for Joseph to have his mother be a part of his sessions, without parental involvement during sessions treatment may not have been as effective in reducing his OCD symptoms.

Helpful and Harmful Family Interactions Affecting Adolescents' Engagement

Parents who know how to balance being a cheerleader for their adolescent and letting their child cope with OCD independently can help maintain therapeutic engagement and treatment progress. This balancing act is the gold standard for the parental role in treatment of adolescent OCD. However, there are times when negative family patterns prevent the parent from taking on this balanced role and the child from engaging in the treatment successfully. March and Mulle (1998) stated that when there are negative family interactions around OCD (e.g., parental involvement in rituals, criticism or familial strife resulting from rituals) or around other daily living activities, sibling issues, or marital conflict, or when parental psychopathology interferes with treatment progress, family involvement in treatment is required. We describe a case that we worked with that illustrates how parental overinvolvement and anxiety can decrease the adolescent's ability to engage in treatment.

Kerry (age 14) was referred to therapy by her mother after her OCD symptoms intensified when she was required to go on an overnight school trip without her mother, Stacey. She had not been in therapy for her OCD, but the stress of the impending trip was overwhelming, and the school suggested that Kerry seek a psychological consultation. Kerry felt compelled to do several rituals before she could fall asleep, including counting to four while looking at each of the four walls of her room, telling her mother that she loved her and hearing that her mother loved her in return, keeping the door open a specific number of inches, checking behind the door, getting into and out of her bed several times until it felt right, and arranging the pillows and blankets on her bed several times. All of these rituals needed to be done with her mother watching. Some were done to keep her mother safe during the night, whereas others were done because she felt anxious if she did not do them. Kerry did not think she could handle going on the trip by herself. Stacey offered to go on the trip, but the school was hesitant about having Stacey accompany Kerry.

Because of Stacey's involvement in Kerry's rituals, both mother and daughter were asked to attend therapy sessions. Stacey and Kerry engaged in the psychoeducation component of treatment. Kerry was taught anxiety management strategies and cognitive strategies to help her cope with OCD. Stacey was given information about OCD and how she could support her daughter. When the exposures were initiated in treatment, Stacey's difficulty tolerating

Kerry's distress began to interfere with treatment. Stacey had difficulty toler-ating her own anxiety and became very distressed when she saw her child become anxious. As a result, she allowed Kerry to engage in rituals at home that she had been able to resist in the therapist's office. The therapist noted Kerry's increase in anxiety and frustration because she was not able to com-plete her exposures at home. With Kerry's permission, Stacey was brought into therapy sessions to help her see that Kerry could complete these exposures and that she could handle the anxiety. Additional parent sessions with the mother were held to help Stacey manage her anxiety when Kerry was com-pleting exposures.

Therapist Style as an Engagement Strategy

The cognitive–behavioral therapist primarily plays the role of coach (March & Mulle, 1998). As a coach, the therapist collaborates with the ado-lescent in developing exposures or opportunities to test hypotheses about OCD. The therapist uses his or her knowledge of OCD and the patient to keep the patient engaged. With this knowledge, the therapist decides how to use validation, flexibility, collaboration, and encouragement in the engage-ment process. Throughout therapy, the therapist checks in with the adoles-cent to monitor engagement. We discuss how these techniques can be used in the assessment, psychoeducation, and exposure phases of treatment.

As early as the assessment phase, the therapist's style is important to engage the adolescent in OCD treatment. During the assessment phase, the therapist has an opportunity to use validation and encouragement in helpful ways. Adolescents in treatment for OCD are often referred by parents and may not exhibit high motivation to change. This must be considered when con-sidering appropriate engagement style. For example, a therapist who trained with Joanna Robin was very eager to start working with adolescents with OCD. However, her excitement prevented her from recognizing and reduc-ing the teen's anxiety during the assessment phase. During the assessment, the adolescent, Sandra, revealed that on the night before the assessment, she had searched the Internet for information on CBT treatment for OCD. When Sandra read that she might have to do E–RP, she became overwhelmed with fear and almost did not attend the initial evaluation. Sandra asked her ther-apist, "Will I have to stop washing my hands like I read online?" This was an opportunity for the therapist to use a validating style about Sandra's fears of E–RP while encouraging her to remain engaged in treatment. This was also a chance to demonstrate to Sandra that the therapist would be a collaborator in treatment, moving at a pace negotiated between therapist and patient. Unfortunately, the therapist instead responded to Sandra's question with factual information about E–RP, suggesting a typical hierarchy that Sandra might follow and minimizing Sandra's fears. As a result, Sandra felt ashamed, nervous, and overwhelmed and reported to her parent that she did not want to return after the assessment.

This example highlights the importance of responding to the adolescent's trepidation about treatment with validation and encouragement. Although it is necessary to be honest with the patient about the components of treatment, this should be done in a way that instills hope in the patient about treatment.

In the psychoeducation phase, the therapist can play a coach role to help the adolescent challenge his or her beliefs about the need to engage in compulsions. This is also an opportunity for the therapist to inject humor into the discussion of OCD and reduce anxiety around refraining from engaging in compulsions. When using humor in therapy, the therapist should ensure that he or she does not make fun of the adolescent and that the adolescent is able to tolerate the use of humor. Following is a dialogue between a therapist and Michael, a 13-year-old adolescent who was having difficulty separating himself from his OCD. The therapist uses humor and an analogy to help Michael become open to the idea of not engaging in his compulsions.

> *Therapist:* So, Michael, I know it has been hard for you to believe that something bad will not happen to your parents if you don't walk down the stairs in the way that OCD tells you to.
>
> *Michael:* Yeah, it's just not worth the risk. I just need to do it so everyone is OK.
>
> *Therapist:* I know it is hard to even think about not doing your ritual, because OCD can feel really scary, trying to bully you around.
>
> *Michael:* Yeah, it always feels that way.
>
> *Therapist:* Well, I can understand why it feels like that. But I see OCD a little differently, more like a nag. Like that kid at school who gets super cautious about *everything* and is always asking, "You sure this is safe, guys?" or "We shouldn't do this." Do you know anyone like that?
>
> *Michael:* [*smiling*] Well, there's this one kid I'm friends with who gets nervous about taking on other kids at the basketball courts.
>
> *Therapist:* That's *exactly* what I mean. Do you and your friends listen to that kid?
>
> *Michael:* [*laughing*] No, because then we'd never play.
>
> *Therapist:* And so then what does your nagging friend do?
>
> *Michael:* Well, he keeps it up for a while. But eventually he gives up.

Therapist:	Hmm. So what do you think would happen if you didn't listen to OCD?
Michael:	[*smiling*] I don't know. Maybe it would quiet down too. I guess I see what you are saying.

When planning exposures, the therapist uses his or her ability to be flexible and collaborate with the adolescent to facilitate engagement. The therapist models flexibility and teaches problem-solving skills that help the patient feel in control while progressing in treatment. For example, Joanna Robin worked with an adolescent with hand-washing compulsions. As part of an exposure, Robin asked her to list "not washing hands after bathroom use" on her hierarchy. She immediately refused. Knowing this teenager, Robin expected her reaction and did not argue with her; instead, they talked about what her OCD was telling her about this exposure. She was able to talk about her anxiety and challenge OCD's rules and became more open to compromising with Robin. An agreement was made: She would not wash her hands with soap at the first exposure, and then 15 minutes later, during her second exposure, she would not wash her hands.

The CBT therapist flexibly uses engagement strategies not only when planning exposures but also when conducting exposures. Indeed, because E–RP requires an adolescent to engage in anxiety-provoking situations, it is crucial for the therapist to constantly monitor the patient's motivation and to apply engagement strategies whenever needed. Joanna Robin worked with a patient with contamination fears who was asked to touch garbage in a garbage can without washing his hands. The adolescent was very nervous about touching garbage and was having difficulty participating in the exposures. Instead of just having him touch garbage by himself, Robin touched the garbage first to help motivate the teen to complete the exposure. She demonstrated flexibility by participating in the exposure with the adolescent, even though it may have been uncomfortable for her as well.

Moving Through the Hierarchy: Keeping Adolescents Engaged in Treatment

Given that treatment for OCD involves the adolescent systematically confronting anxiety-provoking situations, the question becomes, How do you get adolescents to do the things they are afraid of? We discuss strategies that maintain engagement in treatment and reduce symptoms of anxiety, including making exposures "fun," collaborative decision making, and moving through the hierarchy at an effective pace.

Although it may be difficult to make exposures pleasurable, it is important to incorporate some elements of enjoyment into exposure sessions. For example, when working with an adolescent with a rereading compulsion, we practiced not rereading newspaper articles about his favorite baseball team. For a child with excessive self-doubting about decisions, we conducted taste tests with different candy and sodas while he practiced not engaging in his self-doubt and tolerating his anxiety. When an adolescent with compulsive hand washing had difficulty discontinuing washing her hands, we used a stopwatch to time her hand washing, and if she completed washing within a specified time, she earned time on the Internet. By getting to know the adolescent's interests, the therapist can tailor exposures and rewards that motivate the adolescent, maintain treatment participation, and make exposures more tolerable.

When working with young children, the therapist tends to have more control over the exposure hierarchy. When working with adolescents, exposure hierarchy development is often a collaborative effort between therapist and patient. The adolescent should be encouraged to think of possible exposures and feel comfortable talking to the therapist when he or she feels the exposure is too easy or not challenging enough. Following is an excerpt from a dialogue between a therapist and adolescent negotiating future exposures. Notice how the two collaborate in developing the hierarchy.

Therapist:	You have been doing a great job with your exposures at home and in session. You completed all of your low-level exposures. How are you feeling about moving up the hierarchy?
Adolescent:	I am feeling pretty nervous, but I just keep remembering what you told me about how OCD gets stronger when you do what it wants you to do. So, I guess I am ready.
Therapist:	It is understandable that you are nervous, and this stuff can be challenging. We'll take it at a pace that feels comfortable to you. Let's talk about what you think would be the next exposure. What do you want to tackle next?
Adolescent:	Well, I am not sure if you noticed, but I just did my tapping ritual when I came into your office. [*guilty smile*]
Therapist:	Yeah, I did. You know what that means, right? [*smiling*]
Adolescent:	I know, I know. [*laughing*] We have to add this one to the list. It is really a pain and it gets in the way of starting my therapy sessions with you.
Therapist:	That sounds good to me. Let's add it to your hierarchy. What is your fear rating on this one?

When working on completing exposures on the hierarchy, the therapist uses his or her clinical judgment to maintain engagement. Moving too quickly or too slowly up the hierarchy can lead to disengagement. In some cases, the therapist may not be aware that the child is not ready for higher level exposures and may push the child too far without adequate understanding of his or her anxiety. Alternatively, some therapists may not encourage the adolescent to engage in higher level exposures. Therapists need to be aware of how their own anxiety or lack of knowledge about the child's ability to complete exposures may prevent the child from moving up the hierarchy. For example, if the therapist's own anxiety about an exposure (e.g., not washing hands before eating) prevents him or her from setting up exposures for the adolescent, this could hinder treatment progress. Another challenge that the therapist faces is parents' concerns about the pace of treatment. Some parents may become frustrated or anxious about the pace of treatment and ask their child to engage in exposures at home that are too difficult. This is important to address because it could lead to disengagement from treatment. In these situations, the therapist acknowledges the parent's emotions while also explaining the child's individual needs for pacing of exposures.

CONCLUSION

We hope this chapter has highlighted some useful strategies for engaging adolescents and their families in collaborative treatment for OCD. Mental health professionals working with adolescents with OCD face a hard sell in terms of engagement in cognitive–behavioral treatment. The crux of E–RP requires facing fears, increasing anxiety, and managing high distress. This type of treatment requires the adolescent's trust in the therapist's expertise and willingness to endure increased distress in the short term. Moreover, adolescents presenting for treatment may disagree with their parents over the nature of their problem, their need for psychological intervention, or both. Thus, there are many potential roadblocks to engaging adolescents in active treatment for OCD. The six engagement strategies described herein—(a) assessment as engagement, (b) psychoeducation as engagement, (c) focusing on the whole adolescent, (d) role clarification of family members, (e) therapist style, and (f) collaboration in development and pace of hierarchy—are certainly not the only possible methods to enhance committed participation in treatment. Recent work with adults has suggested that incorporating motivational interviewing into E–RP may show promise for increasing commitment to treatment (e.g., Simpson, Zuckoff, Page, Franklin, & Foa, 2008).

It is important to note that although nearly all of the engagement strategies discussed in this chapter are incorporated in empirically supported cognitive–behavioral treatments, there have not been any dismantling studies to examine whether specific engagement strategies are more important than others in predicting attrition, therapeutic alliance, symptom reduction, or overall treatment outcome with adolescent OCD. In fact, Bolton and

Perrin (2008) found that E–RP alone, without inclusion of adjunctive CBT strategies such as psychoeducation or familial involvement, led to clinically and statistically significant improvement in OCD symptoms. Thus, further research is warranted to address these unanswered questions and help streamline the most clinically relevant engagement strategies for adolescents and families affected by this complex and debilitating mental illness.

REFERENCES

American Academy of Child and Adolescent Psychiatry. (1998). Practice parameters for the assessment and treatment of children and adolescents with obsessive-compulsive disorder. *Journal of the American Academy of Child & Adolescent Psychiatry, 37*(Suppl. 10), 27S–45S.

Allsopp, M., & Verduyn, C. (1990). Adolescents with obsessive–compulsive disorder: A case note review of consecutive patients referred to a provincial regional adolescent psychiatry unit. *Journal of Adolescence, 13*, 157–169. doi:10.1016/0140-1971(90)90005-R

American Psychiatric Association. (2000). *Diagnostic and statistical manual of mental disorders* (4th ed., text revision). Washington, DC: Author.

Barrett, P., Healy-Farrell, L., & March, J. S. (2004). Cognitive–behavioral family treatment of childhood obsessive–compulsive disorder: A controlled trial. *Journal of the American Academy of Child & Adolescent Psychiatry, 43*, 46–62. doi:10.1097/00004583-200401000-00014

Benazon, N. R., Ager, J., & Rosenberg, D. R. (2002). Cognitive behavior therapy in treatment naïve children and adolescents with obsessive-compulsive disorder: An open trial. *Behaviour Research and Therapy, 40*, 529–540. doi:10.1016/S0005-7967(01)00064-X

Berg, C. Z., Whitaker, A., Davies, M., Flament, M. F., & Rapoport, J. L. (1988). The survey of the Leyton Obsessional Inventory—Child Version: Norms from an epidemiological study. *Journal of the American Academy of Child & Adolescent Psychiatry, 27*, 759–763.

Bolton, D., & Perrin, S. (2008). Evaluation of exposure with response prevention for obsessive compulsive disorder in childhood and adolescence. *Journal of Behavior Therapy and Experimental Psychiatry, 39*, 11–22. doi:10.1016/j.jbtep.2006.11.002

Chu, B. C., Choudry, M. S., Shortt, A. L., Pincus, D. B., Creed, T. A., & Kendall, P. C. (2004). Alliance, technology, and outcome in the treatment of anxious youth. *Cognitive and Behavioral Practice, 11*, 44–55. doi:10.1016/S1077-7229(04)80006-3

Creed, T. A., & Kendall, P. C. (2005). Therapist alliance-building behavior within a cognitive-behavioral treatment for anxiety in youth. *Journal of Consulting and Clinical Psychology, 73*, 498–505. doi:10.1037/0022-006X.73.3.498

de Haan, E., Hoogduin, K., Buitelaar, J., & Keijsers, G. (1998). Behavior therapy versus clomipramine for treatment of obsessive-compulsive disorder in children and adolescents. *Journal of the American Academy of Child & Adolescent Psychiatry, 37*, 1022–1029.

DiGiuseppe, R., Linscott, J., & Jilton, R. (1996). Developing the therapeutic alliance in child-adolescent psychotherapy. *Applied and Preventive Psychology, 5*, 85–100. doi:10.1016/S0962-1849(96)80002-3

Douglass, H. M., Moffitt, T. E., Dar, R., McGee, R., & Silva, P. (1995). Obsessive-compulsive disorder in a birth cohort of 18 year-olds: Prevalence and predictors. *Journal of the American Academy of Child & Adolescent Psychiatry, 34*, 1424–1431. doi:10.1097/00004583-199511000-00008

Franklin, M. E., Kozak, M. J., Cashman, L. A., Coles, M. E., Rheingold, A. A., & Foa, E. B. (1998). Cognitive–behavioral treatment of pediatric obsessive–compulsive disorder: An open clinical trial. *Journal of the American Academy of Child & Adolescent Psychiatry, 37,* 412–419. doi:10.1097/00004583-199804000-00019

Franklin, M. E., Rynn, M., Foa, E. B., & March, J. S. (2003). Treatment of obsessive-compulsive disorder. In M. A. Reinecke, F. M. Dattilio, & A. Freeman (Eds.), *Cognitive therapy with children and adolescents: A casebook for clinical practice* (pp. 162–184). New York, NY: Guilford Press.

Geller, D. A. (2006). Obsessive compulsive and spectrum disorders in children and adolescents. *Psychiatric Clinics of North America, 29,* 353–370. doi:10.1016/j.psc.2006.02.012

Geller, D. A., Biederman, J., Faraone, S., Agranat, A., Cradock, K., Hagermoser, L., . . . Coffey, B. J. (2001). Developmental aspects of obsessive compulsive disorder: Findings in children, adolescents, and adults. *Journal of Nervous and Mental Disease, 189,* 471–477. doi:10.1097/00005053-200107000-00009

Geller, D. A., Biederman, J., Stewart, S. E., Mullin, B., Martin, A., Spencer, T., & Faraone, S. (2003). Which SSRI? A meta-analysis of pharmacotherapy trials in pediatric obsessive–compulsive disorder. *American Journal of Psychiatry, 160,* 1919–1928. doi:10.1176/appi.ajp.160.11.1919

Goodman, W., Price, L., Rasmussen, S., Riddle, M., & Rapoport, J. (1991). *Children's Yale-Brown Obsessive Compulsive Scale (CY-BOCS).* New Haven, CT: Yale University.

Herjanic, B., & Reich, W. (1982). Development of a structured psychiatric interview for children: Agreement between child and parent on individual symptoms. *Journal of Abnormal Child Psychology, 10,* 307–324. doi:10.1007/BF00912324

Heyman, I., Fombonne, E., Simmons, H., Ford, T., Meltzer, H., & Goodman, R. (2003). Prevalence of obsessive–compulsive disorder in the British nationwide survey of child mental health. *International Review of Psychiatry, 15,* 178–184. doi:10.1080/0954026021000046146

Kovacs, M. (1996). *The Children's Depression Inventory.* Toronto, Ontario, Canada: Multi-Health Systems.

Maina, G., Albert, U., Bogetto, F., & Ravizza, L. (1999). Obsessive–compulsive syndromes in older adolescents. *Acta Psychiatrica Scandinavica, 100,* 447–450. doi:10.1111/j.1600-0447.1999.tb10895.x

March, J. M., & Benton, C. M. (2007). *Talking back to OCD: The program that helps kids and teens say "no way"—and parents say "way to go."* New York, NY: Guilford Press.

March, J. S., Biederman, J., & Wolkow, R. (1998). Sertraline in children and adolescents with obsessive-compulsive disorder: A multicenter randomized controlled trial. *JAMA, 280,* 1752–1756. doi:10.1001/jama.280.20.1752

March, J. S., & Mulle, K. (1998). *OCD in children and adolescents: A cognitive behavioral treatment manual.* New York, NY: Guilford Press.

Merlo, L. J., Storch, E. A., Murphy, T. K., Goodman, W. K., & Geffken, G. R. (2005). Assessment of pediatric obsessive–compulsive disorder: A critical review of current methodology. *Child Psychiatry and Human Development, 36,* 195–214. doi:10.1007/s10578-005-4079-7

Pediatric OCD Treatment Study (POTS) Team. (2004). Cognitive–behavior therapy, sertraline, and their combination for children and adolescents with obsessive–compulsive disorder: The Pediatric OCD Treatment Study (POTS) randomized controlled trial. *JAMA, 292,* 1969–1976. doi:10.1001/jama.292.16.1969

Piacentini, J. (1999). Cognitive behavioral therapy of childhood OCD. *Child and Adolescent Psychiatric Clinics of North America, 8,* 599–616.

Piacentini, J., Bergman, R. L., Jacobs, C., McCracken, J. T., & Kretchman, J. (2002). Open trial of cognitive behavior therapy for childhood obsessive–compulsive disorder. *Journal of Anxiety Disorders, 16,* 207–219. doi:10.1016/S0887-6185(02)00096-8

Piacentini, J., Gitow, A., Jaffer, M., Graae, F., & Whitaker, A. (1994). Outpatient behavioural treatment of child and adolescent obsessive-compulsive disorder. *Journal of Anxiety Disorders, 8*, 277–289. doi:10.1016/0887-6185(94)90008-6

Piacentini, J., Langley, A., & Roblek, T. (2007). *Cognitive–behavioral treatment of childhood OCD: It's only a false alarm, therapist guide.* New York, NY: Oxford University Press.

Renshaw, K. D., Chambless, D. L., & Steketee, G. (2003). Perceived criticism predicts severity of anxiety symptoms after behavioral treatment in patients with obsessive–compulsive disorder and panic disorder with agoraphobia. *Journal of Clinical Psychology, 59*, 411–421. doi:10.1002/jclp.10048

Renshaw, K. D., Steketee, G., & Chambless, D. L. (2005). Involving family members in the treatment of OCD. *Cognitive Behaviour Therapy, 34*, 164–175. doi:10.1080/16506070510043732

Shirk, S. R., & Karver, M. (2003). Prediction of treatment outcome from relationship variables in child and adolescent therapy: A meta-analytic review. *Journal of Consulting and Clinical Psychology, 71*, 452–464. doi:10.1037/0022-006X.71.3.452

Simpson, H. B., Zuckoff, A., Page, J. R., Franklin, M. E., & Foa, E. B. (2008). Adding motivational interviewing to exposure and ritual prevention for obsessive–compulsive disorder: An open pilot trial. *Cognitive Behaviour Therapy, 37*, 38–49. doi:10.1080/16506070701743252

Steinberg, L. (1990). Autonomy, conflict, and harmony in the family relationship. In S. S. Feldman & G. R. Elliot (Eds.), *At the threshold: The developing adolescent* (pp. 255–276). Cambridge, MA: Harvard University Press.

Stewart, S. E., Rosario, M. C., Brown, T. A., Carter, A. S., Leckman, J. F., Sukhodolsky, D., . . . Pauls, D. (2007). Principal components analysis of obsessive–compulsive disorder symptoms in children and adolescents. *Biological Psychiatry, 61*, 285–291. doi:10.1016/j.biopsych.2006.08.040

Storch, E. A., Ledley, D. R., Lewin, A. B., Murphey, T. K., Johns, N. B., Goodman, W. K., & Geffken, G. R. (2006). Peer victimization in children with obsessive–compulsive disorder: Relations with symptoms of psychopathology. *Journal of Clinical Child and Adolescent Psychology, 35*, 446–455. doi:10.1207/s15374424jccp3503_10

Turner, C. M. (2006). Cognitive–behavioural theory and therapy for obsessive–compulsive disorder in children and adolescents: Current status and future directions. *Clinical Psychology Review, 26*, 912–938. doi:10.1016/j.cpr.2005.10.004

Waters, T. L., Barrett, P., & March, J. S. (2001). Cognitive–behavioral family treatment of childhood obsessive–compulsive disorder: Preliminary findings. *American Journal of Psychotherapy, 55*, 372–387.

Williams, T., Salkovskis, P., Forrester, E., & Allsopp, M. (2002). Changes in symptoms of OCD and appraisal of responsibility during cognitive behavioral treatment: A pilot study. *Behavioural and Cognitive Psychotherapy, 30*, 69–78. doi:10.1017/S1352465802001078

7

ENGAGING SUICIDAL MULTIPROBLEM ADOLESCENTS WITH DIALECTICAL BEHAVIOR THERAPY

ALEC L. MILLER, JULIE S. NATHAN, AND ELIZABETH E. WAGNER

Suicide is the third leading cause of adolescent deaths in the United States, accounting for more deaths than all natural causes combined and preceded only by accidents and homicide (Anderson, 2002). The high rates of nonlethal suicide attempts are similarly disconcerting, with suicide attempt rates ranging from 7% to 16% among adolescents (Adcock, Nagy, & Simpson, 1991; Kandel, Raveis, & Davies, 1991; Lewinsohn et al., 1996; Reynolds & Mazza, 1992).

Unfortunately, as many as 50% of adolescents who attempt suicide do not receive follow-up mental health treatment (Spirito, Brown, Overholser, & Fritz, 1989), and up to 77% of those who do receive treatment either do not attend therapy appointments or fail to complete treatment (Trautman, Stewart, & Morishima, 1993). These alarming facts about adolescent suicide attempters indicate the pressing need for effective psychosocial interventions. Unfortunately, no comprehensive empirically supported treatment exists for this population. This is particularly distressing given the high rate of suicidal adolescents diagnosed with borderline personality features (Brent et al., 1994; Crumley, 1979; Marton et al., 1989) and various Axis I disorders (Brent et al., 1994; Shaffer et al., 1996). Clearly, the high rate of treatment dropout among adolescent suicide attempters and the potentially lethal consequences of their failure to attend treatment underscores the critical need for a psychosocial intervention that directly targets commitment to and engagement with treatment.

Dialectical behavior therapy (DBT; Linehan, 1993a), with its focus on engaging suicidal multiproblem patients in treatment, appeared to address this need. Miller, Rathus, Linehan, Weztler, and Leigh (1997) adapted DBT for suicidal adolescents with borderline personality features and comorbid Axis I diagnoses. Pilot studies (Katz, Gunasekara, Cox, & Miller, 2004; Rathus & Miller, 2002; Miller, Wyman, Glassman, Huppert, & Rathus, 2000) have found DBT to be a promising intervention for suicidal adolescents with borderline features. More recently, Miller, Rathus, and Linehan (2007; Miller, Glinski, Woodberry, Mitchell, & Indik, 2002; Woodberry, Miller, Glinski, Indik, & Mitchell, 2002) have emphasized the importance of increased family participation in the treatment. A full review of DBT and its application to adolescents and families is beyond the scope of this chapter. A more detailed review of the modifications is provided elsewhere (Miller et al., 2007).

DBT treats adolescents who present for treatment often feeling as though they do not need treatment. Even those who have made a recent suicide attempt may minimize it as an impulsive act and state that they now feel better. Many of these adolescents have had conflictual relationships with their parents and other authority figures, and being told that they must talk to a therapist because they have a problem leaves many teenagers angry and noncompliant. The high rate of treatment dropout among adolescent suicide attempters underscores the need for therapists to equip themselves with a variety of treatment engagement techniques and strategies. Ultimately, Miller et al. (2007) believed DBT is an effective treatment only if therapists are able to engage these multiproblem patients in treatment.

This article is divided into six parts: (a) a brief overview of the theory and structure of DBT for adolescents; (b) a review of the psychoeducation provided to teens and families during the initial phase of therapy; (c) stylistic strategies used by the therapist; (d) commitment strategies used both to engage teens in treatment and to strengthen their agreement to reduce problem behaviors; (e) dialectical strategies for when one "gets stuck" in the session; and (f) a clinical vignette.

OVERVIEW OF DBT FOR ADOLESCENTS

DBT (Linehan, 1993a, 1993b; Linehan et al., 2006) is the first empirically supported treatment for chronically suicidal and nonsuicidal self-injurious adult outpatients diagnosed with borderline personality disorder. Nonsuicidal self-injurious behaviors are any acute, intentional, self-injurious behaviors resulting in tissue damage but without conscious suicidal intent. DBT blends standard cognitive–behavioral therapy with Eastern philosophy and meditation practices and shares elements with psychodynamic, client-centered, gestalt, paradoxical, and strategic approaches (Koerner, Miller, & Wagner, 1998).

DBT is based on Linehan's (1993a) biosocial theory, in which borderline personality disorder is viewed primarily as a dysfunction of the emotion regulation system. Emotional dysregulation is viewed as a result of the transaction between a biologically emotionally vulnerable individual and an environment that is a poor fit with this vulnerability. The theory suggests that borderline personality disorder behaviors (e.g., nonsuicidal self-injury) result when a child who has difficulty regulating emotion is placed in an invalidating environment, that is, one that pervasively and chronically communicates that the child's responses are inappropriate, faulty, inaccurate, or otherwise invalid (Koerner et al., 1998). Invalidating environments may include families, teachers, therapists, coaches, and peers (Miller et al., 2007). Thus, DBT conceptualizes suicidal behaviors as maladaptive solutions to overwhelming, intensely painful negative emotions, yet it also conceptualizes suicidal behaviors as having several potential functions, including regulating affect and behavior eliciting help from an otherwise invalidating environment.

DBT with adolescents consists of 16 concomitant weekly individual and multifamily skills training group sessions. A dialectical philosophy provides the theoretical foundation of DBT treatment strategies, and the core dialectic in DBT is the emphasis on balancing change and acceptance. Hence, the therapist selectively applies problem-oriented change strategies (i.e., behavioral analyses, exposure to emotional cues, contingency management and cognitive modification, irreverent communication strategies, and consultation-to-the-patient strategies) balanced with acceptance strategies (i.e., validation strategies, reciprocal communication strategies, environmental interventions). Validation requires that the therapist communicate to patients that their responses make sense in their current life context or situation. With suicidal adolescents, the therapist often has to search for the valid aspect in a patient's response that on the whole may have been dysfunctional. For some patients, experiencing validation in the context of their dysfunctional behavior may be unique, which in turn may help to engage and retain them (Linehan et al., 2002).

Effective treatment of suicidal adolescents with multiple problems requires that the therapist provide comprehensive treatment that is structured in such a way that highest order priorities are attended to in a systematic manner. Comprehensive treatment involves five functions (Functions a through c refer to the client; Functions d and e refer to the treatment team and the therapist): (a) learning new skills in a psychoeducational multifamily skills training group; (b) working one-to-one with a therapist to reduce factors that interfere with the ability to use skills (i.e., increasing motivation); (c) ensuring that generalization occurs via in vivo interventions (phone consultation or in vivo therapy interactions when in crisis); (d) participating in a weekly therapist consultation meeting that provides both technical help and emotional support to assist the therapist in performing DBT competently; and (e) providing additional interventions that may be needed to structure the environment, including collateral family sessions or meetings with other treatment providers or school personnel so that the patient does not have to get worse to get additional help.

In DBT with adolescents, the foci of therapy are pretreatment targets (agreement on goals and commitment to change) and first-stage targets (safety, stability, behavioral control of action, and enhancement of basic capabilities). In the first stage of DBT, the therapist structures each treatment interaction to address the following specific targets in a hierarchical order of importance:

- decreasing life-threatening and parasuicidal behaviors;
- decreasing behaviors that interfere with treatment, particularly noncompliance and premature dropout;
- decreasing behaviors that have a severe effect on quality of life, including substance abuse, school truancy, high-risk sex, and those that necessitate inpatient psychiatric care; and
- increasing behavioral skills.

The individual therapist applies the DBT strategies to the highest priority target relevant at the moment. For example, if a parasuicidal act occurred during the week, which should be noted on the patient's diary card, it is always treated first in the next session.

In DBT with adolescents, the therapist takes an active stance early in treatment. Thus, the therapist sets the agenda collaboratively with the patient according to hierarchically ordered behavioral treatment targets and then uses this agenda to guide the session. Other treatment orientation may take a more passive stance at the start of treatment, allowing the patient to freely choose the session topic. In DBT, however, it is the extent of the disordered behavior (e.g., severity of dysfunction, complexity of other problems) that determines the focus of treatment both over the course of treatment and within a given treatment interaction. This adherence to predetermined behavioral targets must be "dialectically" balanced with letting the session unfold and skillfully weaving in the necessary components identified in this chapter. A common mistake of a beginning DBT individual therapist is to force the agenda on the patient; we call this error "following the manual, instead of the moment" (see Table 7.1, http://pubs.apa.org/books/supp/elusive/).

ENGAGEMENT STRATEGIES FOR ADOLESCENTS

DBT therapists use a variety of engagement strategies aimed at strengthening the alliance between the therapist, the teen, and the family.

Conduct Clinical Assessment of DBT Problem Areas and Targets

The individual therapist spends much of the first session gathering history relevant to DBT for suicidal multiproblem teens. Hence, the therapist folds the patient's problems into the five major problem areas (see Table 7.2, http://pubs.apa.org/books/supp/elusive/). This technique helps engage patients by making DBT immediately relevant for them. The five problem areas include confusion about self, impulsivity, emotional instability, interpersonal problems, and adolescent–family dilemmas. For example, the DBT therapist might say,

> When you are feeling OK one minute and then really depressed the next minute, we call that a problem regulating emotions or emotional instability [Problem Area 3 in Table 7.2] and confusion about self [Problem Area 1] because you are seemingly unaware of why your emotions just shifted. If you then start binge drinking without thinking about the consequences, we consider that impulsive behavior [Problem Area 2].

DBT therapists review the other problem domains if the adolescent does not raise them during the first session. Typically, adolescents in our program endorse at least four out of five problem areas. The DBT therapist tells the patient that although she or he may feel overwhelmed by having these problems, there is some good news. "For each of these problem areas that you experience, we will teach you specific skills that you can use to target and reduce your problems." This engagement strategy works by instilling hope in both adolescents and their parents by teaching them concrete and specific skills that can replace their maladaptive behaviors.

The DBT therapist must also obtain a thorough history of suicidal and nonsuicidal self-injurious behaviors and assess current suicidal ideation, plan, and intent (Target 1). Additionally, the therapist must examine the patient's prior treatment history and anticipate treatment-interfering behaviors (Target 2), the patient's current quality-of-life–interfering behaviors (e.g., depression, school failure, substance abuse, binging and purging, and relational problems; Target 3), and finally, the patient's repertoire of behavioral skill capabilities and deficits (Target 4). The therapist might say, for example, "In DBT, we consider your overdose as life-threatening behavior, and your dropping out of two prior treatment programs as treatment-interfering behavior." Reframing these problems in DBT language helps the therapist explain how DBT will target these problems. Sharing a common language may strengthen the therapeutic alliance and facilitate the patient's engagement in treatment.

Present Biosocial Theory and Its Relationship to Borderline Behavioral Patterns

In DBT, therapists explain the biosocial theory of borderline personality disorder to their parents and their families. In addition to helping them understand the etiology and maintenance of borderline personality disordered behaviors, this intervention facilitates treatment engagement in two ways. First, patients and families often feel that the biosocial theory describes their experiences in a nonjudgmental and empathic manner. Creating an atmosphere in which patients and families feel validated and understood is critical to engaging and retaining them in treatment. Second, the use of multimedia approaches such as visual aids (e.g., handouts) to present this information helps keep adolescents interested.

The following dialogue illustrates how the biosocial theory might be discussed with patients and families. The therapist (pointing to a handout that lists the five problem areas) asks the adolescent, "How do you think you developed these particular problems that brought you into treatment?" To help answer this question, the therapist first reviews and defines the two components of the theory: bio and social. The therapist facilitates a discussion (vs. a didactic lecture) with the adolescent, starting with the bio component. "Have you ever experienced yourself as more emotionally (a) sensitive, (b) reactive, and (c) slower in returning to your emotional baseline once you get upset than your siblings or peers?" (Linehan, 1993a). Most of these adolescents admit that little things seem to get under their skin easily and affect them more than their peers. They acknowledge that when they get upset, their emotional reactions are intense and reactive (e.g., not only a little sad but feeling very depressed; not merely irritated but experiencing angry outbursts). Many also endorse a slow return to baseline. Specifically, when an emotion such as anger is triggered in a biologically emotionally vulnerable adolescent, instead of a sharp peak and then a quick return to baseline (e.g., within a 15-minute to 30-minute time period), they take much longer to calm themselves down to their emotional baseline level. This third characteristic can best be explained graphically as the beginning of an arc, which instead of returning back down to "0" remains elevated at a moderate to high level for an extended period (see Figure 7.1, http://pubs.apa.org/books/supp/elusive/). The DBT therapist explains that there is a growing body of research that suggests that the brains of those with borderline personality disorder behavioral patterns appear different on brain scans from the brains of those who do not exhibit these same behaviors (Miller et al., 2007). The implicit message is that in spite of having different biological wiring than their siblings or peers (validation of their emotional distress), these adolescents will need to work extra hard to regulate their emotions with the new DBT skills being taught.

The social part of the theory is described as the "invalidating environment." Once both *validation* and *invalidation* are defined, the therapist immediately provides an example to illustrate the concepts. The therapist attempts to use real-life examples provided by the adolescent, which facilitates the adolescent's engagement in treatment. For example, the therapist says,

> You told me that whenever you feel depressed and have less energy to do your chores in the house, your mother calls you lazy and tells you she should have aborted you. You also told me that when you travel with your family to visit your relatives your father insists that you put on a smile even if you are not happy. These are examples of invalidation, whereby your environment communicates to you that your thoughts, feelings, and actions are wrong, inappropriate, and invalid. Who's to say how you should feel and think? Those are your thoughts and feelings—not theirs!

We find this exercise to be extremely helpful to adolescents in helping them feel understood and not alone. Moreover, they often experience an enhanced sense of hope as the therapist explains that the family will be taught skills to address the chronic invalidation:

> The good news is that now is the time for family members and adolescents alike to learn how to validate one another and to put an end to the invalidating environment as you know it! Each one of you has to take responsibility for becoming more aware of this behavior and practicing the skill of validation, starting today.

Orient to DBT Program and Treatment Philosophy

The therapist orients the adolescent and family to the treatment format and philosophy, including the duration and modalities of treatment, the supportive and collaborative nature of the therapy, and the behavioral philosophy of the treatment, which involves behavioral rehearsal of new skills and telephone coaching to aid in skills generalization (see Miller, Rathus, Linehan, Wetzler, & Leigh, 1997, for a more comprehensive review). The therapist delivers this information in a flexible manner as she or he weaves it throughout the first two sessions.

Review Treatment Agreements

Patient and therapist agreements are presented and discussed at the start of individual therapy to build commitment to treatment. Patient agreements are (a) to enter and stay in therapy for the length of the program, (b) to attend both individual therapy and group skills training (review attendance policy), and (c) to work on reducing specific parasuicidal, therapy-interfering, and quality-of-life interfering behaviors (e.g., substance abuse).

Implicit and explicit therapist agreements are (a) to make every reasonable effort to be effective, including obtaining consultation as needed from supervisors and colleagues attending the therapist consultation meeting; (b) to be available to the patient (both for sessions and by pager); (c) to show respect for the patient; and (d) to maintain confidentiality with the following exceptions: suicidal ideation with plan and intent, to be reported to the legal guardian, and suspected physical or sexual abuse or neglect, to be reported to child protective services as mandated by state law.

The therapist might discuss the patient–therapist agreements with adolescents as follows:

> I think I'm a pretty good DBT therapist. However, I'm not perfect. I make mistakes, and I'll probably do something in the next 16 weeks that will bother you, piss you off, and maybe even cause you to consider leaving therapy. Now, let's be clear, I expect you will also make mistakes; you may do things that piss me off. The point I am making here is that if you are going to get the help you need, we BOTH need to be sure that we keep the therapeutic relationship strong. That requires both of us to be honest with each other if we feel there is a problem; if one of us upsets the other, even accidentally, we have to say to the other person, "Hey, when you said that, you pissed me off!" or "Hey, why didn't you call me when you said you would?"

STYLISTIC STRATEGIES

Stylistic strategies refer to how the therapist communicates information rather than the content of the information, per se.

> Style has to do with tone (warm vs. cool or confrontational), with edge (soft and flowing vs. hard and abrupt), with intensity (light or humorous vs. very serious), with speed (fast, quick-moving, or interruptive vs. slow, thoughtful, and reflective), and with responsiveness (vulnerable vs. impervious). (Linehan, 1993a, p. 371)

DBT therapists rely on an interpersonal style that balances reciprocal and irreverent communication strategies and is intended to keep the patient engaged and the therapy moving (see Linehan, 1993a, for a complete description of all of the dialectical strategies). Reciprocal communication strategies, like those used in client-centered therapy, aim to reduce the power differential and arbitrariness inherent in some standard therapeutic relationships by making the therapist more genuine and more open to the patient's influence.

In our experience, therapists who have had more experience with adult patients may approach teenagers with an authoritarian, doctorlike "one-up–one-down" stance that can alienate adolescents.

Reciprocal communication in DBT means being responsive, warm, and engaged; using self-disclosure; and being genuine. Self-disclosure can be used to provide feedback to the patient about the effect of her or his behavior on the therapist. For example, a therapist might note, "I'm confused, because I can't tell whether you don't understand me or don't want to understand me" or "When you call me for help and then criticize all my efforts to help you, I feel frustrated." Self-disclosure by the therapist can also provide a model of adaptive behavior. For example, in discussing a patient's urge to assault a peer, the therapist might describe a recent event in which she or he experienced a similar urge after being cut off on the highway by another driver. This self-disclosure models acceptance of a painful life event, validates the patient's reactions, and presents the therapist as a vulnerable and imperfect person.

The challenge when using reciprocal communication is to get the adolescent to both like and respect the therapist. In working with adolescents, it is important to communicate a high level of confidence in three domains: one's ability as a therapist, the ability of the patient to improve, and the efficacy of the treatment. Feigning confidence in any one of these domains will likely prove ineffective because teenagers often see through the act and then disengage from the treatment. This can be particularly challenging for new therapists, who may feel less competent. Thus, a therapist should strive for balance between genuinely communicating confidence in all three domains (self, patient, and treatment) in a warm and responsive manner while not overpromoting them.

Irreverent communication strategies, similar to strategies used in Whitaker's (1975) strategic therapy, contrast sharply with reciprocal strategies. Irreverent strategies may be used when the patient, therapist, or both are stuck in a dysfunctional emotional, thought, or behavior pattern. Irreverent communications aim to get the patient's attention, shift the patient's affective response, and help the patient see a different point of view.

Irreverent communication may be unexpected, confrontational, or extreme and usually contrasts with the patient's current affect; it is intended to jolt patients out of their current affective state into a different emotional state. The communication should be genuine and matter of fact, with voice tone and facial expressions consistent with the content of an irreverent communication. Irreverence is never used in a mean-spirited way and is best used when the therapist and client have established a strong relationship and the patient knows the therapist to be caring and compassionate. There are several irreverent communication strategies (e.g., expressing omnipotence and impotence, plunging in where angels fear to tread, oscillating intensity and using silence, and calling a patient's bluff). "Plunging in where angels fear to tread" is an irreverent strategy in which the therapist asks straightforward, unflinching questions about sensitive areas, such as suicidal behavior, sexuality, and therapy-interfering behaviors (Linehan, 1993a). "Do you expect me to believe that?" is the irreverent communication strategy of calling a patient's bluff. For a more thorough review of these strategies, see Linehan (1993a).

The following exchange further illustrates the use of irreverence:

> *Patient:* My sister is really getting me angry because she refuses to help me clean up the house. . . . I swear, one of these days, I am going to cut off her legs and cut out her tongue.
>
> *Therapist:* Well, I guess then you won't be getting any help from her cleaning up in the future.

In this example, the therapist is slightly unorthodox and does not provide the answer the patient is looking for. The irreverent responses are intended to break entrenched patterns of thought in a relatively light manner and shift the patient from the mood that generated the comments into a more questioning, receptive state of mind. The DBT therapist may shift rapidly back and forth between reciprocal and irreverent communication during a single interaction, always balancing the two styles so that reciprocal communication and irreverence become integrated into a unified interpersonal style.

SPECIFIC COMMITMENT STRATEGIES WITH ADOLESCENTS

At the initial stages of therapy, the therapist takes an explicit, verbal commitment from the patient both to participate in DBT for the length of the program and to reduce his or her maladaptive behaviors. Commitment strategies are critical both to obtaining and to maintaining a patient's engagement in the treatment process. In our experience, inadequate commitment from the patient, therapist, or both can lead to therapy failures or treatment terminations. The patient may make an insufficient or glib commitment in the initial stages of the change process or, more often, events within or outside of therapy may dissipate the patient's previous commitments. This is particularly relevant to adolescents, given that they usually reside in their invalidating environments and often feel hopeless about their situation improving. Patient commitment in DBT is both an important prerequisite for effective therapy and, in itself, a goal of the therapy. Therefore, DBT views the patient's commitment to treatment and to change as a behavior itself, which can be elicited, learned, and reinforced. So, for example, rather than assuming the patient is committed to implementing behavioral solutions to old problems, the therapist works collaboratively with the patient to facilitate the patient's commitment to change. When working in a brief treatment model (16 weeks), the therapist must figure this out quickly.

In-session behaviors that are inconsistent with this initial degree of commitment and collaboration include refusing to work in therapy, avoiding or refusing to talk about feelings and events connected with target behaviors, and rejecting all input from the therapist or attempts to generate alternative solutions. It is important that the therapist actively target these in-session problem behaviors. At these moments, the therapist should discuss the adolescent's commitment to therapy itself, with the goal of eliciting a recommitment.

Eliciting commitment necessitates a certain amount of salesmanship—the product being sold is new behavior and, sometimes, life itself. To obtain commitment to DBT, the therapist needs to be flexible and creative while using one or more commitment strategies. Linehan (1993a) identified eight commitment strategies: (a) selling commitment and evaluating pros and cons, (b) playing devil's advocate, (c) foot-in-the-door–door-in-the-face techniques (Cialdini, Vincent, Lewis, Catalan, Wheeler & Darby, 1975; Freedman & Fraser, 1966), (d) connecting present commitments to prior commitments, (e) highlighting freedom to choose and absence of alternatives, (f) using principles of shaping, (g) cheerleading, and (h) agreeing on homework. Several examples are highlighted in this section.

In evaluating the pros and cons of proceeding with treatment, the therapist starts by laying out the counterarguments of pursuing treatment that the patient him- or herself would likely consider. This is followed by a discussion of the advantages of participating in treatment. For example, the therapist might say,

> Now, thinking of the disadvantages of committing to treatment, it is going to take a huge effort, possibly too much effort, to change some of your long-standing behavioral patterns. The time commitment necessary for group and individual sessions, as well as therapy homework assignments and phone consultations, may be too much for you right now. However, by making a commitment to treatment, we will work together to help you achieve your goals of reducing your self-cutting, keeping you out of the hospital, and helping you stay in school so that you can graduate. So we should weigh out the pros and cons before you make a final decision.

In the devil's advocate approach, the therapist argues against a commitment to treatment with the intent that the adolescent will him- or herself make the argument for participating in treatment. The therapist might say, "This treatment requires a huge time commitment, and I am not sure that you are up to it right now." This technique becomes quite useful with teenagers who are more likely to offer quick agreements without thinking through the consequences of those agreements, such as, "Oh, yeah, I definitely want to do this therapy . . . and yes, I will never cut myself again."

The foot-in-the-door–door-in-the-face techniques are well-known procedures from social psychology that enhance compliance with requests. In the foot-in-the-door technique, the therapist makes a request that seems easy, followed by a more difficult request. For instance, a therapist first obtained agreement from a socially phobic patient to attend group skills training. In the next session, the therapist said encouragingly, "OK, now that you are there, can you volunteer to report on your homework, or at least read something from the skills notebook when the skills trainers ask for volunteers?" Another example of the foot-in-the-door technique is first getting commitment to participate in treatment and reduce all target behaviors. Second, the therapist mentions, "Oh, by the way, there's one more little thing I would like you to do for next week; it's called a diary card." At that point, the therapist reviews the card.

In the door-in-the-face technique, the therapist first makes a harder request and then solicits a more easily performed behavior. This strategy proves helpful in obtaining early commitment to treatment. For example, one patient would not agree to stay alive for the entire length of the program (i.e., 16 weeks) but could make a commitment not to end his life on a weekly basis. The therapist said, "How about if you agree to stay alive this week, and we will reevaluate next week to see if you are willing to renew your agreement?"

The strategy of highlighting freedom to choose and absence of alternatives is particularly useful in working with teenagers who are in treatment involuntarily. When people believe they have chosen freely and when they believe there are no alternatives to reach their goal, commitment and compliance are enhanced. In using this strategy, the therapist stresses the patient's freedom of choice while at the same time stressing the lack of effective alternatives. For example, in developing or redeveloping a patient's commitment to stop attempting suicide, the therapist may emphasize that the patient is free to choose a life of coping by suicide, but if she or he makes that choice, another treatment should be found because DBT requires reduction of suicidal behavior as a goal. When using this strategy to strengthen commitment to the treatment program, the DBT therapist lists in detail all the problems the adolescent is currently experiencing and then says,

> So, you can try to manage your suicidality, depression, substance use, probation, suspensions from school, and huge conflicts with your parents on your own, as you have been doing, or the other option is to try this therapy twice per week and see if we can get these problems under control so that you can stay alive, get your parents off your back, and hopefully then won't be kicked out of home and school and sent to residential treatment. Of course, it's totally your choice. What do you think?

Connecting present commitments to prior commitments involves reminding the patient of commitments made previously. It should be used when the therapist believes the patient's commitment is fading or when the patient's behavior is incongruent with his or her previous commitments. For instance, when a patient threatened to use laxatives again, the therapist said, "But I thought you were going to try your best not to do that ever since you made that commitment 6 weeks ago. That's one of the commitments you made on entering therapy with us."

Another strategy is generating hope by cheerleading. One of the major problems confronting suicidal and borderline adolescents is their lack of hope that they can effect change in their lives or their fear that their attempts to change will end in failure or humiliation. In cheerleading, the therapist encourages the patient, reinforces even minimal progress, and consistently points out that the patient has within her or him what it will take to handle her or his problems. For example, one patient was raised by an emotionally abusive alcoholic father who continued to demean and insult her. This patient needed extensive amounts of cheerleading and encouragement to help build a sense of hope that she could actually change herself. These patients can overwhelm the therapist. At these times, the therapist consultation group becomes critical in helping the therapist reestablish commitment, perspective, and balance to engage or reengage the adolescent.

Finally, the same commitment strategies used with the adolescent are used with the families. Having the parents or guardians buy into this treatment approach and participate themselves often requires a fair degree of orienting and commitment by the therapist (Miller et al., 2007). Remember, many of these families are burned out by the adolescent's behaviors and feel pervasively invalidated by prior treatment providers. Thus, validation is a key first strategy before moving toward commitment and change.

DIALECTICAL STRATEGIES

Dialectical strategies permeate the entire treatment and emphasize the tensions elicited by contradictory emotions, cognitions, and behavior patterns, both within the individual and between the individual and her or his environment. The strategies are based on a dialectical philosophy that views reality as an interrelated system, with opposing internal forces and in a state of continuous change. These strategies are used in individual therapy and inform both treatment supervision and therapist consultation meetings (Fruzzetti, Waltz, & Linehan, 1997). We briefly discuss the dialectical stance the individual therapist uses and offer a few examples of specific dialectical strategies. The therapist uses these strategies with the patient to restore movement and flow within the session and to counter getting stuck, which can result in significant breaches in the therapeutic alliance and, ultimately, dropout.

The therapist uses a dialectical focus on two different therapeutic levels. First, within the therapeutic interaction, the therapist consciously monitors the balance of change and acceptance, flexibility and stability, challenging and nurturing, and other dialectics to engage adolescents and maintain a collaborative working relationship in the moment-to-moment interactions. Second, the therapist teaches and models dialectical thinking and behavior in the session by opposing any term or proposition with its opposite or an alternative. This requires the therapist to continually look out for alternatives, including polar opposite alternatives, to help inform current discussions. The therapist helps the patient achieve a synthesis of oppositions rather than verifying either side of an argument. The point is that either extreme of a dialectic is likely not helpful, so the patient is helped to find the middle path by moving from "either–or" thinking to "both–and" thinking. The therapist might say, "I can see why you want more independence than you are allowed, and at the same time, it is important to continue to have some dependence on those around you so that you can obtain nurturance and support when you want it."

The dialectical strategies used in DBT include entering the paradox, using metaphors, playing devil's advocate, extending, activating, "wise mind," making lemonade out of lemons, and allowing natural change (see Linehan, 1993a, for a complete description of all of the dialectical strategies). For example, "making lemonade out of lemons" turns something seemingly problematic, including negative external situations, into an advantage. For example, an adolescent with mild social phobia is told that she has to attend a multifamily skills training group with five other patients. When she tells her therapist, "I can't do that," the therapist responds to the patient's distress by saying lightly or with some humor, "Oh, this is fabulous! We've found an opportunity for you to practice your distress tolerance and interpersonal effectiveness skills." This strategy is best used in the context of a strong therapeutic relationship.

VIGNETTE

To illustrate the various DBT engagement strategies used with suicidal multiproblem adolescents, we present several excerpts from a first session of a composite client (strategies illustrated are presented in brackets). The following case is that of a 15-year-old African American girl living with her maternal grandmother and younger brother who presented to our treatment program. She was referred from a local emergency room following a report of suicidal ideation to her teacher. The first excerpt presents a discussion of the presenting problem.

Therapist: So, you're saying you threatened to self-harm when your teacher couldn't give you the attention you wanted in that moment, and I'm already thinking "Oh, boy," if I'm not giving you the attention you want immediately.

Patient: Not immediately. Because I did wait a long time.

Therapist: Well, however long, it's possible that I may not even realize that you want something from me. I'm hoping that I will, but I sometimes make mistakes. Don't get me wrong—I think I'm pretty good—I run the program. But I make mistakes, too, and it may be possible that there may be a time or a phone call that I miss. You ask for help, and I just don't hear you. [expressing omnipotence and impotence] Did you ever hear the expression "like two ships passing in the night"? [using metaphor] It's possible, wouldn't you say, in the 4 months we're working together that I may miss something. I want you to say to me, "John, I think you are missing something" or "John, when you didn't call me back the other day, I got upset." I don't want to find out after you cut yourself. Let's make a deal now. And, you know, I'll do the same for you. If you make me angry or do something when I say, "Wait a minute. I think she's missing something with me," I'll tell you directly, "I think we have a little problem here." We have to work as a team [therapeutic collaboration], so if one of us is missing something or upset with the other, we're not going to be a good team. So I'd like to shake your hand and agree that if one of us is upset, we're going to let the other person know. Can we make that agreement right now? [patient–therapist agreement]

Patient: Um hmm. [*shake hands*]

* * * * * *

Therapist: So you want to live?

Patient: No.

Therapist: If you could solve some of your family problems, would you want to live?

Patient: No.

Therapist: So, what are you doing here if you don't want to live?

Patient: [*shrugs*]

Therapist: So, you're telling me you want to die? All of the time or some of the time? [irreverence]

Patient: All the time.

Therapist: All the time? Maybe there's a moment, when you are practicing cheerleading, for example, when you are happy to be
living?

Patient: Well, yes. But only when I'm with this new guy. There is
something about him . . . .

Therapist: Listen—here's my question to you. If we can work together
for the next 16 weeks, I am going to ask you not to hurt yourself. [door in the face] If you want to harm yourself after-
wards, that is your choice. [irreverence] But if we are going
to work together, I need a commitment from you today that
you are going to give this therapy a chance. I need a commitment from you because, you know, I can't stop you from
hurting yourself. Don't get me wrong—I hear you. I know
what I'm asking is not easy, and I know things have been
tough for you these past few weeks. [validation and reciprocal communication] If you want to do it, you will. But what
I can do is help you create a life that feels worth living, and
I do that pretty well, actually. I can't stop you from cutting
yourself if you want to, but I need you to commit to try to
stop for the next 16 weeks. Can you give me that?

Patient: [*shakes head no*]

Therapist: Why not?

Patient: Because I go straight for something to cut if I get angry.

Therapist: You mean you are not sure you can stop?

Patient: No, I mean I know I'm not going to stop.

Therapist: Because you don't want to, or you can't?

Patient: Because I can't.

Therapist: OK, but if you could stop hurting yourself, would you?

Patient: I think so.

Therapist: So 16 weeks seems too long of a commitment?

Patient: It's 4 months, right?

Therapist: Yeah.

Patient: Won't work. I have to leave in July for a sleep-away camp.

Therapist: We'll work something out. But that's still months away.
This is my question. You can't give me 16 weeks. Can you
give me 8 weeks? [door in the face, continued] That's half

the time. Can you say in the next 2 months, you will do everything in your power not to harm yourself? Remember, I'm gonna help you. You're not alone in this. We're gonna work out a system so that when you have an urge to cut yourself, you'll call me for coaching and say, "I have an urge to hurt myself. What should I do?" At that point, I will suggest skills for you to use.

Patient: You heard about the thing with Stella?

Therapist: Where you paged Stella from school and you handled the situation without hurting yourself? C'mon now, that was good. [*slaps high five*] That's the idea. [positive reinforcement]

*   *   *   *   *   *

Therapist: You tell me, which of these problem areas relate to you. [*hands sheet to patient*] [allowing patient to identify her own problems and fold them into DBT problem areas]

Patient: All of them.

Therapist: So, okay, do you have trouble knowing what you're feeling when you're feeling it? [*points to sheet*] [visual aids]

Patient: Yes, and I don't know why I'm feeling certain things sometimes.

Therapist: Yes. That's called "confusion about self" on the handout.

Patient: I act sometimes without thinking about it.

Therapist: Uh huh. And that is what we call impulsivity. How true is this next one of you, emotional instability? [*pointing to handout*]

Patient: Well, my mood could change really fast. I could be real happy at one time and then another time be angry and not know why.

Therapist: OK. So your moods change quickly, and you don't know why. Sometimes you are depressed, sometimes you're angry, sometimes you are happy?

Patient: Yeah—sometimes.

Therapist: OK. Fair enough. And what kind of mood are you in when you hurt yourself—cut yourself or try to kill yourself?

Patient: Angry, pissed off, I guess. Maybe confused sometimes.

Therapist: OK—this is good for us to know. What about interpersonal problems?

Patient: I can be happy, smile and somebody notices, and they say I'm their friend. But, I might not get along with them later. Recently, I've been fighting with my friends and family.

* * * * * *

Therapist: See, I don't know if this therapy is going to be right for you. [devil's advocate] Do you know why? Because this therapy is for people who want to stop harming themselves; people who want to create a life that feels worth living. They are willing to come to therapy twice a week. They want to stop drinking and doing drugs. Now, that's a lot.

Patient: Yeah, that is a lot.

Therapist: I know. So what I'm saying is that there's a lot of things that would make sense for you and I to work on, but I'm not sure if you want to work on all this. On the one hand, you're saying you want to stop the behavior, but on the other, you are not sure you want to stop. The thing with this therapy is that there is a lot of focusing on reducing the behaviors that get people into trouble. Not to say when you get older drinking at social events wouldn't be OK, but right now when you are drinking and you have sharps around and you're thinking of killing yourself and you're feeling depressed, that is a dangerous combination. We know alcohol increases the risk of people hurting or killing themselves, so if you drink, you are going to be more likely to harm yourself. But you tell me you don't want to harm yourself, right?

Patient: [*sighs and shrugs*]

Therapist: So what do you think? Do you think this therapy may be too hard for you?

Patient: [*sways side to side in chair*] Yeah.

Therapist: Why would you want to do this therapy when I'm asking you to stop things you don't necessarily want to stop?

Patient: Um. . . . [*looking down*]

Therapist: You know what I mean? Because it is hard work, this therapy. But you are a hard worker from what you tell me. How are your grades in school?

Patient: Good. I study hard, but they're dropping because of all my problems.

Therapist: So you can work hard when you want to. Am I right about that?

Patient:	Yes.
Therapist:	So the question is, can you do the same with this therapy? And maybe you'll have to see—maybe you'll have to see if it is something you want to do. [*moment of silence; both patient and therapist looking at one another*] What do you think?
Patient:	I'd rather see later on in the therapy because if I really, really want to do it, then I know I'll do it, but right now, I'm not paying mind to it.
Therapist:	Well, I'm not sure what to tell you. We really can't do therapy unless you want help with these things. Maybe I should tell you and your grandmother when you feel ready and you really want help with these things, we'll meet then.
Patient:	Wait a minute. I'm saying I want help with my problems now because later in the year it will be too late.
Therapist:	Which problems?
Patient:	Don't know. I don't expect things to be perfect with my family. I just want to leave all this crap behind with them. So, I guess I want help with the future.
Therapist:	So, you want help planning for your future?

The conversation continues, with patient identifying specific problem areas she wants help with while the therapist folds them into DBT Stage 1 targets. Therapist obtains patient's commitment throughout.

SUMMARY

Mental health professionals working with suicidal, multiproblem adolescents face myriad treatment challenges. Primary among these challenges are the tasks of engaging and retaining these adolescents in a psychosocial treatment program that can address their complex needs. The need to more effectively target treatment engagement and retention is made even more urgent by suicidal adolescents' high rate of treatment dropout combined with their high rate of suicide reattempts. DBT for adolescents addresses this need by providing a treatment philosophy and concrete therapeutic strategies that directly target suicidal adolescents' commitment to and engagement with treatment. We hope this chapter proves useful to clinicians working to address the complexity of problems that characterize suicidal adolescents.

REFERENCES

Adcock, A., Nagy, S., & Simpson, J. A. (1991). Selected risk factors in adolescent suicide attempts. *Adolescence, 26,* 817–828.

Anderson, R. N. (2002). Deaths: Leading causes for 2000. *National Vital Statistics Reports, 50*(16). Retrieved from http://www.cdc.gov/nchs/data/nvsr/nvsr50/nvsr50_16.pdf

Brent, D. A., Johnson, B. A., Perper, J. A., Connolly, J., Bridge, J., Bartle, S., & Rather, C. (1994). Personality disorder, personality traits, impulsive violence, and completed suicide in adolescents. *Journal of the American Academy of Child & Adolescent Psychiatry, 33,* 1080–1086. doi:10.1097/00004583-199410000-00003

Cialdini, R. B., Vincent, J. E., Lewis, S. K., Catalan, J., Wheeler, D., & Darby, B. L. (1975). Reciprocal concessions procedure for inducing compliance: The door-in-the-face technique. *Journal of Personality and Social Psychology, 31,* 206–215. doi:10.1037/h0076284

Crumley, F. E. (1979). Adolescent suicide attempts. *JAMA, 241,* 2404–2407. doi:10.1001/jama.241.22.2404

Freedman, J. L., & Fraser, S. C. (1966). Compliance without pressure: The foot-in-the-door technique. *Journal of Personality and Social Psychology, 4,* 195–202. doi:10.1037/h0023552

Fruzzetti, A. E., Waltz, J. A., & Linehan, M. M. (1997). Supervision in dialectical behavior therapy. In C. E. Watkins Jr. (Ed.), *Handbook of psychotherapy supervision* (pp. 84–100). New York, NY: Wiley.

Kandel, D. B., Raveis, V. H., & Davies, M. (1991). Suicidal ideation in adolescence: Depression, substance use and other risk factors. *Journal of Youth and Adolescence, 20,* 289–309. doi:10.1007/BF01537613

Katz, L. Y., Gunasekara, S., Cox, B. J., & Miller, A. L. (2004). Feasibility of dialectical behavior therapy for parasuicidal adolescent inpatients. *JAMA, 43,* 276–282. doi:10.1097/00004583-200403000-00008

Koerner, K., Miller, A. L., & Wagner, A. W. (1998). Dialectical behavior therapy: Part I. Principle based intervention with multi-problem patients. *Journal of Practical Psychiatry and Behavioral Health, 4,* 28–36.

Lewinsohn, P. M., Rohde, P., & Seeley, J. R. (1996). Adolescent suicide ideation and attempts: Prevalence, risk factors, and clinical implications. *Clinical Psychology: Science and Practice, 3,* 25–46.

Linehan, M. M. (1993a). *Cognitive-behavioral treatment of borderline personality disorder.* New York, NY: Guilford Press.

Linehan, M. M. (1993b). *Skills training manual for treating borderline personality disorder.* New York, NY: Guilford Press.

Linehan, M. M., Comtois, K. A., Murray, A. M., Brown, M. Z., Gallop, R. J., Heard, H. L., . . . Lindenboam, N. (2006). Two year randomized trial and follow-up of DBT vs. therapy-by-experts for suicidal behaviors and borderline personality disorder. *Archives of General Psychiatry, 63,* 757–766.

Linehan, M. M., Dimeff, L. A., Reynolds, S. K., Comtois, K. A., Selch, S. S., Heagerty, P., & Kivlahan, D. R. (2002). Dialectical behavior therapy versus comprehensive validation therapy plus 12-step for the treatment of opioid dependent women meeting criteria for borderline personality disorder. *Drug and Alcohol Dependence, 67,* 13–26.

Marton, P., Lorenblum, M., Kutcher, S., Stein, B., Kennedy, B., & Pakes, J. (1989). Personality dysfunction in depressed adolescents. *Canadian Journal of Psychiatry, 34,* 810–813.

Miller, A. L., Glinski, J., Woodberry, K., Mitchell, A., & Indik, J. (2002). Family therapy and dialectical behavior therapy with adolescents: Part I. Proposing a clinical synthesis. *American Journal of Psychotherapy, 56,* 568–584.

Miller, A. L., Rathus, J. H., & Linehan, M. M. (2007). *Dialectical behavior therapy with suicidal adolescents*. New York, NY: Guilford Press.

Miller, A. L., Rathus, J. H., Linehan, M. M., Wetzler, S., & Leigh, E. (1997). Dialectical behavior therapy for suicidal adolescents. *Journal of Practical Psychiatry and Behavioral Health, 3*, 78–86. doi:10.1097/00131746-199703000-00002

Miller, A. L., Wyman, S. E., Glassman, S. L., Huppert, J. D., & Rathus, J. H. (2000). Analysis of behavioral skills utilized by adolescents receiving dialectical behavior therapy. *Cognitive and Behavioral Practice, 7*, 183–187. doi:10.1016/S1077-7229(00)80029-2

Rathus, J. H., & Miller, A. L. (2002). Dialectical behavioral therapy adapted for suicidal adolescents. *Suicide & Life-Threatening Behavior, 32*, 146–157. doi:10.1521/suli.32.2.146.24399

Reynolds, W. M., & Mazza, J. J. (1992, June). *Suicidal behavior in non-referred adolescents*. Paper presented at the international Conference for Suicidal Behavior, Western Psychiatric Institute and Clinic, Pittsburgh, PA

Shaffer, D., Gould, M., Fisher, P., Trautman, P., Moreau, D., Kleinman, M., & Flory, M. (1996). Psychiatric diagnosis in child and adolescent suicide. *Archives of General Psychiatry, 53*, 339–348.

Spirito, A., Brown, L., Overholser, J., & Fritz, G. (1989). Attempted suicide in adolescence: A review and critique of the literature. *Clinical Psychology Review, 9*, 335–363. doi:10.1016/0272-7358(89)90061-5

Trautman, P. D., Stewart, N., & Morishima, A. (1993). Are adolescent suicide attempters noncompliant with outpatient care? *Journal of the American Academy of Child & Adolescent Psychiatry, 32*, 89–94. doi:10.1097/00004583-199301000-00013

Whitaker, C. A. (1975). Psychotherapy of the absurd: With a special emphasis on the psychotherapy of aggression. *Family Process, 14*, 1–16. doi:10.1111/j.1545-5300.1975.00001.x

Woodberry, K. A., Miller, A. L., Glinski, J., Indik, J., & Mitchell, A. (2002). Family therapy and dialectical behavior with adolescents: Part 2, a theoretical review. *American Journal of Psychotherapy, 56*, 585–602.

8

TREATMENT ENGAGEMENT WITH ADOLESCENT SUICIDE ATTEMPTERS

DEIDRE DONALDSON, ANTHONY SPIRITO, AND JULIE BOERGERS

Suicidal adolescents are a difficult population to treat. Research has demonstrated that it is challenging to engage them in treatment, particularly those who have made a suicide attempt. This is problematic because such adolescents remain at elevated risk for affective distress, reattempts, and other risk behaviors (Boergers & Spirito, 2003). Symptoms of distress often associated with suicidality (e.g., hopelessness, loneliness, emotional regulation difficulties, and depression) can be alleviated by psychotherapy (e.g., Pillay & Wassenaar, 1995; Slee, Spinhoven, Garnefski, & Arensman, 2008; TADS Team, 2007). Thus, to effectively treat suicidal adolescents, treatment engagement is an important problem to address. Treatment engagement, or the process of actively participating in treatment, has been operationalized across various literature bases to include session attendance, therapeutic rapport or alliance, openness toward treatment, and satisfaction with treatment (Broome, Flynn, Knight, & Simpson, 2007). Treatment engagement begins with the referral process and involves not only adherence with the initial referral but ongoing treatment attendance.

Suicidal adolescents are challenging in both of these arenas. They are known to exhibit poor adherence with the outpatient referral process, and they exhibit higher treatment dropout rates and drop out sooner than adolescents being treated for other psychological problems (see Boergers & Spirito, 2003, for a review). Estimates in the United States have indicated that between 15% and 20% of adolescents referred for outpatient treatment following an actual attempt never follow through with the referral (i.e., never attend the initial appointment; Brent, Perper, & Moritz, 1993; Trautman & Rotheram, 1987). Trautman, Stewart, and Morishima (1993) found that adolescent suicide attempters attend significantly fewer outpatient treatment sessions than nonsuicidal adolescents receiving treatment (median of three vs. 11 sessions).

Similar rates of treatment refusal have been found outside the United States. For instance, Pillay and Wassenaar (1995) reported that of 40 Indian adolescents who received medical follow-up referral for outpatient care after a suicide attempt, 45% refused treatment. Similar treatment refusal rates have been noted for adolescent suicide attempters in Great Britain (44%; Taylor & Stansfeld, 1984) and France (35%; Granboulan, Rabain, & Basquin, 1995).

An increasing body of literature points to the importance of treatment alliance as a salient component of treatment engagement in suicidal and depressed adolescents (e.g., A. L. Miller, Rathus, & Linehan, 2007; Shirk, Gudmundsen, Kaplinski, & McMakin, 2008) as well as other high-risk groups, such as substance abusers (e.g., Hogue, Dauber, Stambaugh, Cecero, & Liddle, 2006; Robbins et al., 2008). Shirk et al. (2008) found, in their study of 54 adolescents in a manual-guided, cognitive–behavioral therapy for adolescent depression, that an early alliance between an adolescent and his or her therapist predicted the continuation of therapy. When looking at the therapist ratings of alliance, Shirk et al. found a positive association between therapist ratings of alliance and the number of cognitive–behavioral treatment sessions completed as well as treatment continuation.

Karver et al. (2008) examined the relations among therapeutic alliance, client involvement, and therapy outcome in a randomized clinical trial comparing two outpatient treatments for adolescents who had attempted suicide (cognitive–behavioral therapy compared with nondirective treatment). Coded ratings were conducted of audiotaped treatment sessions with 23 attempters for the first four therapy sessions. Results suggested that therapeutic alliance and client involvement were significantly related to client outcome only in the cognitive–behavioral therapy condition. Yet, therapist lapse behaviors (e.g., criticizes, distorts or misunderstands, fails to acknowledge emotion) were related to client outcome in both types of therapy conditions, providing additional support for the importance of therapeutic alliance in the treatment of adolescent suicide attempters.

Hawley and Weisz (2005) found that parents' ratings of their own alliance with the therapist predicted treatment completion better than youth-rated alliance. This finding suggests that the parental relationship with the therapist might influence adolescent treatment adherence. Additionally, Shelef, Diamond, Diamond, and Liddle (2005) found parents' alliance with the therapist to predict treatment attendance.

Treatment satisfaction is also gaining recognition as an important component of treatment engagement. Garland, Haine, and Boxmeyer (2007) studied 143 families who received outpatient mental health care in one of two large community-based clinics. The primary aim of the study was to examine the extent to which parent and youth satisfaction with outpatient mental health care could be accounted for by a wide variety of potential determinants. Fifty-five clinicians provided treatment during the study. Youth satisfaction was positively associated with the therapists' years of experience, and parent satisfaction was positively associated with the number of treatment sessions. In addition, higher parent satisfaction was associated with lower caregiver strain at service entry and improvement in youth-reported functional impairment. Similarly, Nock and Kazdin (2001) found that parents who report very high or low expectations about treatment are likely to attend more sessions and are less likely to drop out of treatment. Burns, Cortell, and Wagner (2008) included clients' perceptions of treatment helpfulness in their study of 85 adolescents who had attempted suicide. They reported that parents rated all forms of treatment to be more helpful than did adolescents and that parent ratings of individual therapy helpfulness for the adolescent were significantly predictive of decreased treatment dropout. In contrast, poor parent–therapist relationship quality has been found to be related to premature treatment termination (Kazdin, Holland, & Crowley, 1997).

Although treatment engagement is emerging as a multifaceted construct reflecting several relevant components, treatment engagement among adolescent suicide attempters continues to be equated mostly with treatment attendance and continuation. Regardless of how treatment engagement is conceptualized, it is acknowledged that to enhance treatment outcomes the process of engagement must be central to the treatment of adolescent suicide attempters.

In this chapter, we outline several known barriers to treatment engagement relevant to suicidal adolescents. This includes discussion of both client (individual, familial) and service barriers. Subsequently, we provide a review of the available literature on enhancing treatment engagement with suicidal adolescents, including our own model derived from clinical research with adolescent suicide attempters. We also propose considerations for mental health professionals to use when addressing treatment engagement with suicidal adolescents and make recommendations for further research on this important topic.

INDIVIDUAL AND FAMILIAL BARRIERS TO TREATMENT AMONG SUICIDAL ADOLESCENTS

In the absence of a comprehensive conceptual model of treatment engagement, the risk factor model of treatment participation outlined by Kazdin (1996) is a useful alternative. This approach emphasizes the importance of identifying risk factors (i.e., barriers) that affect treatment attendance to improve engagement. Borrowing from Kazdin's discussion, this model assumes that multiple risk factors act together to influence outcome, that no single risk factor is sufficient, and that elucidating such factors can guide interventions to improve the desired outcome (i.e., improved treatment engagement).

Kazdin and colleagues (e.g., Kazdin & Mazurick, 1994; Kazdin, Mazurick, & Bass, 1993; Kazdin, Stolar, & Marciano, 1995) have examined the problem of treatment engagement in another high-risk treatment group, namely children and adolescents referred for treatment of conduct problems. Research with this group might be helpful in understanding suicidal adolescents because children and adolescents with conduct problems are similarly difficult to treat and also exhibit problems with treatment engagement. Research on adolescents with conduct problems has elucidated pertinent risk factors and engagement interventions. (The reader is also referred to Chapter 5 of this book, which examines the problem of engagement among adolescents with externalizing disorders and anger problems.)

Much of Kazdin's research on children and adolescents with conduct disorders has focused on individual adolescent and family factors that affect treatment engagement. Several factors have been found to differentiate those who drop out of treatment (i.e., attend fewer than six sessions) from those who complete treatment (see Kazdin, 1996). Individual factors for poor engagement that result in treatment dropout include multiple diagnoses, a more severe and prolonged history of antisocial behavior, cognitive or academic problems, and negative peer influences. Kazdin (1996) reported that multiple diagnoses and more severe and prolonged problems are risk factors because those who fail to engage or to complete treatment actually self-select out as a function of impairment. Burns et al. (2008) examined treatment adherence and satisfaction in 85 adolescents who had attempted suicide. Those with a diagnosis of either conduct disorder or substance abuse (other than alcohol or marijuana) dropped out of treatment earlier than others who had attempted suicide.

Certain characteristics have been found to be related to compliance with an initial outpatient treatment visit among adolescent suicide attempters. Specifically, higher levels of suicidal symptoms and depressed mood predict greater likelihood of follow-through (Taylor & Stansfeld, 1984). Similarly, research has suggested that a history of previous attempts, alcohol use at the time of attempt, and greater planning at the time of attempt are all associated with better treatment adherence (Spirito, Lewander, Levy, Kurkijian, & Fritz, 1994), perhaps because of heightened family or professional concern about the adolescent.

Kazdin (1996) reported that several family factors affect treatment engagement, including socioeconomic disadvantage, parenting challenges (i.e., parenting stress, poor parenting skills, single parenthood), parental history of psychopathology, life events, and ethnicity. Brookman-Frazee, Haine, Gabayan, and Garland (2008) found family sociodemographics (i.e., ethnic minority and low socioeconomic status) and clinical factors (i.e., parent stress, parent psychopathology, severe child behavioral problems, and poor child functioning) to affect treatment follow-through. According to research among adolescents who have attempted suicide, socioeconomic status is not predictive of treatment engagement (Spirito et al., 1994). However, family cohesion, level of family conflict, and parental physical health do predict treatment attendance in this population (Spirito et al. 1994; Taylor & Stansfeld, 1984; Trautman & Rotheram, 1987). Some of these factors impede the parent's day-to-day functioning, which, in turn, affects treatment engagement. Because treatment with children and adolescents relies, in part, on the parents' engagement in treatment, these factors should be considered.

Although limited research has addressed the issue of treatment engagement across ethnic groups, Kazdin et al. (1995) found that predictors of child treatment dropout differ according to ethnicity and need to be addressed accordingly. In their study, for example, they found that African American families dropped out of treatment for child mental health problems in higher numbers and earlier in treatment than Caucasian families. Although several common factors predicting dropout (or failure to engage) emerged, ethnic differences in rates of disengagement persisted even after socioeconomic disadvantage and family factors (which were disproportionately represented among the minority families) were controlled. Another study found that among Latino families, English-speaking families with highly acculturated adolescents were less likely to remain engaged with a school-based preventive intervention (Dillman Carpentier et al., 2007). A growing body of research has suggested the need to culturally tailor interventions to better engage and retain ethnic minority adolescents and their families (e.g., Breland-Noble, Bell, & Nicolas, 2006; Liddle, Jackson-Gilfort, & Marvel, 2006). Cultural and familial factors such as traditions, social norms, acculturation level, mistrust of the health care system, and values (such as interrelatedness vs. autonomy) all have the potential to affect treatment engagement. For example, family-oriented interventions may be more appropriate than individual psychotherapy for suicidal Latina adolescents compared with other ethnic groups because of a cultural emphasis on familism (Zayas & Pilat, 2008).

Treatment expectations that differ from actual experience reportedly affect participation in treatment (e.g. Plunkett, 1984). Historically, brochures, interviews, and videotaped modeling have been used as preparation techniques to influence such expectations (Day & Reznikoff, 1980). This research has focused primarily on parent perceptions. However, child perceptions may play an increasing role with age and may therefore also be relevant. Kazdin (1996) suggested that the congruence of treatment expectations across the child and family and what actually occurs in treatment should be examined empirically. Treatment expectations regarding attendance may be especially important.

In addition to these findings, transportation difficulties and stigma are factors worth mentioning with respect to adolescent suicide attempters. Studies with other patient groups experiencing transportation problems have suggested that a history of transportation difficulties (e.g., availability of vehicle, number of family members dependent on available transportation) may be useful in predicting follow-through with appointments (Yang, Zarr, Kass-Hout, Kourosh, & Kelly, 2006). Indeed, suicidal adolescents often experience transportation barriers. Sometimes this is a function of the adolescent's socioeconomic status. Other times, however, transportation is available but influenced by those who have control over its use (e.g., parents, relatives, friends).

Stigma is cited by adolescents as a barrier to help seeking in general (Gilchrist & Sullivan, 2006). It is also the most cited reason for avoiding psychotherapy (Vogel, Wade, & Aschcman, 2009). In addition to the potential for stigma from suicidality and suicidal behaviors, stigma seems a likely barrier to treatment engagement among suicide attempters (e.g., Moskos, Olson, Halbern, & Gray, 2007). However, further investigation is warranted.

Kazdin et al. (1997) tested the relation between parent report of barriers to treatment and premature treatment termination in a study of 242 children seen in a child psychiatry service where 10 clinicians served as therapists. The overall findings indicated that perceived barriers to treatment participation, including stressors and obstacles associated with coming to treatment, perceptions that treatment was not very relevant, and a poor relationship between the parent and the therapist, were all related to premature treatment termination. Among adolescents who attempt suicide, approximately 55% of those referred for outpatient services reportedly experience individual or family barriers to treatment (Spirito, Boergers, Donaldson, Bishop, & Lewander, 2002). Approximately 14% of adolescents report treatment resistance, 5% of parents report ambivalence toward treatment, and 3% of families report transportation problems and scheduling difficulties that interfere with treatment attendance, all of which affect treatment engagement. Family barriers to treatment are significantly negatively correlated with the number of outpatient treatment sessions adolescent suicide attempters actually attend ($r = .62, p < .001$; Spirito, Boergers, et al., 2002). Individual and family barriers relevant to suicidal adolescents are summarized in Table 8.1 (http://pubs.apa.org/books/supp/elusive/).

SERVICE BARRIERS TO TREATMENT AMONG SUICIDAL ADOLESCENTS

The role of service barriers seems to be at least as significant as family barriers to treatment engagement among suicidal adolescents. Approximately 58% of the families of adolescent suicide attempters we have studied report that service barriers affect treatment engagement throughout the treatment process (Spirito, Boergers, et al., 2002). Other surveys of adolescent treatment have reported similar results (e.g., Tolan, Ryan, & Jaffe, 1988). Although a significant proportion of those families also experience individual barriers, family barriers, or both, service barriers often fall outside the direct control of the adolescent or family referred for treatment. Moreover, service barriers persist even when families have access to the assistance of a trained mental health professional to help them navigate such barriers (Spirito, Boergers, et al., 2002).

Research has suggested five specific service barriers among suicidal adolescents (Spirito, Boergers, et al., 2002). These include delays in getting an appointment once referred, being placed on a waiting list, problems with insurance coverage or concerns about the cost of treatment, inability to switch therapists when requested, and language compatibility with the treatment provider. Being placed on a waiting list and scheduling difficulties were two prevalent (34% and 21%, respectively) factors found in one study (Spirito, Boergers, et al., 2002). These factors were followed by problems with insurance coverage or the cost of treatment (17%), mismatch with treatment provider (14%), and language compatibility (7%). The first two predominantly affect the adolescent's or family's adherence with the initial appointment. The others could presumably affect the initial appointment, ongoing treatment attendance, the therapeutic alliance, and treatment satisfaction.

Delays in obtaining an initial appointment or being put on a waiting list can be influenced by the availability of providers, receiving insurance authorization for treatment, and the volume of patients on clinic waiting lists. Although community mental health providers typically prioritize cases on the basis of acuity, suicidal adolescents still experience referral difficulties. For example, when mental health clinics use a crisis service model and suicidal teens are referred to this time-limited service, therapy may be terminated after one or two sessions if the adolescent no longer reports suicidal symptoms. These patients are then typically referred to a general outpatient therapy service. However, there is often subsequently a long period of time between the referral and first appointment, decreasing the likelihood of treatment follow-through and successful engagement (Spirito, Boergers, et al., 2002).

Sometimes the family's ambivalence toward treatment is manifested in their reported difficulty receiving treatment. For instance, suicidal adolescents present with many restrictions on their appointment schedules because of what they consider more important commitments (e.g., adolescent work schedules, sports, preferences for time of day). Family concerns about the cost of treatment persist, regardless of insurance type. Although families may see the need and benefit of treatment, some families weigh the perceived financial costs of treatment as greater than the hope of any benefits, particularly at the time of referral and onset of treatment. Insurance coverage or payment for services further affects the ability to find treatment resources, not to mention a provider with whom the family feels comfortable. Families have also reported that their insurance plan or therapist availability determines more about their choice of treatment than they do. Perhaps this perceived lack of control over treatment further compromises the engagement process.

Referral dissatisfaction, or mismatch with the provider, tends to arise after the adolescent has attended at least one appointment. Interestingly, research has also suggested that suicidal adolescents show different rates of adherence to outpatient treatment, depending on the type of treatment provided. For example, King, Hovey, Brand, and Ghaziuddin (1997) found that suicidal adolescents demonstrated the highest compliance rates with outpatient psychiatry (medication) visits (67%), followed by individual psychotherapy (51%), and family therapy (33%). Spirito, Boergers, et al. (2002) reported that some families who followed through with the initial appointment and subsequently requested a therapist transfer proceeded to drop out of therapy when the agency failed to accommodate the request.

Bilingual families, particularly parents, often report that they would feel more comfortable working with a therapist who speaks their native language. In instances when this is not possible, therapists either need to involve an interpreter, which involves more time and effort for everyone involved, or, less preferably, rely on an English-speaking family member, both of which may affect the engagement process and the development of the therapeutic alliance. Clinical experience has indicated that language preference may be reflective of satisfaction with the treatment provider or related to consistency with treatment expectations.

Although not formally examined as a service barrier among attempters, it has been documented that providers report anxiety, stress, and discomfort treating suicide attempters (Hellman, Morrison, & Abramovitz, 1987;

Kleespies & Ponce, 2009). Suicidal behavior of all types has been found to have an emotional impact on clinicians, and the impact increases with the severity of suicidal behavior (from ideation to attempt to completion; Kleespies, Penk, & Forsyth, 1993). Coupled with the fact that the suicide accounts for a high proportion of lawsuits filed against mental health clinicians (Baerger, 2001), clinician attitudes toward suicidal behavior may manifest as a service barrier for this population (e.g., difficulty obtaining a provider) or affect treatment engagement directly (e.g., therapist discomfort, lack of training). More research specifically regarding the relation between therapist attitudes toward suicidal behaviors and engagement with suicidal adolescents is needed.

Service barriers exist within the context of mental health care delivery and may require systemic solutions because they are such prominent factors affecting a number of adolescents referred for outpatient treatment. Service barriers were so substantial among adolescent suicide attempters in our study that our treatment protocol, as described in detail in the Structured Disposition Approach section, was limited in its effectiveness to the extent that service barriers were present (Spirito, Boergers, et al., 2002). The Surgeon General highlighted this problem in *Call to Action to Prevent Suicide*, by requesting the elimination of "barriers in public and private insurance programs for provision of mental and substance abuse disorder treatments" (U.S. Public Health Service, 1999, p. 7), a call that largely continues unanswered to the present. In 2002, the Institute of Medicine's Committee on Pathophysiology and Prevention of Adolescent and Adult Suicide released a report titled *Reducing Suicide: A National Imperative* (Goldsmith, Pellmar, Kleinman, & Bunney, 2002). It emphasized, among other factors, the need to reduce treatment barriers such as poor doctor–patient communication, stigma, and financial coverage of treatment.

APPROACHES TO ENGAGING SUICIDAL ADOLESCENTS

There have been at least four intervention studies targeting treatment engagement with suicidal adolescents. Each of these has demonstrated success using different but related methods focusing on a few of the many barriers to treatment engagement described earlier.

Deykin, Hsieh, Joshi, and McNamara (1986) examined adolescent adherence with outpatient treatment following random assignment to either an outreach program or standard care. The outreach approach was based on a social work model and included both a direct service component and a community-based education about suicidal behavior.

The service component consisted of support and advocacy for the adolescent, as well as assistance for financial difficulties. The social worker also checked in with adolescents to encourage them to attend their scheduled psychotherapy appointments. The program served participants who presented to a hospital emergency room for treatment of self-inflicted injuries. A small randomized trial showed promise in that the experimental group was significantly more likely to adhere to treatment recommendations than those who were simply provided with a referral.

Rotheram-Borus, Piacentini, and Cantwell (2000) conducted an extensive, system-level intervention for a group of Latina suicide attempters and their families seen in an emergency department. Emergency department staff attended a 2-hour training workshop on suicidality and treatment engagement. The workshop followed a detailed manual that trained staff in how to foster positive interactions with patients, reinforce the importance of outpatient treatment, and emphasize the seriousness of suicide attempts. During their emergency department visit, adolescent suicide attempters and their families viewed a videotape about suicidality and what to expect in psychotherapy. In addition, an on-call family therapist was available. Latina attempters ($n = 140$) were sequentially assigned to receive either the specialized emergency department intervention or routine emergency department care. The specialized intervention significantly increased attendance at the first outpatient therapy appointment (95% to 83%). In addition, those who received the emergency department intervention were somewhat more likely to attend more outpatient therapy sessions (5.7 sessions vs. 4.7 sessions).

Summerville, Kaslow, and Doepke (1996) reviewed assessment data, discussed family problem solving, and provided information regarding treatment with no effect ($N = 20$). Summerville et al.'s preliminary data suggested that improved maternal problem solving increased the likelihood of adolescent treatment attendance at and adherence with therapy appointments.

In general, these studies show promise in focusing on parent concerns about treatment and preparing the adolescent and family for treatment in a manner that improves engagement. Our own work has attempted to address a broader range of barriers known to affect treatment engagement among adolescent suicide attempters, or the *structured disposition approach* (SDA; Donaldson, Spirito, Arrigan, & Aspel, 1997; Spirito, Boergers, et al., 2002). This term is derived from our efforts with suicidal adolescents, which typically begin during disposition treatment planning in the general medical hospital following a suicide attempt. Several components of this approach are also relevant to treatment referrals regardless of where they emanate as well as throughout the treatment process. The methodology outlined here is easily transportable and could be used by adolescents presenting with varying levels of suicidal symptoms in both medical and psychiatric hospital settings. Disposition for adolescent suicide attempters most often involves referral to outpatient psychological treatment, and this process varies considerably from one clinician to another. Thus, we developed a highly structured methodology consisting of a set of core components outlined in Exhibit 8.1 (http://pubs.apa.org/books/supp/elusive/).

When developing this approach, we sought core components that would be flexible enough to address the wide range of potential barriers previously reviewed, as well as factors known to improve treatment adherence in general. Specifically, literature regarding treatment adherence suggests that specific information about treatment given ahead of time (e.g., during disposition planning) improves subsequent outpatient treatment adherence (e.g., Jellinek, 1978).

The first core component of the SDA addresses the patient's and family's treatment expectations. As discussed previously, misconceptions about treatment, or the possibility that expectations for therapy will not be met, can act as a barrier to treatment engagement. We first discuss this separately with the adolescent and his or her parents, when possible, and review it subsequently with everyone together. The goal is to elicit and discuss as many different expectations as possible. Helpful questions include "What do you think about going to therapy or counseling?" "What do you think usually happens in therapy/counseling?" or "When you think about the problems you are experiencing, how many visits to a therapist or counselor do you think it would take to get better?" Note that discussion of expectations may also elicit information about other barriers, which can also be addressed.

Once the family's expectations have been elicited, information is provided about what might actually happen in treatment. We divide this into three types of information: (a) treatment objectives, (b) treatment methods, and (c) the treatment process. Presenting treatment objectives helps the adolescent and family know what to expect in treatment and helps eliminate potential treatment misconceptions. Because treatment for suicidal adolescents can take many forms, depending on the provider's theoretical orientation, reviewing treatment objectives can help reconcile the family's expectations with what is actually likely to transpire and what the expected outcomes will be, which may reduce the risk of poor engagement.

Information about treatment methods includes how visits will be organized, with whom the adolescent and parents will meet, how long sessions will typically last, and the content of sessions. Regardless of the type of treatment provided, there should also be some discussion of what to expect from the treatment process. For example, if the disposition is to cognitive–behavioral treatment, we would provide information regarding the interactive nature of treatment, the use of assignments, the use of session agendas, and so on. If the adolescents and their parents have any remaining questions about the treatment methods, they are addressed accordingly. This thorough discussion about treatment expectations and information is conducted at the outset of treatment, throughout the referral process if possible, or both. It is important to continue to address these issues because failure to do so may create a subsequent treatment barrier. For example, in subsequent treatment sessions, we provide reminders of the number of sessions that remain and review what has been accomplished to date in treatment as well as progress toward treatment objectives.

The second core component of the SDA is the use of problem solving to address treatment barriers. We concurrently discuss barriers with the adolescent and parents as they arise and target at least one primary barrier, using cognitive problem solving.

It is helpful to prompt for barriers by stating, "We know that sometimes things come up that make it difficult for adolescents to go to therapy appointments. What are some things you can think of that make it hard for teenagers to go to counseling?" Then we ask the family members to brainstorm about all of the possible ways that a person in that situation, with that problem, might respond to the problem. Because this may be the first time the family has been exposed to problem solving, the therapist is actively involved in assisting the family to generate options. For example, if the family only lists a couple of options, the therapist would offer one (e.g., "What you said made me think of another thing that someone in that situation might do"). The therapist may also need to help the family brainstorm additional viable alternatives. At this point, any of the potential barriers listed in Table 8.1 (http://pubs.apa.org/books/supp/elusive/) that are not mentioned by the family may be reviewed as examples. Subsequent discussion follows about the plan to use a minimum of one of the options until the barrier is eliminated to enhance treatment engagement.

With suicidal adolescents in particular, the stigma surrounding not only mental health treatment but suicidal behavior in particular is significant and interferes with treatment engagement to the extent that suicidal behavior is denied. As a consequence, we have found it useful to reframe suicidal behavior as a failure in problem solving (Donaldson, Spirito, & Overholser, 2003). For example, we suggest to adolescents and their families that suicidal behavior seems to them to be the only current option (or alternative in problem-solving language) that would help them escape life's problems. We often summarize the experience using the following types of statements: "So, basically, you felt stuck and decided that the only way you could get out of this situation was to hurt yourself" or "You couldn't think of anything else to do that you thought would be helpful. So, you thought you would solve the problem by escaping it or hurting yourself." We might also state, "We can help you to learn how to get yourself 'unstuck' without having to hurt yourself." This is consistent with research showing that 55% of adolescents who actually attempt suicide report doing so as a method of escape from what they perceive to be an unbearable situation (Boergers, Spirito, & Donaldson, 1998). In our experience, this reframing takes the pressure off of the fear of mental illness (even if that is known to be present), decreases the shock and blame around the behavior, and is accepted by most adolescents and parents as an understandable target for how to improve the adolescent's life situation and engage in treatment.

Finally, our expectation for poor treatment attendance is addressed directly by contracting with the patient and family for treatment attendance. Specifically, we let families know that suicidal adolescents often have low rates of treatment follow-through, we review the importance of or rationale for treatment, and we contract with the family for a minimum number of sessions. In doing this, we include statistics on the severity of suicidal symptoms (e.g., statistics about rates of reattempts following an attempt) and emphasize the severity of the adolescent's symptoms. We provide the expectation that therapy involves work and takes time to have an effect. For example, we might state,

> We find that it takes time for therapy to help. Treatment usually doesn't help anyone if they go only one or two times. It takes time for you and the therapist to get to know each other. Because of this, we recommend that people go to treatment at least six times to increase the chance that it will be helpful.

Research has indicated that adolescent suicide attempters generally drop out quickly and attend, on average, fewer than five treatment sessions. Thus, we contract for six sessions of treatment and then discuss the need for further treatment with the therapist as necessary. The SDA has been shown to increase attendance to an average of nine sessions (Donaldson, Spirito, & Esposito, 2005). Most follow through with the six-session contract and, in our experience, often request more sessions.

A pilot test of SDA components in conjunction with a phone follow-up program involving 23 adolescent suicide attempters was first conducted (Donaldson et al., 1997). Participants received three phone calls focusing on the reduction of ideation and improved treatment adherence. Engagement was measured by comparing follow-through with initial referral and ongoing treatment attendance in those receiving the intervention with a sample of 78 adolescent attempters who received standard care following an attempt at the same hospital a few years prior. Results indicated that those receiving the SDA and follow-up phone calls exhibited fewer treatment no-shows in response to the initial referral (9% vs. 18%) and attended more sessions once initially engaged in treatment (5.5 vs. 3.9).

This pilot trial was followed by a larger, randomized trial ($N = 63$) comparing adolescents who had attempted suicide and were referred for outpatient psychotherapy in the community and who received the SDA and subsequent telephone follow-up with those who received no such approach or follow-up (Spirito, Boergers, et al., 2002). Results of this larger trial suggested that the SDA was effective in increasing ongoing treatment attendance (8.4 sessions for the experimental group vs. 5.7 for the comparison group), but only when service barriers to treatment were controlled. When service barriers existed, the intervention approach did not significantly affect treatment attendance. This occurred despite the fact that the intervention specifically targeted such barriers, as well as family barriers. Essentially, some service barriers (e.g., waiting list, problem with insurance coverage) proved to be impenetrable, possibly because of the inability of people outside the treatment center to have control over certain service barriers (e.g., request for a different therapist).

SUMMARY AND CONCLUSIONS

Research with suicidal adolescents has clearly demonstrated the problem of treatment engagement with adolescent suicide attempters. Given the high-risk nature of this group, enhancing treatment engagement is critical to addressing the problem of adolescent suicide. It is apparent that research with other patient groups has expanded and clarified the concept of treatment engagement. Studies involving adolescent suicide attempters have primarily equated engagement with treatment attendance or completion. Greater consideration of the relational aspects of the therapeutic enterprise (e.g., alliance, satisfaction) seems indicated.

The known studies addressing treatment engagement with adolescent suicide attempters to date have targeted patient-identified barriers to treatment and patient expectations and knowledge about treatment to improve treatment engagement, as indicated mostly by treatment attendance and adherence. These studies support the notion that the elimination of barriers to treatment is a useful method of improving treatment engagement among this population. Most of this work, however, targets only a select few individual and family barriers to treatment. Service barriers may be as important, if not more so, than individual and family barriers. Thus, a unified model addressing individual and family factors as well as service barriers may help enhance treatment engagement with suicidal adolescents. The SDA is useful in this regard. It represents a standardized model flexible enough to address a range of individual, family, and service barriers and treatment-relevant information and planning.

It is acknowledged that some barriers, especially service barriers, are not easily addressed and may require systemic changes within the health delivery system. We turn again to the call to action put forth by the Surgeon General in

1999 (U.S. Public Health Service, 1999) to eliminate service barriers. Change at all levels of intervention within the health care delivery system (i.e., clinicians, researchers, policymakers) is needed to systematically address the problem of treatment engagement from both a patient and a service perspective and to improve access to quality mental health care for all individuals in need.

We approach the problem of treatment engagement with adolescent suicide attempters using a problem-solving approach. An alternative or complementary approach that might be useful in enhancing treatment engagement in this population is motivational interviewing (W. R. Miller & Rollnick, 1991). This approach was developed to address addictive behaviors. Theory and research have indicated that any attempt to increase motivation to change behavior should use an empathic, nonjudgmental style; personalized feedback on future risk; and increased confidence in the client's ability to change (W. R. Miller & Rollnick, 1991). Motivational interviewing has already been found to have utility in improving adolescent drinking and smoking behaviors (Colby et al., 1998; Monti, Colby, & Barnett,1999; Spirito et al., 2004) and, more recently, treatment engagement in these same populations (Stein et al., 2006). To our knowledge, this model has not been tested with suicidal adolescents, although its tenets are certainly applicable.

As we aim to enhance treatment engagement among suicidal adolescents, it becomes increasingly important to improve access to empirically supported treatments for this population. This process has advanced more quickly for adolescents suffering from depression than it has for suicidal adolescents, especially those who have attempted suicide. When we surveyed adolescents who had attempted suicide regarding their experiences in outpatient treatment (Spirito, Stanton, Donaldson, & Boergers, 2002), more than three fourths of the sample stated that they talked about whatever they wanted in treatment. Most described their therapist using supportive or dynamic treatment methods (e.g., made connections between emotions and childhood experiences, clarified and expressed feelings in session). About half the sample reported that they were taught cognitive techniques, and approximately one third of the sample reported learning behavioral techniques (e.g., relaxation) in their sessions. In a separate study of adolescents who had attempted suicide and were referred for outpatient psychotherapy in the community, 39% reported treatment was not at all helpful (Donaldson et al., 1997). There is still no gold standard for treatment of adolescent suicide attempters.

If what constitutes effective treatment is uncertain, then the effects of enhancing treatment engagement may be limited. Conversely, engaging adolescents in treatments that work may actually improve treatment engagement. Further research on effective treatments is needed, and enhancing treatment engagement should certainly constitute an important component of effective treatment for suicidal adolescents.

REFERENCES

Baerger, D. R. (2001). Risk management with the suicidal patient: Lessons from case law. *Professional Psychology: Research and Practice, 32*, 359–366. doi:10.1037/0735-7028.32.4.359

Boergers, J., & Spirito, A. (2003). The outcome of suicide attempts among adolescents. In A. Spirito & J. Overholser (Eds.), *Evaluating and treating adolescent suicide attempters: From research to practice* (pp. 261–276). San Diego, CA: Academic Press. doi:10.1016/B978-012657951-2/50013-3

Boergers, J., Spirito, A., & Donaldson, D. (1998). Reasons for adolescent suicide attempts: Associations with psychological functioning. *Journal of the American Academy of Child & Adolescent Psychiatry, 37*, 1287–1293.

Breland-Noble, A. M., Bell, C., & Nicolas, G. (2006). Family first: The development of an evidence based family intervention for increasing participation in psychiatric clinical care and research in depressed African American adolescents. *Family Process, 45*, 153–169. doi:10.1111/j.1545-5300.2006.00088.x

Brent, D. A., Perper, J. A., & Moritz, G. (1993). Psychiatric risk factors for adolescent suicide: A case control study. *Journal of the American Academy of Child & Adolescent Psychiatry, 32*, 521–529. doi:10.1097/00004583-199305000-00006

Brookman-Frazee, L., Haine, R. A., Gabayan, E. N., & Garland, A. F. (2008). Predicting frequency of treatment visits in community-based youth psychotherapy. *Psychological Services, 5*, 126–138. doi:10.1037/1541-1559.5.2.126

Broome, K. M., Flynn, P. M., Knight, D. K., & Simpson, D. D. (2007). Program structure, staff perceptions, and client engagement in treatment. *Journal of Substance Abuse Treatment, 33*, 149–158. doi:10.1016/j.jsat.2006.12.030

Burns, C. D., Cortell, R., & Wagner, B. M. (2008). Treatment compliance in adolescents after attempted suicide: A 2-year follow-up study. *Journal of the American Academy of Child & Adolescent Psychiatry, 47*, 948–957. doi:10.1097/CHI.0b013e3181799e84

Colby, S. M., Monti, P. M., Barnett, N. P., Rohsenow, D. J., Weissman, K., Spirito, A., . . . Lewander, W. J. (1998). Brief motivational interviewing in a hospital setting for adolescent smoking: A preliminary study. *Journal of Consulting and Clinical Psychology, 66*, 574–578. doi:10.1037/0022-006X.66.3.574

Day, L., & Reznikoff, M. (1980). Social class, the treatment process and parents' and children's expectations about child psychotherapy. *Journal of Clinical Child Psychology, 9*, 195–198. doi:10.1080/15374418009532987

Deykin, E. Y., Hsieh, C. C., Joshi, N., & McNamara, J. J. (1986). Adolescent suicidal and self destructive behavior: Results of an intervention study. *Journal of Adolescent Health Care, 7*, 88–95. doi:10.1016/S0197-0070(86)80002-X

Dillman Carpentier, F. R., Mauricio, A. M., Gonzales, N. A., Millsap, R. E., Meza, C. M., Dumka, L. E., . . . Genalo, M. T. (2007). Engaging Mexican origin families in a school-based preventive intervention. *Journal of Primary Prevention, 28*, 521–546. doi:10.1007/s10935-007-0110-z

Donaldson, D., Spirito, A., Arrigan, M., & Aspel, J. W. (1997). Structural disposition planning for adolescent suicide attempters in a general hospital: Preliminary findings on short-term outcome. *Archives of Suicide Research, 3*, 271–282. doi:10.1080/13811119708258279

Donaldson, D., Spirito, A., & Esposito, C. (2005). Treatment for adolescents following a suicide attempt: Results of a pilot study. *Journal of the American Academy of Child & Adolescent Psychiatry, 44*, 113–120. doi:10.1097/00004583-200502000-00003

Donaldson, D., Spirito, A., & Overholser, J. (2003). Treatment of adolescent suicide attempters. In A. Spirito & J. Overholser (Eds.), *Evaluating and treating adolescent suicide attempters:*

From research to practice (pp. 295–321). San Diego, CA: Academic Press. doi:10.1016/B978-012657951-2/50015-7

Garland, A. F., Haine, R. A., & Boxmeyer, C. L. (2007). Determinates of youth and parent satisfaction in usual care psychotherapy. *Evaluation and Program Planning, 30,* 45–54. doi:10.1016/j.evalprogplan.2006.10.003

Gilchrist, H., & Sullivan, G. (2006). Barriers to help-seeking in young people: Community beliefs about youth suicide. *Australian Social Work, 59,* 73–85. doi:10.1080/03124070500449796

Goldsmith, S., Pellmar, T. C., Kleinman, A. M., & Bunney, W. E. (2002). *Reducing suicide: A national imperative.* Washington, DC: National Academies Press.

Granboulan, V., Rabain, D., & Basquin, M. (1995). The outcome of adolescent suicide attempts. *Acta Psychiatrica Scandinavica, 91,* 265–270. doi:10.1111/j.1600-0447.1995.tb09780.x

Hawley, K. M., & Weisz, J. R. (2005). Youth versus parent working alliance in usual clinical care: Distinctive associations with retention, satisfaction, and treatment outcome. *Journal of Clinical Child and Adolescent Psychology, 34,* 117–128. doi:10.1207/s15374424jccp3401_11

Hellman, I. D., Morrison, T. L., & Abramowitz, S. I. (1987). Therapist experience and the stresses of psychotherapeutic work. *Psychotherapy: Theory, Research, Practice, Training, 24,* 171–177.

Hogue, A., Dauber, S., Stambaugh, L. F., Cecero, J. J., & Liddle, H. A. (2006). Early therapeutic alliance and treatment outcome in individual and family therapy for adolescent behavior problems. *Journal of Consulting and Clinical Psychology, 74,* 121–129. doi:10.1037/0022-006X.74.1.121

Jellinek, M. (1978). Referrals from a psychiatric emergency room: Relationship of compliance to demographic and interview variables. *American Journal of Psychiatry, 135,* 209–213.

Karver, M., Shirk, S., Handelsman, J. B., Crisp, H., McMakin, D., Gudmundsen, G., & Fields, S. (2008). Relationship processes in youth psychotherapy: Measuring alliance, alliance-building behaviors, and client involvement. *Journal of Emotional and Behavioral Disorders, 16,* 15–28. doi:10.1177/1063426607312536

Kazdin, A. E. (1996). Dropping out of child psychotherapy: Issues for research and implications for practice. *Clinical Child Psychology and Psychiatry, 1,* 133–156. doi:10.1177/1359104596011012

Kazdin, A. E., Holland, L., & Crowley, M. (1997). Family experience of barriers to treatment and premature termination from child therapy. *Journal of Consulting and Clinical Psychology, 65,* 453–463. doi:10.1037/0022-006X.65.3.453

Kazdin, A. E., & Mazurick, J. L. (1994). Dropping out of child psychotherapy: Distinguishing early and late dropouts over the course of treatment. *Journal of Consulting and Clinical Psychology, 62,* 1069–1074. doi:10.1037/0022-006X.62.5.1069

Kazdin, A. E., Mazurick, J. L., & Bass, D. (1993). Risk for attrition in treatment of antisocial children and families. *Journal of Clinical Child Psychology, 22,* 2–16. doi:10.1207/s15374424jccp2201_1

Kazdin, A. E., Stolar, M. J., & Marciano, P. L. (1995). Risk factors for dropping out of treatment among White and Black families. *Journal of Family Psychology, 9,* 402–417. doi:10.1037/0893-3200.9.4.402

King, C. A., Hovey, J. D., Brand, E., & Ghaziuddin, N. (1997). Prediction of positive outcomes for adolescent psychiatric inpatients. *Journal of the American Academy of Child & Adolescent Psychiatry, 36,* 1434–1442. doi:10.1097/00004583-199710000-00026

Kleespies, P. M., Penk, W. E., & Forsyth, J. P. (1993). The stress of patient suicidal behavior during clinical training: Incidence, impact, and recovery. *Professional Psychology: Research and Practice, 24,* 293–303. doi:10.1037/0735-7028.24.3.293

Kleespies, P. M., & Ponce, A. N. (2009). The stress and emotional impact of clinical work with the patient at risk. In P. Kleespies (Ed.), *Behavioral emergencies: An evidence-based resource for evaluating and managing risk of suicide, violence, and victimization* (pp. 431–448). Washington, DC: American Psychological Association. doi:10.1037/11865-019

Liddle, H. A., Jackson-Gilfort, A., & Marvel, F. A. (2006). An empirically supported and culturally specific engagement and intervention strategy for African American adolescent males. *American Journal of Orthopsychiatry, 76*, 215–225. doi:10.1037/0002-9432.75.2.215

Miller, A. L., Rathus, J. H., & Linehan, M. M. (2007). *Dialectical behavior therapy with suicidal adolescents* (pp. 130–150). New York, NY: Guilford Press.

Miller, W. R., & Rollnick, S. (1991). *Motivational interviewing: Preparing people to change addictive behaviors.* New York, NY: Guilford Press.

Monti, P. M., Colby, S. M., & Barnett, N. P. (1999). Brief intervention for harm-reduction with alcohol-positive older adolescents in a hospital emergency department. *Journal of Consulting and Clinical Psychology, 67*, 989–994. doi:10.1037/0022-006X.67.6.989

Moskos, M. A., Olson, L., Halbern, S. R., & Gray, D. (2007). Barriers to mental health services among adolescents who complete suicide. *Suicide & Life-Threatening Behavior, 37*, 179–186. doi:10.1521/suli.2007.37.2.179

Nock, M. K., & Kazdin, A. E. (2001). Parent expectancies for child therapy: Assessment and relation to participation in treatment. *Journal of Child and Family Studies, 10*, 155–180. doi:10.1023/A:1016699424731

Pillay, A. L., & Wassenaar, D. R. (1995). Psychological intervention, spontaneous remission, hopelessness and psychiatric disturbances in adolescent parasuicides. *Suicide & Life-Threatening Behavior, 25*, 386–392.

Plunkett, J. W. (1984). Parents' treatment expectations and attrition from a child psychiatric service. *Journal of Clinical Psychology, 40*, 372–377. doi:10.1002/1097-4679(198401)40:1{372::AID-JCLP2270400169}3.0.CO;2-Q

Robbins, M. S., Mayorga, C. C., Mitrani, V. B., Szapocznik, J., Turner, C. W., & Alexander, J. F. (2008). Adolescent and parent alliances with therapists in brief strategic family therapy with drug-using Hispanic adolescents. *Journal of Marital and Family Therapy, 34*, 316–328. doi:10.1111/j.1752-0606.2008.00075.x

Rotheram-Borus, M. J., Piacentini, J., & Cantwell, C. (2000). The 18-month impact of an emergency room intervention for adolescent female suicide attempters. *Journal of Consulting and Clinical Psychology, 68*, 1081–1093. doi:10.1037/0022-006X.68.6.1081

Shelef, K., Diamond, G., Diamond, G. S., & Liddle, H. A. (2005). Adolescent and parent alliance and treatment outcome in multidimensional family therapy. *Journal of Consulting and Clinical Psychology, 73*, 689–698. doi:10.1037/0022-006X.73.4.689

Shirk, S. R., Gudmundsen, G., Kaplinski, H. C., & McMakin, D. L. (2008). Alliance and outcome in cognitive-behavioral therapy for adolescent depression. *Journal of Clinical Child and Adolescent Psychology, 37*, 631–639. doi:10.1080/15374410802148061

Slee, N., Spinhoven, P., Garnefski, N., & Arensman, E. (2008). Emotion regulation as mediator of treatment outcome in therapy for deliberate self-harm. *Clinical Psychology & Psychotherapy, 15*, 205–216. doi:10.1002/cpp.577

Spirito, A., Boergers, J., Donaldson, D., Bishop, D., & Lewander, W. (2002). An intervention trial to improve adherence to community treatment by adolescents after a suicide attempt. *Journal of the American Academy of Child & Adolescent Psychiatry, 41*, 435–442. doi:10.1097/00004583-200204000-00016

Spirito, A., Lewander, W., Levy, S., Kurkijian, J., & Fritz, G. (1994). Emergency department assessment of adolescent suicide attempters: Factors related to short-term follow-up outcome. *Pediatric Emergency Care, 10*, 6–12. doi:10.1097/00006565-199402000-00003

Spirito, A., Monti, P., Barnett, N., Colby, S., Sindelar, H., Rohsenow, D., . . . Myers, M. (2004). A randomized clinical trial of a brief motivational intervention for alcohol positive adolescents treated in an emergency department. *Journal of Pediatrics, 145*, 396–402. doi:10.1016/j.jpeds.2004.04.057

Spirito, A., Stanton, C., Donaldson, D., & Boergers, J. (2002). Treatment as usual for adolescent suicide attempters: Implications for the choice of comparison groups in psychotherapy research. *Journal of the American Academy of Child & Adolescent Psychiatry, 31*, 41–47.

Stein, L. A., Colby, S. M., Barnett, N. P., Monti, P. M., Golembeske, C., & Lebeau-Craven, R. (2006). Effects of motivational interviewing for incarcerated adolescents on driving under the influence after release. *American Journal on Addictions, 15*, 50–57. doi:10.1080/10550490601003680

Summerville, M. B., Kaslow, N. J., & Doepke, K. J. (1996). Psychopathology and cognitive and family functioning in suicidal African-American adolescents. *Current Directions in Psychological Science, 5*, 7–11. doi:10.1111/1467-8721.ep10772673

TADS Team. (2007). The Treatment for Adolescents With Depression Study (TADS): Long-term effectiveness and safety outcomes. *Archives of General Psychiatry, 64*, 1132–1144. doi:10.1001/archpsyc.64.10.1132

Taylor, E. A., & Stansfeld, S. A. (1984). Children who poison themselves—II: Prediction of attendance for treatment. *British Journal of Psychiatry, 145*, 132–135. doi:10.1192/bjp.145.2.132

Tolan, P., Ryan, K., & Jaffe, C. (1988). Adolescents' mental health service use and provider process, and recipient characteristics. *Journal of Clinical Child Psychology, 17*, 229–236. doi:10.1207/s15374424jccp1703_6

Trautman, P. D., & Rotheram, M. J. (1987). *Referral failure among adolescent suicide attempters.* Poster presented at the annual meeting of the American Academy of Child Psychiatry, Los Angeles, CA.

Trautman, P. D., Stewart, N., & Morishima, A. (1993). Are adolescent suicide attempters non-compliant with outpatient care? *Journal of the American Academy of Child & Adolescent Psychiatry, 32*, 89–94. doi:10.1097/00004583-199301000-00013

U.S. Public Health Service. (1999). *The surgeon general's call to action to prevent suicide.* Washington, DC: Department of Health and Human Services, Public Health Service.

Vogel, D. L., Wade, N. G., & Ascheman, P. L. (2009). Measuring perceptions of stigmatization by others for seeking psychological help: Reliability and validity of a new stigma scale with college students. *Journal of Counseling Psychology, 56*, 301–308. doi:10.1037/a0014903

Yang, S., Zarr, R. L., Kass Hout, T. A., Kourosh, A., & Kelly, N. R. (2006). Transportation barriers to accessing health care for urban children. *Journal of Health Care for the Poor and Underserved, 17*, 928–943. doi:10.1353/hpu.2006.0137

Zayas, L. H., & Pilat, A. M. (2008). Suicidal behavior in Latinas: Explanatory cultural factors and implications for intervention. *Suicide & Life-Threatening Behavior, 38*, 334–342. doi:10.1521/suli.2008.38.3.334

CONCLUSIONS: LOOKING AHEAD—FUTURE DIRECTIONS IN TREATMENT ENGAGEMENT WITH HIGH-RISK ADOLESCENTS

DAVID CASTRO-BLANCO, MARC S. KARVER, AND JOSEPH CHIECHI

There is widespread agreement that access to health care is a linchpin to the overall well-being of a nation. Access is determined by both availability and a mechanism to ensure the use of available resources. These are exciting times for clinicians working with adolescent patients. In recent years, there have been improved measures for assessing and recognizing adolescent psychopathology, there has been an explosion of evidence-based treatments for youths, and laws have been passed or are being considered that may lead to reform of mental health care organization and financing policies, leading to more adolescents who may be able to receive higher quality mental health services. Most relevant to this book has been the opening up of the black box of youth treatment and youth mental health services over the past 10 years.

When Bordin (1979) proposed the universality of the therapeutic alliance as a determining factor in treatment outcome, he did so with adult outpatients in mind. However, even as recently as the late 1990s, there were only a handful of child–adolescent treatment researchers who were examining treatment processes. Outside of these researchers, investigations of youth treatment processes were conducted in a sporadic manner, often as an add-on to a treatment study being conducted to examine other major hypotheses. Most treatment researchers at that time still did not even attend to what went on in the delivery of a treatment aside from the name of the treatment and how that treatment was related to outcomes. The 1990s were dominated by a rapid increase in the discovery of a large number of evidence-based youth treatments, much as was seen in the adult treatment literature in the prior decade. However, despite this being good for the field, there was the danger that this discovery of evidence-based treatments would cause an overemphasis on techniques and the forgetting of therapist behaviors that would be considered more in the realm of stylistic strategies. This emphasis misses the point that a therapist can have a great set of evidence-based techniques targeted at specific areas of youth psychopathology; however, these techniques may be useless if the adolescent client does not like the therapist, does not think the therapist has something worthwhile to say, does not listen to the therapist, and so forth. However, Shirk and Karver (2003) published a meta-analysis on the handful of assorted studies that had been conducted on youth treatment processes. Following the publication of this study, the field was awakened and there was an explosion of studies focusing on not just the interpersonal processes that occur within treatment but even the processes that occur before treatment that can affect whether a youth and his or her family will come to treatment, stay in treatment, and participate in treatment.

One can see that significant progress has been made in understanding the processes of adolescent engagement in therapy. Each chapter of this book contains a strong examination of a specific area of study relative to service and treatment processes with adolescent clients and their families. We are grateful for the authors' contributions to this book and to the field of adolescent treatment. Their work has helped advance the cutting edge on how to get adolescents into treatment and then maintain them in such treatment. Our goal in this final chapter is to identify themes and challenges that emerged across the various chapters. As with any exploration, the real measure of progress is less what has been discovered and more what we now know we have yet to learn and understand relative to adolescent treatment processes.

CLARIFYING ADOLESCENT ENGAGEMENT: CONCEPTUAL CONFUSION

Adolescent engagement, therapeutic alliance, treatment attendance, participation in therapy, patient involvement, and related terms all appear to be very important yet challenging constructs because throughout the youth treatment process literature (and even in the chapters of this book), the terms are either not defined or used interchangeably when they do not have the same meaning. Thus, it is important that the field clarify its terms and then consistently use them in the same manner. Without such clarification, readers of this literature will not be able to understand what is being studied, and thus the literature will be less able to inform clinical practice.

As noted by several authors, an important clarification needed is that treatment attendance should not be considered treatment involvement or engagement (Shirk, Caporino, & Karver, Chapter 2; Gallagher, Kurtz, & Blackwell, Chapter 5). Just because a youth or his or her family shows up for treatment does not mean they will participate in therapeutic activities during a session. This attempt at conceptual differentiation is helpful; however, even more clarification and differentiation is needed when referring to what happens when adolescents and their families are present in a therapy room.

When adolescents and their families are present in the therapy room, terms such as the *therapeutic alliance, therapeutic relationship, treatment participation, treatment involvement, treatment engagement, bond,* and *agreement* have been used. The therapeutic alliance and therapeutic relationship constructs appear to refer to an umbrella treatment process term that includes some of the other constructs as domains. The meta-analysis by Karver, Handelsman, Fields, and Bickman (2006) revealed that most measures of the therapeutic alliance or therapeutic relationship in the youth treatment literature contained a bond or attachment or emotional connection domain. However, beyond this domain, the therapeutic relationship construct varied on other domains, with half of the measures used containing a cognitive component suggesting client agreement with the therapist on goals, tasks, or both or willingness to work with the therapist and half of the measures containing a domain representing client behavioral participation in treatment. Chu, Suveg, Creed, and Kendall (Chapter 3 of this volume) also point out that treatment involvement and alliance definitions have often overlapped; however, they suggested that the therapeutic alliance construct should be separated from the behavioral involvement construct, which represents actual participation during a treatment session. If this recommendation were to be followed, the therapeutic alliance would be more of an experiential emotional–cognitive connection construct (attachment and social contract as suggested by Shirk et al. in Chapter 2 of this volume) that could perhaps be studied as a potential predictor of actual in-session behavioral involvement in treatment. The popular Bordin (1979) definition of the therapeutic alliance as containing domains of bond and agreement on goals and tasks would fit within an emotional–cognitive connection definition of the alliance. As suggested by Shirk et al. (Chapter 2 of this volume) and Chu et al. (Chapter 3 of this volume), further examination of the subdomains of the therapeutic alliance within the youth treatment process literature may not be useful because research has suggested that adolescents may not be able to distinguish between the hypothesized components of the alliance.

Chu et al. (Chapter 3) define *involvement* as client verbal self-disclosure, initiation of difficult topics, observable client participation, homework completion, and clients actively shaping therapeutic tasks. Shirk et al. (Chapter 2) also support the use of the term *involvement* instead of the term *engagement*. In fact, they suggest that the term *engagement* should be reserved for therapist behaviors meant to build or enhance a therapeutic alliance. Chu et al. also include willingness to engage in the therapeutic relationship in their definition; however, we suggest that this area should not be included in the definition of *involvement* because it fits more closely with the idea of a cognitive–motivational connection seen in the therapeutic alliance construct than as the equivalent of actual behavioral involvement. Research on the theory of planned behavior (e.g., Armitage & Conner, 2001) has consistently shown that even if people have favorable attitudes toward engaging in a behavior (such as participating in treatment), other elements (social pressures such as views on what is normative or stigma, perceived ability or barriers to performing the requested behavior) may prevent these favorable attitudes from turning into actual behavior.

Shirk et al. (Chapter 2) also note the presence of treatment-defeating client behaviors and hostility in some alliance measures. Not a lot of research has been done on these terms in the youth treatment literature, and we suggest that these behaviors, which could fit under the umbrella term *treatment resistance*, need further study to understand how they are related to the therapeutic alliance and treatment involvement. Treatment resistance may be a predictive client characteristic brought into treatment, a response to therapist behaviors, the inverse of positive constructs such as the therapeutic alliance or treatment involvement, or all of these. In summary, there is excellent potential for definitional clarity in the youth treatment process literature; however, further research of a consistent nature remains to be done to clarify the boundaries between the various treatment process constructs.

ALLIANCE MEASUREMENT

Even after clearly defining and conceptualizing the therapeutic alliance, measuring that alliance poses both an opportunity and a challenge. Constantino, Castonguay, Zack, and DeGeorge (Chapter 1 of this volume) point out that clinicians cannot just use their clinical judgment to monitor the alliance because it is not clear that clinicians naturally attend to the alliance, especially in the current mental health services climate, which emphasizes the use of diagnosis-specific evidence-based treatments. Thus, they recommend that clinicians learn to monitor the alliance using existing alliance measurement tools. Chu et al. (Chapter 3) also emphasize monitoring interventions for positive and negative signs of involvement in therapy. Alliance and involvement measurement provides clinicians with the opportunity to be guided on when to adjust what they are doing in therapy. This type of feedback on what works and when is likely to be an essential part of any effective model of treatment with adolescents. For example, the therapist using Miller, Nathan, and Wagner's (Chapter 7) dialectical behavior therapy (DBT) adaptation with a suicidal and high-risk adolescent could determine the impact of humorous, irreverent communications as opposed to validation with the teen. The ability to turn on a dime is a hallmark of DBT with adult patients. Constantino et al. (Chapter 1) and Gallagher et al. (Chapter 5) all suggest that brief alliance measures could be practically used in clinical practice. Being able to measure how treatment engagement strategies work with younger patients offers promise to researchers and clinicians alike.

The challenge lies in accurately measuring the therapeutic alliance in adolescent treatment. As shown by Shirk et al. (Chapter 2), participant and observer measures of the alliance have literally exploded in the past decade, with numerous studies introducing new alliance measures. It has also been pointed out that many measures in the adolescent treatment literature are downloads from the adult treatment literature (Chapters 1 and 2) and thus may not be appropriate for adolescent clients. Not surprisingly, no model or measure has yet been settled on as the gold standard or clear choice for adolescent alliance measurement; however, most measures appear to have some combination of affective–relational comfort–conflict, cognitively oriented task or goal agreement, collaborative involvement, or all of these. However, Shirk et al. point out that several studies have found only a unitary alliance–collaborative bond construct. Although challenging to accomplish, a large study using varied alliance measures with proposed differing domains may be needed to answer the question of what subconstructs truly matter in the adolescent therapeutic alliance. Moreover, one should keep in mind that what a healthy therapeutic alliance looks like could differ depending on what mental health problem is being treated and by what treatment. Shirk et al. suggest that it may be worth considering other models for measurement of the alliance that include subconstructs such as facilitation of adolescent autonomy, confidence in the therapist and therapist credibility, and so forth. The challenge pointed out by Shirk et al. in validating an alliance measure is that there is no alliance gold-standard measure or objective criterion. More studies are needed of theory- or model-driven measures to collect better evidence of support such as predictive validity; convergent, divergent, and discriminant validity; and consistency with hypothesized models of the alliance. Constantino et al. (Chapter 1) and Chu et al. (Chapter 3) also point out that timing is an added challenge because it is not clear whether alliance measurement would be most useful by looking at it on a moment-by-moment basis during sessions, looking at segments of sessions or globally looking over an entire session or sessions, or looking at patterns across sessions. Finally, given that Constantino et al. and Shirk et al. point out that there are only low to moderate associations across alliance perspectives when evaluating a single relationship, the field still needs to determine how to evaluate multiple alliance perspectives across entire families because therapy with an adolescent and his or her family involves not only the alliance between the therapist and adolescent but that between the therapist and other family members, as well as between each of the family members.

MECHANISMS OF CHANGE

Figuring out how to engage adolescents and their families in treatment would be much easier if we understood the mechanisms by which the therapeutic alliance and treatment more broadly work. Constantino et al. (Chapter 1) point out that this is challenging because the mechanisms may not be what is theorized in specific treatments, and in fact, therapists may not be doing what they believe they are doing. Several of the authors emphasize that the research literature has demonstrated a moderate alliance-to-outcome relationship (Chapters 1–3). However, this does not tell us what the mechanism of change is. Figuring that out has proven to be quite complicated. Shirk et al. (Chapter 2) suggest that the use of certain early engagement strategies may help build the affective alliance, which may motivate treatment involvement, which then increases adolescent receptivity to treatment techniques. Participation in treatment techniques then results in positive client changes that reverse or replace pathological mechanisms, resulting in improved client outcomes. Support for this is that adolescent alliance as measured by bond and task components has been found in a number of studies to be related to willingness to commit to therapy and treatment participation, involvement, or collaboration, which have been found to be related to lower attrition and positive treatment outcomes (Chapters 1–3). However, Shirk et al. also suggest the possibility of the alliance serving an alternative or second role as a relational change mechanism that changes relational variables (e.g., interpersonal schemas, skills, coping strategies) to contribute to symptom change. This mechanism has been unexplored.

Moreover, Chu et al. (Chapter 3) and Shirk et al. (Chapter 2) point out that the mechanism may be even more complicated because the alliance and involvement in treatment have been found to not be stable over treatment, with both large positive and negative shifts occurring. Chu et al. found some evidence that large shifts in treatment involvement may be related to positive or negative outcomes, depending on the direction of the shift. Constantino et al. (Chapter 1) and Chu et al. point out that alliance ruptures (typically affective strains or disagreements in therapy) have been found to be related to premature treatment termination. Thus, successful use of treatment engagement strategies at times when a client is at risk of treatment failure (such as the therapist apologizing for and exploring a treatment rupture; Chapter 1) may be an important part of successful treatment. Furthermore, Chu et al. point out that different patterns of alliance and involvement have been found to have different relationships to outcome in the adult treatment literature. It may be that treatment works best when therapists can recognize certain alliance or involvement patterns and respond with treatment engagement strategies that lead to patterns with adolescents and their families that result in positive treatment outcomes. To further complicate the search for a unifying model, it may be that the treatment mechanisms vary depending on the problem being treated and the treatment being used (e.g., Karver et al., 2008). Add to this that treatment with adolescents often involves treatment with parents and other family members. Caron and Robin (Chapter 6) and Gallagher et al. (Chapter 5) indicate that parent–family involvement has been found to be related to better treatment outcomes in their respective treatments of obsessive–compulsive disorder and externalizing problem behaviors. Thus, as suggested by Shirk et al., it is apparent that the field would benefit from studies examining alternative alliance models to discover the role of various treatment process constructs in successful treatment.

THERAPIST ENGAGEMENT STRATEGIES

Across the various chapters, one sees a growing list of suggested strategies for initially engaging adolescents and their families in treatment or reengaging clients when an alliance rupture has occurred. The most common themes recurring throughout this text are the need to establish an emotional, trust-based connection and to establish a collaborative cognitive (agreements) and behaviorally (participation) based working connection with the adolescent client and the family. These points are reiterated throughout this text, whether the discussion focuses on adolescents with mood, suicidal, anxiety, or disruptive behavioral disorders. The clinician's challenge is to quickly use these strategies to enlist both the teen and the family as participants in the treatment process, or they may drop out before they are exposed to the working components of the intended treatments. Quick, effective alliance building with the high-risk adolescent improves the chances for a productive, goal-directed collaboration between therapist and adolescent. However, as noted by several of our chapter authors (Constantino et al., Chapter 1; Gallagher et al., Chapter 5; Caron & Robin, Chapter 6), many in the clinical literature have made a number of engagement suggestions on how to build the alliance, but these suggestions are often not based on empirical work that has attempted to find a relationship between therapist behaviors and their impact on treatment processes or outcomes with clients.

One recommended engagement strategy across many of the chapters for establishing or repairing a ruptured emotional or trust-based connection is the use of empathy and validation. Constantino et al. (Chapter 1), Chu et al. (Chapter 3), Gallagher et al. (Chapter 5), and Miller et al. (Chapter 7) suggest that it can be particularly helpful to engage reluctant adolescent clients by carefully paying attention to the client and finding the kernel of truth in what the client says or to in some way verify that the experience of the adolescent makes sense given past experiences, current circumstances (such as acknowledging that conflict may be because others are struggling with accepting that the adolescent is developing and becoming more autonomous), or both. This could mean that instead of arguing with a skeptical client, the therapist could listen and validate the skepticism that the client feels relative to the therapist, the therapy, the teaching of a skill, the completion of therapy homework, and so forth. Caron and Robin (Chapter 6) add that a clinician can validate the difficulty a client may have in answering questions, participating in therapy, and in completing homework. Miller et al. add that acknowledging to teens that they have been invalidated likely engages them by making them feel more understood and like they have someone advocating for them, which may in turn instill youths with hope that treatment will work to make their situation better and thus make them more likely to work with the therapist. Caron and Robin, Chu et al., and Miller et al. suggest that therapist behavior can go beyond mere words and that therapist actions with parents can be very validating for adolescent clients. For example, the therapist advocating for the teen to the teen's parents about what is normative behavior or to decrease criticism of the teen can go a long way toward making the teen feel validated.

In addition, several of the chapter authors recommend taking a strength- or reinforcement-based approach of looking for small indicators of progress, praising and supporting teen efforts, and getting parents to do the same because this builds hope and positive connection with a therapist and maintains behavioral participation in treatment (Castro-Blanco, Chapter 4; Gallagher et al., Chapter 5; Caron & Robin, Chapter 6; Miller et al., Chapter 7). More research is needed on this set of therapist behaviors, especially validation, but several of the chapter authors noted that there is some empirical support for eliciting and attending to the client's subjective experience (Shirk et al., Chapter 2; Gallagher et al., Chapter 5) and what are called the *counselor facilitative behaviors*—accurate empathy, warmth, genuineness, and responsiveness (Constantino et al., Chapter 1; Chu et al., Chapter 3; Gallagher et al., Chapter 5). Moreover, Chu et al. and Gallagher et al. point out that treatment attendance has been found to be poor when clients do not feel understood. In addition, nonsupportive, nonvalidating therapist behaviors such as the therapist failing to acknowledge adolescent expression of emotion, criticizing adolescents, pushing the adolescent to talk when not ready, and misunderstanding adolescent statements have been found to be related to poor ratings of therapeutic alliance and client treatment collaboration (Constantino et al., Chapter 1; Chu et al., Chapter 3; Gallagher et al., Chapter 5).

However, balance is needed in therapist engagement behaviors with adolescents (Constantino et al., Chapter 1; Miller et al., Chapter 7). Efforts to invite and enlist the adolescent in treatment through validation and acceptance strategies should be balanced with the establishment of clearly agreed-on goals (Castro-Blanco, Chapter 4; Gallagher et al., Chapter 5; Caron & Robin, Chapter 6) and active collaboration and agreement on treatment behavior change tasks, or the result could be an adolescent who likes his or her therapist but does not participate in treatment. Attending to and respecting adolescent autonomy needs in making decisions in therapy (what goals to pursue, what issues to talk about, what pace therapy proceeds at) has been emphasized across chapters as particularly important given typical adolescent development and that adolescents, unlike adults, are not typically self-referred for treatment (Constantino et al., Chapter 1; Shirk et al., Chapter 2; Chu et al., Chapter 3; Caron & Robin, Chapter 6).

To establish a collaborative relationship with the adolescent client and his or her parents, therapist emphasis on negotiation-based skills has been suggested as a good initial engagement strategy; as a means to set goals collaboratively between the adolescent, parents, and therapist; and as a means to resolve therapeutic ruptures (Chu et al., Chapter 3; Castro-Blanco, Chapter 4; Gallagher et al., Chapter 5; Caron & Robin, Chapter 6). It is worth noting that the use of negotiation fosters an atmosphere in which the adolescent is an active part of the treatment rather than the focus. Gallagher et al. and Shirk et al. (Chapter 5) suggest viewing the adolescent, his or her family members, and the therapist as players or allies on the same treatment team. Moreover, instead of maintaining a mindset of fixing something broken, the use of a negotiation-focused intervention permits the adolescent and family members to demonstrate the legitimacy of their goals, to regard and respect the wants of every member of the family, and to learn to cooperate with rather than compete against one another to achieve beneficial change for all. Among the potential strategies for accomplishing these tasks are learning to reframe the apparently conflicting goals of the adolescent and parents, through synthesis or bridging, into one common goal (Gallagher et al., Chapter 5). Parents may enter treatment complaining that their adolescent does not listen, is not respectful, will not observe curfew, and is oppositional. The adolescent may well respond with countercomplaints that the parents are too strict, do not respect the teen or his or her friends, are too demanding, and do not trust or recognize trustworthiness. The therapist seeking to engage the adolescent through collaboration may use some of the techniques suggested by Constantino et al. (Chapter 1), Castro-Blanco, Chu et al., Donaldson, Spirito, Boergers (Chapter 8), or Miller et al. (Chapter 7): reframing the conflicting complaints with the synthesized goal of promoting trust on both parts, collaborative agenda setting, having discussions with instead of lecturing at family members, openness to discussing and repairing problems in the therapy relationship, and the client committing to the therapist but also the therapist committing to the client. Rather than appearing to take sides, the therapist's task as a true collaborator and facilitator of change is to demonstrate that the adolescent, family members, and therapist all contribute to treatment success and are on the same side, not competing sides.

Another important part of getting adolescents and other family members to join the treatment team is convincing them that the treatment team is worth joining. Several of the chapter authors have approaches (Miller et al., Chapter 7; Donaldson et al., Chapter 8) or recommendations (Chu et al., Chapter 3; Gallagher et al., Chapter 5) incorporating aspects of motivational interviewing (e.g., examining pros and cons of change), emphasizing reconciling incorrect treatment expectations, or fitting client problems into the treatment framework that provides the good explanations that serve to decrease the barriers and increase the desirability or hopefulness of participating in the treatment. Donaldson et al. point out that motivational interviewing approaches have shown past effectiveness in engaging adolescents with addictive behaviors. Several of the chapter authors have noted that therapist use of collaborative goal setting, well-explained treatment rationales, and therapy task engagement strategies has been found to be related to better treatment attendance and alliances (Constantino et al., Chapter 1; Shirk et al., Chapter 2; Chu et al., Chapter 3; Gallagher et al., Chapter 5). Constantino et al. and Chu et al. point out that rigid adherence to a treatment, which tends to be less flexible (not adapting sessions to meet client needs, inputs, interests, or all of these) and collaborative, has been found to be related to the occurrence of alliance ruptures and ratings of a poor client–therapist alliance.

It is interesting that Miller et al.'s approach (Chapter 7), which includes the use of irreverence, at first glance does not seem consistent with a book about alliance formation with adolescents. Irreverence appears to be a therapeutic style that would threaten the therapeutic alliance, but Miller et al. suggest that irreverence, humor, and dual-edged statements can actually make an adolescent client who is initially not disposed to cooperate or participate in treatment more receptive to therapy. A similar perspective is also presented in other chapters as well (Chu et al., Chapter 3; Gallagher et al.,

Chapter 5; Caron & Robin, Chapter 6;). Constantino et al. (Chapter 1) suggest that these disarming strategies work because the therapist acts opposite to what the adolescent client expects, which may make the therapist seem more "real" and may also break the adolescent out of his or her negative mind-set relative to therapy and the therapist. Of course, these more shocking statements likely need to be balanced with a healthy amount of validating-type comments. However, what this balance should be is unknown. As several of the chapter authors state (Chu et al., Chapter 3; Gallagher et al., Chapter 5), given that there have only been a few preliminary studies of alliance-fostering techniques (Constantino et al., Chapter 1), there is still plenty more that needs to be learned about what specific therapist behaviors and combination of these, in what quantity, and at what time during therapy are needed to build an alliance with an adolescent client, repair alliance ruptures, and maintain participation in treatment.

ENGAGING PARENTS

A strong alliance leading to adolescent participation may be necessary for treatment gains to occur, but it is not sufficient. Parents facilitate treatment for their adolescents in many ways: scheduling appointments and providing transportation, giving information to clinicians as part of ongoing assessment, participating as critical treatment partners in youth interventions, encouraging youth adherence to clinician suggestions, and promoting generalization of youth treatment gains (Gallagher et al., Chapter 5; Caron & Robin, Chapter 6; Miller et al., Chapter 7). If the adolescent's parents dislike the clinician and do not bring the youth to therapy, the therapeutic alliance with the youth becomes irrelevant. The effective involvement of the parents may require a recognition of their importance to the process and a sensitivity to the myriad barriers they face that can potentially compromise the parents' or family's active participation in treatment. The clinician working with an adolescent and parents may need to carefully balance advocating for the youth with not neglecting the importance of empathy for the parents, validating the parents' concerns and acknowledging parental competencies, or risk a rupture of the parent–therapist alliance (Gallagher et al., Chapter 5; Caron & Robin, Chapter 6; Miller et al., Chapter 7). In addition, it is suggested that the clinician be collaborative with parents and clear in explaining the rationale behind treatment suggestions, or parents can lose confidence in the credibility of the therapist (Gallagher et al., Chapter 5; Miller et al., Chapter 7). However, the therapist must also balance parental desire for involvement in treatment, which can be very helpful, with validating adolescent desire for parents to not be involved and thus allowing more adolescent autonomy (Chu et al., Chapter 3; Caron & Robin, Chapter 6). In looking across the chapters of this book, it becomes clear that parental involvement is a severely understudied area. Despite most of the authors emphasizing the importance of engaging parents, it appears that little research has been done to find what therapist behaviors actually do successfully involve parents in treatment, and more research is needed on the optimal level or role of parental involvement in adolescent therapy, especially keeping issues of adolescent autonomy in mind.

EXTRATHERAPY SITUATIONAL AND SYSTEMIC PROCESSES

In addition, getting an adolescent and parents to engage in treatment also involves examining variables beyond the relationships that occur within the therapy room. Problems with lack of transportation (noted by Chu et al., Chapter 3; Donaldson et al., Chapter 8), prohibitive costs of treatment (Chu et al., Chapter 3; Donaldson et al., Chapter 8), stigma (Castro-Blanco, Chapter 4; Donaldson et al., Chapter 8), pejorative labeling, referral of poor and minority persons to the criminal justice system (Gallagher et al., Chapter 5), and being blamed for broader problems may serve as imposing barriers against adolescent and family attendance and involvement in treatment, even when there is a recognition of problems and the need for intervention. Gallagher et al. suggest that treatment barriers such as these may tax limited time, energy, and financial resources and thus may explain the relationship between low socioeconomic status and minority status and treatment dropout. Donaldson et al. point out that service providers, particularly in community clinics, often face difficulty in setting up timely appointments and commencing services, which is extremely concerning when the potential adolescent client has been referred for issues of suicide risk. Gallagher et al. also point out that therapy support staff and how they treat families when they come in for an appointment can have an impact on family involvement in treatment. Furthermore, Donaldson et al. point out that being placed on a waiting list or having problems with insurance authorization or coverage of mental health treatment can serve to minimize problem significance to families and hurt clinician engagement attempts. Even when families do get in to treatment, Donaldson et al. point out that lack of sufficient providers in the mental health service system can leave families with an inability to switch therapists when a mismatch with a treatment provider is perceived (e.g., language compatibility problems, different interpersonal styles, different preferred therapeutic approach). In addition, Donaldson et al. point out that treatment sessions are often seen as competing for time with outside interests, such as family obligations, meetings, and school activities. Given these barriers, even if we do learn the best techniques to engage youths and families in treatment, forming strong alliances, it may not matter if service barriers prevent families from reaching the therapist's office.

EXTRATHERAPEUTIC TREATMENT ENGAGEMENT INTERVENTIONS

Given the existence of the aforementioned service barriers and high percentages of troubled adolescents who are not using mental health services, many of the chapter authors suggested the need for programmatic, policy, and systems change to reduce barriers and increase service accessibility (Gallagher et al., Chapter 5; Donaldson et al., Chapter 8). Interventions that have been found to be successful at reducing barriers to treatment attendance have included components such as meeting families in their homes at times convenient for them, high availability of clinicians to families, swift scheduling of appointments with clients at the height of crisis when treatment motivation is high, and having clinicians with low caseloads (Gallagher et al., Chapter 5; Donaldson et al., Chapter 8). In addition, frequent contact by mental health professionals has been found to result in higher treatment attendance (Donaldson et al., Chapter 8). The professionals encourage adolescents and other family members to attend appointments using engagement behaviors similar to those that might be used by a therapist trying to build and maintain an alliance, such as providing support and advocacy. Furthermore, Donaldson et al. found that training those who refer adolescents and families to mental health services in engagement strategies, such as addressing adolescent and family beliefs about what to expect from treatment, stating an expectancy of helpfulness, discussing priorities that compete with therapy, and contracting with families for treatment attendance, has been shown in several studies to lead to increased attendance. This parallels Gallagher et al.'s emphasis on providing pretherapy preparation materials to families to address treatment expectations to increase first-session attendance and Miller et al.'s (Chapter 7) use of creative commitment strategies to get adolescents to commit to engaging in treatment. These strategies may work because they address families' incorrect expectations about treatment, create positive expectancies for change, and prepare families to be more likely to agree with a therapist on treatment goals and treatment tasks (Donaldson et al., Chapter 8).

Of course, Gallagher et al. (Chapter 5) emphasize that mental health professionals should not make assumptions and should go through a process of trying to first understand family treatment barriers on a case-by-case basis. Once these barriers are understood, then the mental health professional can alter and explain treatment in such a way so as to match family needs and culture so that treatment can be acceptable and practical to get engagement. Many of the chapter authors (Chu et al., Chapter 3; Gallagher et al., Chapter 5; Donaldson et al., Chapter 8) propose that using problem-solving strategies would be important in overcoming treatment barriers. They suggest that the key to getting youths to treatment and keeping youths in treatment is to understand their problematic barriers and then come up with related solutions. Donaldson et al. also propose the use of reframing and validation as a means to address stigma, which is an important barrier to treatment for suicidal teens and likely for youths with other mental health difficulties. However, it is concerning that Donaldson et al. report that their engagement intervention only worked on treatment attendance when controlling for service barriers. This points out that service barriers need to be attended to more by researchers and policymakers because they affect whether families can even access mental health services. In addition, the field may need to determine the unique challenges to engaging different challenging adolescent populations. Barriers and engagement strategies may vary by psychopathology, ethnicity, race, age, and so forth.

QUO IMUS?

Treatment process research with youths has come a long way from the early days. Back in the 1940s, Sigmund and Anna Freud suggested that the therapeutic relationship with youth clients was very important, but they did not measure it or empirically examine how to change it (Freud, 1946). This type of examination of the therapeutic alliance with adolescents did not occur with any regularity until the past 10 to 15 years. Since then, the field has changed quickly and dramatically, with an explosion of studies in recent years on treatment process with adolescent clients. The chapters in this text have highlighted some of the more promising, cutting-edge clinical research with adolescents in which the therapeutic alliance and treatment engagement have been highlighted.

In this final chapter, we note several important promising areas in which therapeutic alliance research is taking off, including the development of measures, increased understanding of treatment mechanisms, and the discovery of strategies to overcome barriers to treatment and strategies to engage adolescents and parents at the beginning of and throughout treatment. One point remains central to all the chapters in this text. The recognition that the treatment relationship holds a special and important place in therapeutic work with adolescents is a critical contribution to the discussion. Regardless of the multifaceted developments in the field, one point will remain vital in any study of treatment outcome with adolescents: Without engagement, there will be no therapy. Even with the most sophisticated, empirically based, and finely nuanced treatment protocol, without effective engagement there will be no therapeutic gain. With all due respect to Fritz Perls, founder of the Gestalt model of treatment and proponent of the empty chair exercise, an empty chair is only effective if the one next to it is occupied by a client. Being the best therapist in an empty office is an exercise in futility.

Nevertheless, the work reported herein also offers a glimpse at areas in which more work is needed. We have noted that across even the experts and leaders in the field, there is conceptual confusion on treatment process constructs. It would seem that the field would benefit from the experts coming to consensus on the use of treatment process terms. Relatedly, there are a lot of measures of the alliance and other treatment processes. The field would benefit from further conceptual work based on what we know of adolescent development and adolescents' involvement in treatment and to have this guide the field toward gold-standard treatment process measures as opposed to the current state of the literature in which there is a lack of standard measurement tools for treatment researchers to turn to. As for treatment mechanisms, most of what we know is based on theory and broad correlations between constructs. Richer measurement of treatment constructs more frequently throughout therapy is needed for us to have a better understanding of treatment response trajectories and how the therapeutic alliance works in therapy. As we learn more about these processes, we should also try to learn more about therapist engagement behaviors. As of now, we are starting to learn more about therapist behaviors that are related to treatment processes, but we need to eventually move toward more empirically rigorous studies such as randomized controlled trials in which causal conclusions can possibly be made about the use of treatment engagement strategies. Moreover, as we learn more, we may also learn that treatment processes may vary depending on the characteristics of clients, characteristics of clinicians (suggested by Constantino et al., Chapter 1; Miller et al., Chapter 7; Donaldson et al., Chapter 8), the match between clinician and client characteristics (Constantino et al., Chapter 1), or the type of treatment that is being delivered. Initial research has suggested that the alliance varies depending on client and family characteristics such as diagnosis, level of functional impairment, interpersonal skills, history of self-harm behavior, substance use, level of education, barriers to treatment, family cohesion, family conflict, treatment and outcome expectations, and hopelessness (Constantino et al., Chapter 1; Shirk et al., Chapter 2; Chu et al., Chapter 3; Gallagher et al., Chapter 5; Donaldson et al., Chapter 8). We may eventually learn that treatment engagement strategies that work may depend on matching strategies to clients and their therapists and on a treatment's being delivered to an adolescent client and his or her family at the appropriate time. Furthermore, in the youth treatment literature, besides some studies showing that culture, ethnicity and race of client and therapist have a relationship to treatment attendance (Donaldson et al., Chapter 8), we know very little about how these characteristics or matching on these characteristics may be related to the treatment alliance and to effective engagement strategies.

The interventions reported in this text have been developed expressly to help the clinician working with troubled, high-risk adolescents in the real world. They offer great possibilities for the future; however, these ideas now need to be put to tougher tests so that the youth treatment field can be guided on how best to work with such a challenging population. Given recent and proposed changes in mental health care reform, clinicians working with adolescents stand at the forefront of helping some of the most vulnerable and promising members of our society who previously did not have access to mental health services. We owe them our best. We owe the clinicians working with them no less.

REFERENCES

Armitage, C. J., & Conner, M. (2001). Efficacy of the theory of planned behaviour: A meta-analytic review. *British Journal of Social Psychology, 40*(Pt. 4), 471–499. doi:10.1348/014466601164939

Bordin, E. S. (1979). The generalizability of the psychoanalytic concept of the working alliance. *Psychotherapy: Theory, Research, and Practice, 16,* 252–260.

Freud, A. (1946). *The psychoanalytic treatment of children.* New York: International Universities Press.

Karver, M. S., Handelsman, J., Fields, S., & Bickman, L. (2006). Meta-analysis of common process factors in youth and family therapy: The evidence for different relationship variables in the child and adolescent treatment outcome literature. *Clinical Psychology Review, 26,* 50–65. doi:10.1016/j.cpr.2005.09.001

Karver, M. S., Shirk, S., Handelsman, J., Fields, S., Gudmundsen, G., McMakin, D., & Crisp, H. (2008). Relationship processes in youth psychotherapy: Measuring alliance, alliance-building behaviors, and client involvement. *Journal of Emotional and Behavioral Disorders, 16,* 15–28. doi:10.1177/1063426607312536

Shirk, S. R., & Karver, M. S. (2003). Prediction of treatment outcome from relationship variables in child and adolescent therapy: A meta-analytic review. *Journal of Consulting and Clinical Psychology, 71,* 452–464. doi:10.1037/0022-006X.71.3.452

INDEX

Hope, 197
Hopelessness, 32
Hormonal fluctuations, 108
Horvath, A. O., 65
Hsieh, C. C., 215–216
Hudson, J., 115
Humor, 177
Hyperactivity, 148

ICT (integrative cognitive therapy), 44
Identity formation, 113–114
Inattentiveness, 148
Independence, 173
Individual barriers, 210–213
Individualized treatment plan, 169–170
Information-gathering approach, 36
Information processing, 110–111
Initial assessment, 85–86, 163–167
Initial meeting, 36, 150
Initial symptomology, 98
Insurance coverage, 213
Integrative cognitive therapy (ICT), 44
Intelligence quotient (IQ), 71–72
Intentional behaviors, 170–171
Interdependence, 34
Internalizing disorders, 103
Interpersonal confrontation, 106
Interpersonal dynamics, 27, 39
Interpersonal relations, 103
Interpersonal rifts. See Alliance ruptures
Interpersonal theory, 34
Interpersonal variables, 32–35
Interviewing, motivational, 152, 236
Intrapsychic variables, 32–35
Introjection, 32, 45
Invalidating environments, 191
Invalidation, 191
Involvement (alliance formation), 63, 96, 98–105, 230
Involvement change scores, 101
Involvement–outcomes relations, 100
Involvement shifts, 95–96, 101–102
IQ (intelligence quotient), 71–72
Irreverence, 236–237
Irreverent communication, 192–193

Jackson-Gilfort, A., 74
Johnson, S., 75
Joshi, N., 215–216

Karver, M., 76, 103, 208
Karver, M. S., 12, 63
Kazdin, A. E., 6–7, 210–212
Kendall, P. C., 100–101, 115
Kroll, L., 72

Lambert, M. J., 142
Language compatibility, 213, 214
Late-maturing adolescents, 109
Lawsuits, 215
Liddle, H. A., 74, 75
Linehan, M. M., 186, 187
Listening techniques, 39–46
Low socioeconomic status, 146–147
Luborsky, L., 67

Magic phrase, 135–136
Manualization, 11
Manuals, treatment, 10, 11, 16
March, J. S., 171
Martin, D. J., 102–103
McNamara, J. J., 215–216
MCS. See Menninger Collaboration Scale
Measures and measurement, 78
    adult-derived, 24
    for alliance/involvement, 231–232
    informal use of, 27–28
    involvement, 98–99, 231
    observational, 73–78, 82
    participant, 65–72
    of therapeutic alliance, 23–28, 64–78
    of treatment constructs, 241
    trends in, 83–84
Mechanisms of change, 232–233
Medication treatment, 149, 170
Menninger Collaboration Scale (MCS), 68, 71–72
Mental health, of client, 31–32
Mental health care
    crisis service model in, 213–214
    delivery of, 26, 215
    reform of, 10, 227
    system of, 238–239
Meredith, L. S., 7
Miller, A. L., 236
Minorities. See Ethnic minorities
Mismatched therapist/client, 29–30
Misunderstandings, 143–144
Monitoring of involvement, 98–105
Mood irregularities, 105, 108

Pretreatment targets, 188
Proactive behavior, 132
Problem domains, 189
Problem-solving approach
    in SNAP, 129
    strategies for, 240
    in structured disposition approach,
        218–219
    in TEEN, 135–136
Process variables, 21–22
Prochaska, J. O., 113
Psychoeducation, 162, 167–170
Psychological inclination, 29
Psychosocial development, 109
Psychotherapy, adolescent. *See* Adolescent
    psychotherapy
Psychotherapy engagement, 21–23
Puberty, 109–110
Public health perspective, 14–17, 140
Purposeful behaviors, 170–171

Questioning, 153

Racial minorities. *See* Ethnic minorities
Realistic expectations, 169
Reciprocal communication, 192–193
Recommitment, 195
Reflective listening, 153
Reframing, 145, 235–236
Refusal of treatment, 96–97, 208
Reinforcement, social, 134
Reinforcement-based approach, 234
Relational barriers, 7–8, 12–15
Relational bond, 12
Relational change mechanisms, 232–233
Relationship variables, 46–47
Replicability, 13
Report of the 2005 Presidential Task Force
    on Evidence-Based Practice, 11
Research, on adolescent treatment, 23,
    83–86, 227–228
Resistance, to treatment. *See* Treatment
    resistance
Retention, 106
Rigidity, 38–39
Risk taking, 124
Rituals, 174–176
Robbins, M. S., 145
Roberts, C., 4–5
Roberts, R. E., 4–5
Role clarification, 171–176

Role exploration, 113–114
Role-play activities, 135
Roles, of family members, 134–135
Rotheram-Borus, M. J., 128–129, 216
Rules and Roles cards, 134–135
Rupture–repair strategies, 40–44
Ruptures, in therapeutic alliance. *See*
    Alliance ruptures
Rynn, M., 171

Safran, Jeffrey, 42, 43
Saiz, S., 61
SASB (structural analysis of social
    behavior), 24
Scheduling difficulties, 213
SDA (structured disposition approach),
    216–217
Self-control, 148–149
Self-disclosure, 193
Self-injurious behaviors, 186–187
Service barriers, 12–13, 213–215
SES (socioeconomic status), 146–147, 211
Setting characteristics, 144
Severity of symptoms, 31–32, 98, 210–211
Shirk, S. R., 61, 63, 69, 76, 103, 231
Single time-point assessments, 99
Situational processes, 238–239
Skeptical clients, 234
SNAP (Successful Negotiation/Acting
    Positively), 129
Social–cognitive abilities, 111
Social development, 111–113
Social problems, 14
Social reinforcement, 134
Socioeconomic status (SES), 146–147,
    211
Spear, L. P., 8
States of change model, 113
Status changes, 111
Stigma, 7, 212, 218
Strassle, C., 37–38
Strategic therapy, 193
Strength-based approach, 234
Strengths, of client, 130
Structural analysis of social behavior
    (SASB), 24
Structured disposition approach (SDA),
    216–217
Strupp, H. H., 73, 75
Stylistic strategies, 192–194

ABOUT THE EDITORS

David Castro-Blanco, PhD, ABPP, is the director of the doctoral program in clinical psychology at the Adler School of Professional Psychology in Chicago, where he also teaches courses on cognitive–behavioral intervention and research design. He received his doctorate in clinical psychology at St. John's University in New York and completed a National Institute of Mental Health–sponsored postdoctoral fellowship at New York State Psychiatric Institute, where he specialized in adolescent suicide prevention. His research focuses on identifying and treating anxiety in young people and enhancing treatment engagement with adolescents at risk for treatment dropout. He has written extensively on mental health issues facing college students and young adults, and he has developed a treatment manual and protocol combining mindfulness meditation practice and study skills training for students experiencing academic anxiety. Before joining the faculty at the Adler School, Dr. Castro-Blanco served on the psychology faculties of the Philadelphia College of Osteopathic Medicine, Long Island University, and St. John's University. In addition, he served as a senior clinician at the American Institute for Cognitive Therapy in New York for 2 years. He holds the Diploma in Clinical Psychology from the American Board of Professional Psychology and has served as an editor or reviewer for several professional journals.

Marc S. Karver, PhD, is a licensed clinical psychologist and an associate professor of psychology at the University of South Florida, Tampa. He received his doctorate in clinical psychology from Vanderbilt University, Nashville, Tennessee. His research interests include the evaluation and improvement of the quality of real-world mental health services for children and adolescents. He has focused on addressing the three areas that define quality mental health services: structure (characteristics of health organizations and service delivery systems that lead to positive outcomes—e.g., prevention services increasing access to mental health services), measurement of treatment processes (what goes on inside of mental health services that leads to positive outcomes), and outcomes (both positive and maladaptive). His work has focused on studying the provision of mental health prevention and intervention services to at-risk populations, such as suicidal adolescents. He has a number of highly cited publications focused on the measurement of treatment engagement processes. Dr. Karver has designed or collaborated on numerous studies involving assessment, treatment decisions, intervention, or prevention services delivered to suicidal youths. His research has been supported by the National Institute of Mental Health and the Substance Abuse and Mental Health Services Administration.